ADVANCED NEGOTIATION AND MEDIATION
THEORY AND PRACTICE

A Realistic Integrated Approach

SECOND EDITION

ADVANCED NEGOTIATION AND MEDIATION THEORY AND PRACTICE

A Realistic Integrated Approach

SECOND EDITION

Paul J. Zwier

Professor of Law
Emory University School of Law

Thomas F. Guernsey

President and Dean
Thomas Jefferson School of Law

NATIONAL INSTITUTE FOR TRIAL ADVOCACY

Address inquiries to:

Reprint Permission
National Institute for Trial Advocacy
1685 38th Street, Suite 200
Boulder, CO 80301-2735
Phone: (800) 225-6482
Fax: (720) 890-7069
E-mail: permissions@nita.org

ISBN 978-1-60156-479-5
eISBN 978-1-60156-513-6

FBA 1479

Library of Congress Cataloging-in-Publication Data

    Names: Zwier, Paul J., 1954- author. | Guernsey, Thomas F., author. | National Institute for Trial Advocacy (U.S.)

    Title: Advanced negotiation and mediation theory and practice : a realistic integrated approach / Thomas F. Guernsey, Paul J. Zwier.

    Description: Second edition. | Boulder, Colorado : National Institute for Trial Advocacy, 2016.

    Identifiers: LCCN 2015041096 (print) | LCCN 2015041152 (ebook) | ISBN 9781601564795 | ISBN 9781601565136 (e-ISBN) | ISBN 9781601565136 ()

    Subjects: LCSH: Dispute resolution (Law) | Negotiation. | Mediation.

    Classification: LCC K2390 .Z85 2016 (print) | LCC K2390 (ebook) | DDC 347/.09—dc23

LC record available at http://lccn.loc.gov/2015041096

Printed in the United States.

To

Lucia Wren Klare Guernsey
TFG

Marlene, Kara, John, and Erin
PJZ

CONTENTS

Chapter Four: Preparing and Planning for the Negotiation Involving the Client

Chapter Five: Opening Discussions: Ice-Breaking and Setting the Agenda

Chapter Six: Information Bargaining

Chapter Eight: Crisis and Outcome

Chapter Nine: Negotiators and Mediators

CHAPTER ONE

NEGOTIATING STRATEGIES AND STYLES

Many authors have attempted to describe negotiation in one all-inclusive theory. For example, academics in the forties, fifties, and sixties began using game theory and other mathematical models to describe behavior during a negotiation. More recent approaches include an economic theory of negotiation and social-psychological theories of negotiation. President Jimmy Carter urged lawyers in the eighties that they could learn much from international negotiators. Other theories on negotiation include attempts to determine whether race, gender, and culture affect the negotiation process and dispute resolution outcomes. These varied theories each suggest different strategies to take in the negotiation.

Interdisciplinary Approaches to Studying Negotiation

- Game Theory
- Economic Theory $\quad$ > two general approaches.
- International Politics
- Ethnic Differences
- Gender Differences
- Social Psychology

While a full discussion of these theories is beyond the scope of this book, you should realize that on a practical level these theories suggest that there are two general approaches (and combinations of these approaches) that are used in negotiation. The game and economic theories view negotiation as an adversarial, position bargaining, zero-sum process. As its name indicates, the problem-solving theory incorporates the learning from international conflict resolution and other conflict resolution structures. It views negotiation as a problem-solving or interest-based "win-win" process. This book's approach to negotiation combines these two theories, suggesting that while an adversarial strategy is appropriate in some circumstances,

Problem solving
v.
adversarial strategy.

a problem-solving strategy may be appropriate in others. Moreover, understanding the different strategies involved in negotiation can help you better counsel your clients. In addition, it will help your client not only choose what kind of mediation she might engage in, but also think strategically about the mediation process.

1.1 Adversarial Negotiation—An Economic Theory and Strategy of Negotiation

Under the economic theory, you can picture every negotiation as involving one or more fungible or interchangeable items, such as money, and the negotiation can be represented in graphic terms. The item being negotiated, damages, for example, is placed on a continuum. The negotiators take positions along the continuum until their positions meet: adversarial bargaining is also referred to as position bargaining. If we take, for example, negotiating over the settlement of a medical malpractice action, the continuum starts with the physician's insurer paying nothing and moves to an infinite number of dollars. The plaintiff and defendant each make a decision about where they will begin negotiating along this continuum—their opening offer (OO). They each will choose places along that continuum where they will move to (their commitment point (CP) and/or target point (TP)) and a place beyond which they will not go—their bottom line (BL).

The area between each side's opening point and bottom line is referred to as their "bargaining range." In the malpractice example, a settlement range exists where the plaintiff's bargaining range overlaps with the defendant's bargaining range. By definition, any settlement that occurs will be within this settlement range. Under this scenario, any settlement will be between $500,000 and $700,000.

See how this framework is based on economics and applies equally well to deals. It attempts to look at ways of placing economic value on a combination of tangible and intangible items. Think about the deal reached between an employer and employee. The same charting lays out the positions of the parties and helps them make choices to arrive at their deal.

[handwritten margin note:] BATNA MLATNA & WATNA ?

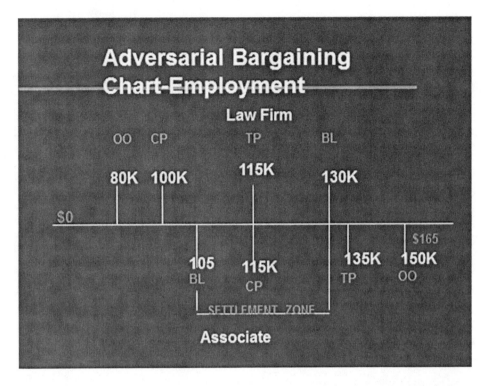

Viewing negotiation in this manner has several practical advantages and suggests certain basic elements of the negotiating process. First, this graphic approach suggests that early in any negotiation you must determine your own bottom line. Second, the graph suggests that you spend much of your time in a negotiation trying to determine the other side's bottom line. While this may seem obvious, what is not obvious—and what the graph suggests—is that your bottom line is the result of rational decision-making. Likewise, if your bottom line is rationally based, then your working assumption should be that your opponent's bottom line is also rationally based. If this is the case, you should spend much of the negotiation seeking information that will allow you to recreate the other side's decision-making perspective and, hopefully, their bottom line. As we will discuss later, not only does this inform your counseling session with the client, but it also informs what you should look for when getting information from the other side, namely economic, psychological, and social relationship data about the opponent and his client that led to a particular bottom line.

you want to be able to predict the other sides

This zero-sum or adversarial approach, however, has obvious disadvantages. It suggests negotiation is a contest in which participants stake out positions and then go through a process of concession and compromise. This adversarial model also suggests that there is a winner and a loser. For example, if one side gains a dollar, the other side loses a dollar. *LOL!*

This adversarial approach may well be contrary to the goodwill you are trying to maintain or develop in a particular negotiation. For example, if you are negotiating a peaceful merger of two hospitals, such an adversarial approach may doom the negotiations before they even begin.

This approach also does not consider the fluid nature of negotiation. For example, it assumes that a negotiator determines a bottom line early in the negotiation and sticks to it. In reality, of course, the negotiator's view of an acceptable solution to the negotiation may change as she gets more information from the other parties to the negotiation.

1.2 Problem-Solving Negotiation as a Strategy

A second theory views negotiation from a problem-solving perspective. Under this theory, the negotiators are engaged in joint problem-solving. Problem-solvers, just as adversarials, are certainly interested in their own needs, interests, and desires. True problem-solvers, however, are just as interested in the other party's needs, interests, and desires. Problem-solvers can be thought of as bargainers of *interests* rather than *positions*. As such, problem-solvers eschew positions and seek to have the parties openly express their needs, interests, and desires so that the parties may jointly create an appropriate solution to the issue being negotiated. Problem-solvers see the "position" of the adversarial negotiator as only one of many solutions to the underlying problem.

Three examples help make the point. Imagine that two parties are sent to a late-night grocer shortly before closing. Both want an orange. They each reach for the orange at the same time and each establishes a firm grip on the orange. How do they resolve who gets the orange? Their option seems to be to resort to violence. The stronger or the more ruthless will be the only one getting the orange.

Now imagine, instead that the parties talk to each other. One wants the orange for its juice, to make a cake. One wants the orange for the rind, to make a garnish for a drink. If they are able to find out why each wants the orange, the problem-solver will be able to suggest a win-win solution to the problem. They split paying for the orange, and one peels it and takes the rind, and the other goes home with the rest—each gets the part she needs.

found out why their position

Remember the Orange

- Positions versus Underlying Needs
- International Problem-Solving
- Building Trust during the Process

Here lies the key, according to those attempting to solve the problem of Middle East peace. The Israelis say: *We get Jerusalem.* The Palestinians say: *No, we get it.* The only resolution seems to be to resort to violence. If however, the parties could get past their positions, if they could describe why they want Jerusalem—to worship in their holy sites, to raise their children in safety and security, to learn their traditions and sacred beliefs, to grow into all that God/Allah intended them to be—then the goals and underlying needs that each side has may be met with win-win solutions. Consider then how a modern map of Jerusalem evidences a problem-solving approach to what otherwise seems an intractable dispute.

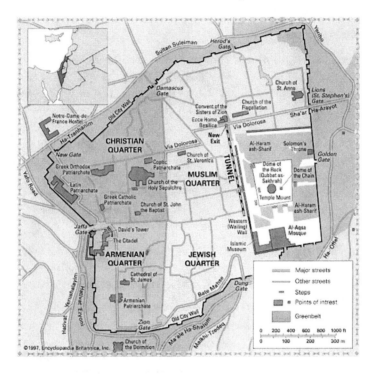

The map shows a number of gates that give Armenian, Christian, Jew, or Muslim choices to enter directly into their Quarter of the Old City. Within their quarter, each experiences sovereignty, ownership, security, religiously and culturally significant sites, and markets predominated by their group. Assuming some joint security force can insure the safety of each group, the problem of how to share the Old City is largely solved.

A primary advantage to problem-solving is that by addressing the underlying needs of the parties (i.e., the reason or interest behind the position), other—perhaps more creative—solutions can be developed. Ownership issues can be transformed from the concept of exclusive control to that of sharing different economic benefits, tax breaks, and income streams from tourism, as well as sharing different times and dates of possession and costs of securing, maintaining, and protection of key cites; such an arrangement uses the benefits of sharing to create possibilities for the exchanges, rather that violence. Lawyers have used creative problem-solving in a number of contexts (e.g., family law and child custody, real estate, mergers and acquisitions) to the point where the approach has become institutionalized within different segment of the profession.

A third such example is in medical malpractice actions. For years, plaintiff's lawyers would demand a set amount of money, such as one million dollars. Defense counsel would offer, if anything, a lower amount. The parties would then move toward some middle ground by a series of concessions and compromises. This was classic adversarial negotiation.

But lawyers in the med-mal field, however, have begun using problem-solving approaches, asking, for example, what underlies the plaintiff's need to have one million dollars? If they could identify those needs and solve them, it might cost less money. If the plaintiff claims he needs the money to ensure long-term medical treatment, to educate his children, and to compensate for lost wages and the like, the insurer can structure a payment schedule that guarantees those things. Not only may the ultimate cost under this structure may be far less than the plaintiff's adversarial demand, but the parties have the flexibility to devise a variety of payment methods other than a single lump-sum payment. Hence, structured settlements have become more popular.

There are many other examples of common uses of problem-solving strategies. Some joint child custody arrangements are essentially problem-solving solutions. Rather than a negotiation premised on dividing time between parents, many parties are asking how to create a living arrangement that accommodates all parties' legitimate needs.

The power of creative problem-solving is particularly evident in situations where adversarial negotiation might lead to deadlock. Remember that for adversarial negotiators to agree, their bargaining ranges must overlap. If the ranges do not overlap, adversarial negotiators will not reach settlement. Take a nonlegal example. In the late 1970s, mortgage interest rates were in the upper teens. The banking industry's negotiation with the borrowing public had been basically adversarial, and business suffered. In that negotiation with the public, the industry staked out a bottom line position of 17–18 percent on home mortgages. The public's bottom line, however, was somewhere near 12 percent. The bargaining ranges did not overlap.

adversarial can lead to dead locks

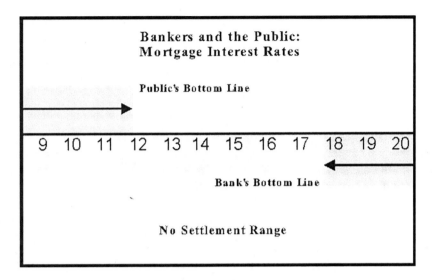

The above graph clearly illustrates that if the parties remained adversarial, they could not agree. The banking industry, however, switched strategies. Rather than continuing adversarial negotiation, banks asked themselves what was underlying the customer's position. What were the needs, interests, and desires that led to the position that the public would only pay 12 percent? If the banks could discover the customer's underlying needs, interests, and desires, then perhaps they could find some appropriate solution other than 12 percent or 17 percent.

Of course, banks quickly recognized that the customer's position was based on her inability to pay the higher rate. Further, customers feared that even if they could afford 17 percent, rates could soon fall and they would be stuck with a 17 percent mortgage. The industry set about trying to meet its own needs to lend money to make money and the public's need for affordable payments and protection from being stuck with a high interest rate. The banking industry, of course, came up with adjustable rate mortgages, giving lower payments and protection against falling interest rates.

Lawyers can use the same techniques in more mundane negotiations as well. In property settlement negotiations associated with divorce, it might be that both parties want the same object—a china cabinet, for example. If there is only one cabinet, adversarials are going to have a problem reaching an agreement if each sticks to his position that he gets it. A problem-solver, however, will explore why each side wants the item. If he wants it because of a perceived inequity in who is already getting the most out of the property whereas she wants it because it is a family heirloom, then giving it to her and compensating him with other property may break the deadlock. Indeed, problem-solvers may find that the reason each wants it is to keep the other from having it! If that is the case, a number of solutions present themselves, including selling it and splitting the proceeds, giving it to the children, or giving it to charity.

In addition to creating multiple solutions, one of problem-solving's advantages is that it is generally more conciliatory. The atmosphere is usually, though not always, more cooperative and, therefore, perhaps more protective of long-term relationships.

The biggest drawback to problem-solving is basically one of trust. A premise of problem-solving is that each side must be able to express his or her needs, interests, and desires. Problem-solvers must generally share more information than adversarials. The needs, interests, and desires that are the working material for a problem-solver may be the type of information an adversarial fears will weaken his position. An adversarial negotiator who doesn't want to disclose information might consider revealing underlying needs, interests, and desires a mistake. Indeed, in a situation where you are a problem-solver and the other side is a clear adversarial negotiator, there is a real risk that you, as the problem-solver, will reveal information that will help the other side assess your client's vulnerabilities without correspondingly gaining information about the other side's vulnerabilities.

be careful

Take, for example, the common experience of buying an automobile. In the past, when you bought a car, you offered a certain price (took a certain position) and the salesperson immediately took another position. You would make concessions and compromise until you reached a middle ground—classic adversarial negotiation. Today it is more common for you to take a position—"I'll give you $15,000 for the car"—and for the salesperson come back and take what appears to be a problem-solving approach: "What were you looking for in a monthly payment?" This is a classic problem-solving question. The salesperson has assumed, usually correctly, that the price you quoted was your perceived solution to your underlying need—that is, the need for a car you can afford. This, of course, is the risk of problem-solving. If you tell the salesperson that your position is based on your ability to pay only $300 a month, the "problem-solving" salesperson can think of all kinds of ways to solve that problem without selling you the car for $15,000. For example, he or she can sell it to you for $18,000 and extend the term of the loan from thirty-six to forty-eight months. This "problem-solving" is done, of course, without the salesperson sharing equivalent information about his underlying need. You, the customer, do not get to find out such things as what the car cost the dealer, whether the salesperson needs to sell this car to earn a bonus or increase a monthly commission, whether the dealer is getting any factory incentives, or any other information that you could use to help decide if the dealer would take a lower price.

While in situations of trust, where parties perceive the need to develop a long-term relationship and empathetic understanding will greatly redound to the benefit of the parties, problem-solving techniques will operate effectively and efficiently.

However, where parties are in short-term relationships or perceive it to their advantage to block and conceal to gain a transactional advantage, then position-bargaining techniques are safer, even if there is a greater risk of deadlock. At the heart of the matter is a view of human nature. Will bargainers be able to set aside selfish concerns and bargain more altruistically for the long-term good of their opponent? Or will bargainers only fake these more altruistic concerns to position themselves to take advantage of the other?

Our approach is to take a realistic integrative approach—to see bargaining in stages. We will take the approach that position-bargaining and problem-solving are not mutually exclusive. At the heart of the matter is information exchange. Position bargaining can lead to information that will test the good faith of the opposition. If the parties develop trust in each other, they can quickly move to problem-solving strategies. If not, bargainers can still move to problem-solving if position bargaining fails. In these situations of deadlock, the parties can try to overcome the deadlock through active listening, restatement, and reflection techniques that may lead to more win-win solutions. Integrative bargaining can bridge the gaps and lead to creative solutions with skills and techniques for problem-solving and monitoring; or, if necessary, further test the positions the opposition has taken with position-bargaining techniques.

[margin note:] realistic integrative approach

1.3   Styles of Negotiation

Besides the two general approaches to negotiation we have referred to as strategy, researchers have identified two styles that are commonly seen in negotiation: competitive and cooperative.[1] Competitive negotiators are aggressive and assertive, and the pitch, pace, tone, and volume of their voices will reflect that style. Cooperative negotiators have a correspondingly different approach. Cooperative negotiators, as the term indicates, take a more cooperative approach, and the pitch, pace, tone, and volume of their voices will be controlled accordingly.

[margin note:] competitive & cooperative

Once you recognize that both strategies and styles have two extremes, you begin to see the range of possible combinations that you can adopt in a negotiation. Competitive adversarials tend to be rigid and demanding. Cooperative adversarials tend to view the negotiation process as a series of concessions and compromise. Competitive problem-solvers tend to be careful and engage in limited problem-solving, often hesitant to reveal too much information because of lack of trust. Cooperative problem-solvers tend to be open and trusting.

[margin note:] variations of strategy & style

Statistically, nothing indicates that one type of negotiator is more likely to be successful than any other. As discussed earlier, however, there are specific advantages

---

1. G. Williams, *Effective Negotiation and Settlement* (1981). *See also* Andrea Kupfer Schneider, *Shattering Negotiation Myths: Empirical Evidence on the Effectiveness of Negotiation Style*, 7 Harv. Negot. L. Rev. 143 (2012).

to each. A particular negotiator may be naturally more cooperative, albeit adversarial, with an opposing counsel she works with regularly, but with the lawyer she meets for the first time, she may become a competitive adversarial.

Many people intuitively move from one combination of style and strategy to another. For example, you may have experienced a frustrating negotiation apparently not going anywhere when someone finally said something like: "[EXPLETIVE DELETED] I can't stand this! What is it you really want out of this deal?" That person has moved from being a cooperative adversarial to a competitive adversarial to a competitive problem-solver. In fact, some would argue that the natural place to switch to problem-solving strategy is where adversarial bargaining has only produced deadlock. In these situations, it is important for the bargainer to remember our early example of the orange. Switching the language to one of goals and objectives may save the bargainers despite apparent deadlock.

Combining Style and Strategy: Adversarial and Problem Solving Competitive and Cooperative		
	Adversarial Strategy	**Problem Solving Strategy**
Competitive Style	Rigid and Risky	Limited Needs and Solutions
Cooperative Style	Concession and Compromise	All Needs and Solutions

One way to get a better perspective on these strategies and styles is to see them in combinations that highlight various strengths and weaknesses.

1.4   Blending Strategies and Styles

We take the approach that both the adversarial strategy and the problem-solving strategy have distinct advantages, and, as with all aspects of negotiation, a choice should be made whether a particular negotiation should proceed from an adversarial perspective or a problem-solving perspective. The following examples suggest how bargainers might combine styles and strategies to reach various results.

1.4.1 The Caring and Compassionate Grandmother

You are five years old. You go to visit your grandmother. First, you attempt to negotiate a second cookie, and then as evening draws, a later bedtime. How might your grandmother choose the best style and strategy to deal with your five-year-old self? She might be very cooperative in style. "Oh honey, come here and give Grandma a hug and kiss. But no, you have already had enough cookies. It is time for bed. Lights out." Grandma has chosen a position-bargaining strategy with a cooperative style. It is firm. It tolerates no discussion of reasons or underlying needs.

1.4.2 The Family's Used Car Negotiator

You are called on to shop for cars for your family members. Before you go, you put on a black T-shirt with white lettering that says, "That's *Mr.* Asshole to You." You walk into the used car dealership and up to the car you've been told to buy. When the salesperson approaches, you say the following: "You used car salespeople, I hate you! I want to spend as little time with you as I can. Here is the deal—you have fifteen minutes to prove to me your costs in this car, what you paid for it, what repairs you made and for how much, and I'll pay you $400 above that amount, plus sales tax, that's it. That means $400 to you for fifteen minutes' work. Now that is the deal. Fifteen minutes, take it or leave it."

Here you have chosen a problem-solver's strategy with a competitive style. You appeal to your underlying goal: to spend no more than fifteen minutes to reach a fair price. You appeal to the salesperson's underlying need: to get paid a fair price for their time. The style is *in your face*. It also depends on the dealer's willingness and ability to reveal their costs in a form that satisfies your requirements for proof.

Indeed, you may now face a choice of whether you should move from one approach to the other within the same negotiation. As with many aspects of negotiation, we intuitively make such moves. However, you will become a better negotiator by choosing to make the moves.

PROBLEM 1.1

Potter v. Cal Ford

Plaintiff, Ms. Potter, decedent, and her husband, Jeffrey, were involved in auto accident when the two-year-old Ford Jeffrey had purchased from Cal Ford suddenly veered off the road into a steel pole with a steel base, killing Ms. Potter. Mr. Potter alleges the expressed warranty he had with Cal Ford, which limited the warranty on the car's steering to sixteen months, violated the Magnuson-Moss Warranty Act. He is seeking damages for wrongful death and compensatory and punitive damages.

- Would you use an adversarial or problem-solving strategy in this negotiation?

- Would you use a competitive or cooperative style?

- Is there any additional information you need before you can answer these questions?

There is, of course, no one correct answer to these questions regarding representation of Mr. Potter. The problem is designed to start you thinking about the multitude of issues you will face when selecting an appropriate strategy or style. Looking at the strategy decision, an adversarial approach might work. After all, if a complaint has been filed asking for damages, you are dealing with a fungible item—money. To the extent the plaintiff gets more, the defendants have less. The risk of such an approach, however, is that if defense counsel takes an adversarial approach also and their bargaining range does not overlap with plaintiff's bottom line, the parties may not agree. For example, if defendants want to pay no more than $500,000, but the plaintiff has decided she will accept no less than two million dollars, there will be no agreement. Therefore, you must premise your decision to take an adversarial approach, at least in part, on your confident expectation that the opposing side's bargaining range will overlap your bargaining range.

[handwritten margin note: take adversarial approach only when you think the ranges overlap]

Also, if you represent the plaintiff, does five million dollars sought in the complaint adequately represent what your client wants out of the lawsuit? Have you determined through counseling that the dollar amount is less important than other intangible issues such as reputation, feelings of anger, or humiliation? Is the real issue not a fungible item at all? Or does the client really want a combination of both money and social and psychological vindication? If the client's goals lean toward the latter, then you should take a creative problem-solving approach.

Of course, by starting out as a problem-solver, implying "there is more at stake than money," you incur two risks: 1) revealing important information about the relative importance of money and 2) not getting as much money in the final deal.

You might, therefore, start off as an adversarial negotiator, stake out a position, and then—using the techniques described in the chapters that follow—gather sufficient information to determine if the defendant is willing to make a concession. If this strategy does not work, you might then shift to problem-solving. You might accomplish this shift to problem-solver by saying:

> Look, this doesn't appear to be working. Let me tell you, I need a break on this dollar amount. My client simply can't take the amount you are offering. And let's be frank—there is no way that $500,000 sends the message that your clients are truly sorry about what occurred. Now, I understand you are limited by the precedent you are setting in settling the case, but let's see if there is some way to meet my client's needs as well as yours. What do you think? Is there some way this remorse can be communicated?

This example clearly communicates the need underlying the monetary position and invites a problem-solving approach in return. In response, defense counsel might offer to apologize. At that point, as plaintiff's counsel, you should pursue other solutions of this type, move on to other issues, or even return to the money issue by saying something like:

> Well, that's a step in the right direction, but the dollar amount is still too low.

Of course, in a specific negotiation none of these scenarios may be effective. The point is, however, that however a scenario unfolds, it may be worth exploring the possibility of a creative, problem-solving solution.

The issue of which style you select requires equally complex decisions. As a professional, your immediate reaction may be to cooperate. After all, law has become a business, and there is nothing to make you competitive. Indeed, long-term relationship issues may exist, at least for the lawyers. Are these lawyers you deal with on a regular basis? Do you rely on a good relationship to the benefit of your respective clients? If yes, the negotiation will naturally take on a cooperative tone.

The point is simply that you must consider the circumstances of the particular negotiation and consciously select the strategy and style best suited to the situation. Also, as with most choices you make, these choices need not—indeed, often should not—be immutable. As circumstances change, so might your strategy or style. One can easily imagine situations where you might want to start out as a competitive, aggressive individual. Imagine a situation in which you represent a child in a short-term state psychiatric facility (average stay six weeks). You discover that your client, an emotionally disturbed thirteen year old in the custody of social services, has been in this institution for two years. Your experts tell you that the child could function in a group home and that clearly contrary to state and federal law, the child has not been involved in an appropriate educational program.

[handwritten margin note: strategy & style depends on situation]

In these circumstances, you could choose between two quite different courses. You could easily conclude that the long-term interests of this child require serious cooperative problem-solving by the very people who have apparently been ignoring the child for at least the past two years. Alternatively, you could just as easily conclude that trying to cooperate and problem-solve with people who have callously disregarded the child will be ineffective. You might, therefore, decide that the best approach is to start out as a competitive adversarial—threatening, perhaps even filing a lawsuit, calling for a meeting of lawyers and interested social service and educational providers, and communicating that you are angry and prepared to go to the mat for a client who has been ignored in the past. At some point, however, you would probably have to shift into a problem-solving approach to encourage the relevant service providers to think of creative ways to get the client the services he needs.

As a reminder of how strategy affects the language and stages of negotiation, we will provide at the end of each chapter a side-by-side chart that describes these differences. The first one of these follows:

Language of Position Bargaining	Language of Problem-Solving
My offer is non-negotiable.	Shall we first agree on a process that will lead to a fair resolution of the questions on the table?
I'm sorry, that is off the table.	
I'm not going to answer that.	Help me understand why you take that position?
I moved last, it is your turn to counter.	
Is that your bottom line?	What needs do you have and let's see if any of them are shared by both of us.
I'll split the difference.	
Can we trade off on those two items?	I think there is a win-win solution in this for everyone.
	It might be most helpful for you to go first and tell me what you want and what your goals are. After I make sure I understand how you see it, then I'll tell you our point of view. Then we can brainstorm and see if there are any creative solutions we can come up with that are fair to each side's legitimate concerns and yet produce the best solution for both sides.

Classic Stages of Position Bargaining	Classic Stages of Interest Bargaining
• Strategic icebreaking • Agenda bargaining • Questions and follow-up • Opening offers and persuasive statements • Concessions • Agreement or deadlock • If deadlock, subsequent offers and concessions till resolution • Write-up and wrap-up	• Icebreaking that is revealing, recognizes and respects the opponent, and evidences trust and goodwill • Exchange of full information, no blocks • Brainstorming—identifying all possible creative solutions • Identifying shared needs, independent needs, needs in conflict • Selecting best solution • Monitoring solution for fair implementation

Now that we have discussed the various strategies and styles of negotiators, the next chapter will introduce the various stages of a negotiation.

CHAPTER TWO

THE ELEVEN-STAGE NEGOTIATION MEDIATION

2.1 Phases and Stages

Theorists tell us that regardless of the strategy or style used, each negotiation is made up of three phases: assessment, exchange, and persuasion.[1] Each of these phases, in turn, involves a number of apparently discrete tasks. Assessment, for example, involves—among other things—acquiring information and evaluating what it means to your goals and the likely goals of the person with whom you are negotiating. The exchange phase typically involves acquiring more information, disclosing information, and presenting a position or proposed solutions. In the persuasion phase, the parties attempt to convince each other to accept a particular proposal. These phases clearly overlap. For example, acquiring information is central to the negotiating process and cuts across each of the phases.

assessment

exchange
persuasion

The approach suggested here takes these phases and their associated tasks and breaks the negotiation process into ten interrelated stages. We then add an eleventh (to our original ten) by describing how mediation might fit in. These stages are roughly, though not always, chronological.[2] Just as the three phases overlap, these stages overlap as well. If you think about the last negotiation you engaged in, you can probably identify each of these stages. We will address each of the stages in detail in the chapters that follow, but for now this brief overview will be helpful.

---

1. R. BASTRASS & J. HARBAUGH, INTERVIEWING, COUNSELING, AND NEGOTIATION (1990).
2. Note that if you engage in an early problem-solving mediation, the stages are in the main, reversed. (Position bargaining becomes the fall back if deadlock occurs after attempting problem-solving. But in the majority, we will proceed from distrust to trust, or from more strategic position bargaining to problem-solving.)

Eleven-Stage Negotiation or Mediation

(Assessment)

1. Preparation and planning

2. Ice breaking

3. Agenda control

(Exchange and Assessment)

4. Information bargaining

5. Proposals, offers, demands

(Persuasion)

6. Persuasion/justification

(Assessment, Exchange, Persuasion)

7. Concessions/reformulation

8. Crisis: resolution or deadlock

9. If deadlock: using an evaluator or facilitator mediator

10. Closing or wrap-up

11. Memorialization or write-up

The first stage of any negotiation is preparation and planning. Whether they prepare for hours or only as a disgruntled colleague walks into their office, most people give some thought to an upcoming negotiation. In the preface, we pointed out that choice is critical to success in negotiation. By maximizing your preparation and planning, you will increase your ability to anticipate the choices you will need to make.

Having prepared as much as circumstances allow, you move to the next stage, which involves some type of interpersonal contact, or ice breaking. The amount of time you spend on ice breaking may vary, but it virtually always occurs.

The third stage involves agenda setting. Fairly early in the process you and the other party will decide what is subject to negotiation. Are you there, for example, to discuss a merger, settlement of a defamation action, the terms of pretrial stipulations, or jury instructions? At this stage, you should be concerned with establishing how you will negotiate. For example, how will you get the negotiation to move through these eleven stages in the order you want?

Handwritten margin notes:
- 1. preparing & planning
- 2. ice-breaking
- 3. agenda setting

Following a discussion of the purpose of the negotiation, you and the other party will exchange information, a process often referred to as information bargaining. During this stage you will seek information, reveal information, and even hide information from each other.

4. information bargaining

After information bargaining series of stages involving persuasion and exchange typically follow. One party makes a proposal, offer, or demand and then provides a persuasive statement or justification of why the proposal, offer, or demand should be acceptable to the other side. This process will repeat itself, and counterproposals, offers, or demands may be presented, also followed by a persuasive statement or justification. Concessions (if you are an adversarial negotiator) or reformulation of the proposals (if you are a problem-solver) then may follow until ultimately a crisis occurs; the point at which the parties either agree or break off discussions. It is here that the parties might think to involve a third-party evaluator or neutral to help resolve areas of disagreement. Then there follows a closing and the parties memorialize the agreement—or lack of agreement—in some manner, usually in writing.

5. proposals, offers, demands
6. persuasion/ justification
7. concessions
8. crisis resolution/ deadlock
9. evaluator
10. closing
11. write-up

To reemphasize the comments in the preface, you must recognize that this is not an inflexible framework. In fact, viewing negotiation as a series of stages is useful only if it is flexible. This framework's value is that it lays out in a straightforward manner the myriad of choices that we must make in a negotiation. Once we understand that a face-to-face negotiation generally proceeds through these stages, we can then alter how we engage in that negotiation in a given circumstance, even combining stages.

Agenda setting is a good illustration of why this framework is only roughly chronological. The parties may have set the agenda by letter before the initial personal contact. Or in a negligence action when plaintiff and defense counsel sit down to talk, both already know that the agenda will include duty, breach, causation, and damages.

As another example, an important stage in the negotiation is the exchange of information. Although first in importance, it is not the first stage in a face-to-face negotiation. Many other things must first occur. In a given negotiation, however, you will choose to move the information exchange stage or major parts of it because of circumstances unique to that particular negotiation.

In a negligence action, serious negotiations to settle the case may not take place until after extensive formal and informal discovery. Counsel will obtain most of the historical facts of the action before the formal negotiation. Indeed, to wait until the face-to-face negotiation would be incompetency at its worst. But some information may be available only during settlement negotiations, given the state of the suit at that particular time, such as the real needs of the parties, economically, socially, and psychologically.

2.2   A Note on Plea Bargaining

Two types of plea bargaining take place in criminal proceedings. The first, charge bargaining, involves—as its name implies—negotiating over the crimes with which the defendant will be charged. Prosecutors have a wide range of crimes (burglary, grand larceny, breaking and entering, etc.) with which to charge a defendant found outside a home at night with a stereo in his hands, so charge bargaining involves negotiating the charge to which the defendant will ultimately plead guilty. The second, sentence bargaining, involves negotiating the sentence the prosecution will recommend the defendant receive in exchange for a guilty plea.

Charge bargaining

Sentence bargaining

Within each of these types, there will often be issues unrelated to either the specific crime charged or the sentence that will be received. For example, in negotiating a recommended sentence, the defendant may have authorized defense counsel to trade his testimony against a co-conspirator.

Recent statutory developments have made charge bargaining increasingly important. Mandatory minimum sentences and other sentencing guidelines often leave little discretion to the prosecutor if the focus is on sentence reduction.

Does any of this discussion of the stages of negotiation apply to plea bargaining? Yes. Prosecutors and defense counsel have the same variety of styles as do civil attorneys. Plea bargainers experience the same stages of the negotiating process as other negotiators. Criminal attorneys must prepare and plan. Prosecutors must choose the appropriate relationship with opposing counsel. Both negotiators agree on an agenda. Acquiring information concerning the strength of the prosecution's case is just as important to criminal defense counsel as the strength of plaintiff's case is to civil defense counsel.

Prosecutors and defense counsel also have various combinations of styles and strategies. Some defense counsel, for example, will be adversarial, staking out a position and viewing the process as a series of concessions and compromises: "My guy didn't do it and you can't prove it, but he wants to get this over with so he'll agree to the misdemeanor charge." Defense counsel are also just as likely to be problem-solvers: "Look, he's just a kid and needs help. The real problem is not that he shop-lifted the goods; it's that he doesn't have the home structure he needs. How about we hold the charges and see if we can't get him into . . . ."

There are, however, a number of factors that affect the plea bargaining process in a way that does not always affect transactional or civil litigation disputes. Two factors, for example, significantly affect information bargaining in plea negotiations. First, favoring the prosecution, is the fact that it has the resources of the state at its disposal. While clearly the state does not always choose to overwhelm the defendant with these resources, the fact remains that the state, if it so chooses, can outspend almost all defendants. Second, favoring the defendant, is that in most jurisdictions, discovery in criminal actions clearly favors the defendant, with the prosecutor having a greater responsibility for turning over evidence than the defendant.

2.3 Transactional Bargaining

Transactional lawyers are most often bargaining about the language in documents. In a merger, for example, it seems that the investment bankers have had all the fun in setting the price, and all the lawyers do is slow down the process and think of reasons why the parties ought not do the deal.

One might think that because transactional lawyers represent buyers and sellers who are selling tangible items that they would most likely be adversarial position bargainers. They would be drawn to the tactics of the "bazaar" and haggle until they move each other into a range of settlement. However, deal lawyers, while worried about value and risk, are also worried about control. Moreover, most deals require some ongoing relationship. At a minimum, payment may be made over a period of time, and the success of the deal itself may depend on the future viability of the new business. So, like other bargainers, transactional lawyers need to be able to problem-solve—to understand the underlying goals of the deals they are drafting to know when to fight about the language or think creatively to draft in a way that each side wins. Transactional lawyers must remember the mantra of deal-makers during the negotiation of the deal: *The person who understands the deal controls the deal.* This is true whether the fight is about tax formulations, representations and warranties, management structure, or contingent liabilities. Deal lawyers and litigators have more in common than they think is when they plan for and conduct negotiations.

In addition, transactional bargainers must understand that the parties may not have enough information at the time of the closing to give value to later risks. In these situations, they might draw on evaluative or meditative processes to solve the disputes when they arise. They must think ahead to the litigation that might arise and lay out a process now that will fairly resolve different later-arising disputes.

With this general overview, we will now turn to a detailed discussion of each of the stages. As we discuss each stage, keep in mind that we will want to identify not only what you need to do, but how to do it. We also want to ask whether how you do it differs depending on which style and strategy you use.

CHAPTER THREE

THE SOCIAL PSYCHOLOGY OF NEGOTIATION

Researchers have long recognized that a social/psychological dynamic permeates all stages of the negotiation process. This "social psychology" can have a significant impact on the negotiation. Our personal observations confirm the fact that people do things in a negotiation for reasons that may not comport with rational business or economic judgment. If you can identify these potential pressures at work on the other party, you can then use them to help "persuade" that party to accept your proposal. Also important, if you recognize these other pressures at work on you, you can choose to either allow yourself to be influenced by them or let them influence the negotiation.

Social psychological pressures occur in a variety of circumstances. The Dollar Auction game makes a number of these points. Ask a group of lawyers to participate in a dollar auction with the following rules and watch what happens:

Dollar Auction

- First bid greater than fifty cents.

- At least five cent increments.

- You owe me your last bid.

You will routinely get an opening bid of fifty-five cents. Or sometimes someone will bid ninety-five cents. But low and behold, the auctioneer can get another bid at one hundred cents. It is at this point that the group becomes aware of the real meaning of the last rule: *you owe me your last bid.* Often then, to save face, the other bidders will bid more than a dollar for the dollar. It becomes a matter of winning the dollar rather than whether it makes sense to bid as much as they bid. When the bidding stalls, the auctioneer can often provoke higher bids by:

- interviewing the bidders and getting personal information out to the group that may raise the embarrassment factor;

- simply telling the bidder that they *really need* another bid to make a point.

Whenever the Dollar Auction is played with these move, the psychological effect on the audience is quite palpable and predictable. The audience tends to look at the auctioneer with suspicion. They feel tricked. Yet they recognize that what has happened is not that far removed from a typical litigation setting negotiation.

The audience learns about sunk costs—that a party is willing to spend more than a dollar for a dollar because if they give up bargaining, they will lose all they have already invested in the outcome. To avoid losing what they have already invested for nothing, they are willing to pay even more to get something. This is the analytical and economic lesson of the auction. The other lessons are psychological and social.

We are all familiar with situations in which a person has taken a position that can only be justified by their desire to "save face." With perhaps more worthy motivations, you may recall situations in which you or another person in the negotiation "gave" the other side a concession because you "wanted to be nice" or "to avoid a fight." The lawyer who agrees to a day off for a member of the staff because she likes the staff member may have an economic motivation (keeping a good employee happy), but the lawyer also may just feel good by waiving a policy that might otherwise prohibit the day off.

Organizations are also subject to social psychological pressures. We sometimes read in the newspapers about the social and psychological aspects of major negotiations. One need only read about a bank—or any other business merger—in which the two entities are going to combine names or create an entirely new name. Certainly combining the two names may have an economic justification—taking advantage of name recognition—but people involved in these types of negotiations will also tell you that combining names provides a soothing compromise for people with an emotional attachment to the original name.

Let's review of some of the more common social psychological influences to illustrate how these pressures work to facilitate or inhibit acceptance of an opponent's particular position.

3.1   Audiences to the Negotiation

Researchers point out that an audience can significantly impact a negotiation. By audience, we do not mean simply the people who may be in the room watching the negotiation. What we mean by audience is the people somewhere who, directly or indirectly, are observing the negotiation or its results.

The types of audiences are quite broad. They run from the obvious—"the folks back home for whom you are negotiating" or a colleague sitting in on the negotiation—to the more subtle—your spouse when you discuss your day at the office. Audiences to a negotiation involving a lawyer include, for example:

- the lawyer's supervisors or superiors;

- the lawyer's professional peers, colleagues, or co-workers;

- the lawyer's spouse;

- the current client in whose interest the lawyer is negotiating;

- other clients;

- potential clients.

Psychologists tell us that the existence of an audience motivates negotiators to seek positive evaluations from the audience. This is common sense. No one wants to go back to the office and reveal to his colleagues that he has just made the worst agreement of the year.

Of course, different audiences will evaluate a negotiation differently. A supervising partner may evaluate the associate-bargainer from a profitability (to the firm) and quality standpoint—did the lawyer get a good deal in a difficult negotiation? The client might evaluate the bargainer in light of factors such as speed or profitability to them (as opposed to the firm). The one common denominator, however, is that if the negotiator is accountable to an audience, this accountability provides a means to control the negotiator.

In blunt terms, if you can give the negotiator what her influential audience desires, you can manipulate her into accepting what the audience wants rather than perhaps what she wants. The clearest example of this, of course, is the client as audience. In our products liability action for Mr. Potter we will spend a great deal of time trying to figure out what the audience/client really wants to make up for the loss of his wife. If you can figure out what the client wants, more likely than not, the desires of the lawyer with whom you are negotiating become irrelevant. Give the lawyer what the client wants and the lawyer should ultimately go along.

PROBLEM 3.1

Refer to Problem 1.1, where plaintiff's lawyer is negotiating with defendant, Cal Ford, the dealer of new Ford automobiles. Plaintiff alleges breach of warranty.

- What audiences would there be for the negotiation?

- How, if at all, would your overall strategy be affected by those audiences?

- Is there any additional information you need before you can definitely answer these questions?

The client is not the only audience. In Problem 3.1, for example, the defendants Cal Ford also have the Ford Motor Co. as an audience. If the plaintiff Potter's attorney can identify how Cal Ford views that audience, she can use that information to her advantage. For example, is the existence of the lawsuit generally known in the community? If not, the threat of continuing the suit and risking exposure with a resultant loss of prestige may have considerable influence on the dealership's willingness to settle and thus on the negotiation. Conversely, the fact that the existence of the suit is already generally known could conceivably make settlement harder. For example, the defendants may feel that settling the case will have a significantly negative impact on Ford's reputation if a settlement is interpreted as an admission of liability. The reputation of Ford may be better served by going to trial and suffering a defeat than by appearing to admit responsibility. Putting together an acceptable settlement package under these circumstances will be particularly difficult if the plaintiff's own goals include seeking precisely the kind of public recognition of liability that the firm seeks to avoid.

As with all aspects of the negotiation process, the pressure of an audience must also be evaluated from the negotiator's perspective. The negotiator with the audience looming in the background must try to avoid being manipulated by that audience. For example, a common question for lawyers is whether the client should attend the actual face-to-face negotiation with opposing counsel. As with most issues related to negotiation, there is no one right answer. This audience dynamic, however, is certainly an important consideration when deciding whether the client should be present.

In a negotiation involving a business transaction that requires a high level of technical expertise, there is often little question that having a client with that expertise attend could be helpful. The value of that expertise must, however, be weighed against the fact that opposing counsel will have direct access to your most important audience. If the client is unable to control his reactions to opposing counsel's negotiation ploys, you may be at a serious disadvantage.

We should quickly add that the cooperative problem-solver must be as aware of these dynamics as the competitive adversarial. For example, lawyers are constantly subject to scrutiny by colleagues. Human nature being what it is, the lawyer probably prefers to be respected by her colleagues as opposed to being held in low esteem. If the general wisdom among opposing counsel's colleagues values aggressive negotiations, the lawyer will likely behave accordingly. Recognizing this, the competitive adversarial should take steps to avoid exacerbating that characteristic. For example, the cooperative problem-solving defense attorney should probably try to avoid plea bargaining with the competitive adversarial prosecutor in the hallways of the court where other prosecutors or police officers are present.

3.2 Restraints on Communication

Researchers also tell us that restrictions on communication can have a significant impact on the negotiation. These restrictions may be between either the negotiators or the negotiator and the negotiator's own people. For example, communication isolation imposes constraints on developing cooperation and promotes distrust and suspicion. A party who is unable to contact her own support group (colleagues, supervisor, secretary) may be more distrustful.

The lesson seems obvious that when trying to work out a joint venture, if you are dealing with a person who is generally distrustful to begin with, it may be to your advantage to ensure that this type of isolation does not occur. You might propose meeting at the other lawyer's or other client's place of business. Or if you meet at your office, try to ensure your counterpart has frequent opportunities to take breaks and use the telephone privately.

PROBLEM 3.2

Assume you are a lawyer for Cal Ford in the breach of warranty case describe in Problem 1.1. You wish to set up a meeting to discuss possible settlement with plaintiffs' counsel. You have now called three times leaving messages. The attorney for the Potters has returned your calls twice, but you have been out of the office.

- How is the Potter's attorney likely to feel?

- How would you feel under these circumstances?

- What steps might you take to deal with the communication problem?

- Does the communication problem give you any insight into other aspects of the negotiation?

Restrictions on verbal communication between negotiators also can have a negative impact on the process. When verbal communication is eliminated, effectiveness often suffers. All too frequently, this occurs when you play telephone tag with someone. As your frustration develops over your inability to contact a lawyer, your anxiety or anger may increase, making it less likely that you will develop the relationship necessary to complete the deal. It may seem obvious, but using a letter at this point can be extremely helpful. Likewise, voice mail is underutilized as a means not just of leaving a message requesting a call in return, but actually to engage in a discussion by leaving a detailed message that outlines needs, interests, and the like. Leaving a message that the lawyer should return your call at a specific time when you will be in your office can also be very effective.

Keep in mind that if you feel frustration and anger, the other person may feel it as well. Directly confronting these feelings may help maintain or develop an appropriate relationship.

3.3 Respect and Anger

One of the most difficult emotional forces at work that prevents conflict resolution and, in fact, may escalate the conflict is anger. The reactions to the Dollar Auction exercise often proves this. When a person feels isolated and embarrassed, he may become angry and just "shut down," say nothing, and refuse to move.

To see how this is so, think first about a conflict that arises between a parent and child and how it informs our understanding of disputes, generally.

Imagine being the parent of a fifteen-year-old daughter. You, your wife, and your other children are all waiting for your fifteen-year-old daughter get home from school so you can leave on your long-anticipated family vacation. You are making the trip by car and need to leave at 4:00 p.m. to be able to stop for dinner and arrive at your vacation cottage by 10:00 p.m. When your daughter left that morning for the last day of school, you made sure she knew to be home by 4:00 p.m. so you could leave on time. Your last words to her were: "Don't be late." Now it is 4:30 p.m. and still no daughter. Might your anger be on the rise?

Conflict resolution theorists tell us that what is likely to happen next is a problem inherent when anger and feelings of lack of respect converge—you will attribute a motive to your daughter's lateness that may produce a significant long-standing effect on your relationship with your daughter and your ability to resolve your conflict with her.

Imagine that when she shows up you let your anger take over. You might even yell and scream at her for her behavior because you attribute her behavior to lack of respect for you and the family. You might even further attribute her behavior to character defects—she is inconsiderate, routinely late, and self-centered. These are character traits that come from you (or her mother), and you were afraid they would surface in her, and now they have and she has this flaw in her character.

She gets angry and cries. She says she was with her friends and has a right to be! She says you are too compulsive, and what difference does it make if we get to the cottage a few minutes later. She says that she is afraid of you and that you can't control your temper. That she hates you and hates living in this family. She runs into her room, slams the door, and locks it.

This likely scenario is what conflict resolution theorists describe as the volatile combination of attribution error and anger.[1] Attribution is the process whereby a harmdoer and the harmed party assign responsibility for the harmdoer's behavior. Each confronts the other with their judgment about who is responsible for the

---

1. Keith G. Allred, *Anger and Retaliation* in CONFLICT: THE ROLE OF ATTRIBUTION, IN EDS. MORTON DEUTSCH & PETER T. COLEMAN, THE HANDBOOK OF CONFLICT RESOLUTION: THEORY AND PRACTICE, 236–245 (2000).

National Institute for Trial Advocacy

harm. The judgment of responsibility turns on the nature of the harmdoer's excuses and motives for causing the harm.

What conflict resolution theorists tell us next is of utmost importance. They tell us that they can predict how anger and loss of respect lead to predictable judgments about the appropriate responsibility that the injuring party will bear. The common judgments of appropriate responsibility can be safely laid out as follows:

- *intentional harmful behavior* leads to an apology, punishment, and the need to repay a fair amount;

- *negligent harmful behavior* leads to a different kind of apology and a change in behavior over those things the harmdoer can fairly control, as well fair compensation;

- *excusable harmful behavior* leads to no apology and no compensation.

Where, however, the judgment of appropriate responsibility is at odds with the injuring party's feelings, the following are the likely effects on the parties:

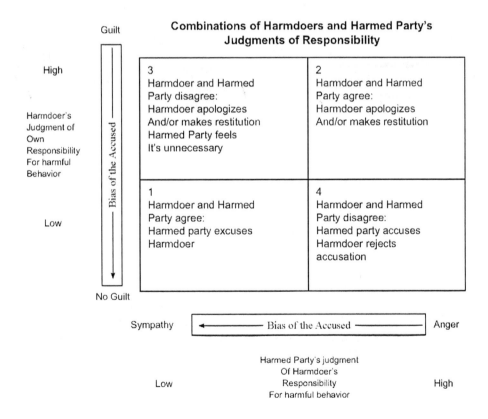

Of course, most of the time there is some combination of behavior or there is a disagreement about the nature of the excuses and whether they are controllable.

Consider, for example, how differently you feel about the family trip situation when your daughter reports the following story: she was approached by a good friend in tears who asked for her help. Her friend's stepfather was approaching her sexually, and she wanted some help about what to do. She did not know where to turn and wanted your daughter to talk to her and help her figure out what best to do.

Do you see what has happened? A paradigm shift has just occurred.[2] It is inappropriate for you to have been angry because your daughter's excuse relates to circumstances beyond her control. You would have been disappointed in her if she had not taken the time to talk to her friend. (You might have preferred for her to have called and explained the situation, but still you do not blame her, nor is it fair to attribute responsibility to her that would require the same level of apology, punishment, and compensation that you and she might otherwise feel is appropriate.)

Moreover, there is more at stake here. Because of your anger, you have attributed her behavior to disrespect at best self-centeredness and, more likely, an intentional motive to harm the family. These attribution errors can cause the most damage to the ability of the parties to resolve the conflict. If the parties are not able to fairly assess what excuses are really available and whether they are beyond the control of the harmdoer, the parties are likely to attribute the behavior to intent, disrespect, and character flaws, provoking not guilt, but a righteous sense of being wronged, harmed, and unfairly blamed. These feelings will likely provoke an escalating angry response, as you gave in your reaction.

These are the same feelings that are in play when an opponent bargainer refuses to return phone calls, laughs at your opening offer, rejects out of hand your client's injury, stereotypes your client along with fakers, or all uncaring arrogant institutions.

As shown by the unreturned phone calls, while these psychological forces operate between the parties, they also operate between the lawyers. How often does a lawyer get angry during a negotiation? How often is anger a result of the lawyer perceiving that her opponent or client does not respect either the lawyer or lawyer's client? The lawyer attributes the behavior of the opponent and/or opponent's representative to an intention to harm or to a character flaw in the opponent/client or industry they represent. When they get angry, the negotiators tend to say things that reflect how they have attributed the worst motives—greed and disrespect to the harmdoer or to the harmed party—to their opposition, and these things can destroy a dispute resolution. The lawyers tend to exaggerate the dispute by taking extreme positions.

---

2. STEVEN COVEY, SEVEN HABITS OF HIGHLY EFFECTIVE PEOPLE. *See* Habit 5, where Covey argues that effective people should try not to react in anger, but seek first to understand before being understood. He otherwise refers to this habit as the habit of "courageous compassion." *See* STEPHEN R. COVEY, PRINCIPLED-CENTERED LEADERSHIP 45 (1992).

Then their opponents can point to these exaggerations as evidence of that the lawyer is a liar. As a result, the opponent justifies tactics that obfuscate and deny responsibility; the opponent will also take further extreme positions because she fears that any admission will be used to unfairly punish and exact retribution. Conflict escalates and can lead to deadlock, unless cooler heads prevail.

What does it mean in this context for cooler heads to prevail? If you find yourself in this escalating conflict, you must think strategically to find ways to deal with your own anger as well as ways to deal with your opponent's anger. The first problem is one that is related to self-control and can be managed very much like any self-control issue. Like an addiction, the problem with anger is that, to some, it feels good, it is born of an instinct to fight, is related to adrenalin and feelings of power, and, for some, is very hard to control. You may often confuse it with the legitimate role that you must play to passionately and zealously represent your clients within the bounds of law.

Because our opponents may be cowered by anger and "flee" rather than fight if they think the anger is irrational enough, the effect may be that the negotiator's anger accomplishes the goal: an outcome in his client's favor. After all, for a threat to be effective, it must be heard, understood, and believed. The emotion and passion of the speaker communicate a willingness to back up his position with violence, if necessary, and, at times, aid in the "believability" part of making a threat effective.

At risk, however, are escalation, deadlock, and permanent damage to the relationship. Interestingly, expressing a position in anger may make you more wedded to it and less willing to see the weakness in the position. In addition, a skilled opponent may see anger as weakness, not strength, and related to the flight instinct. They may also see the failure of self-control as a character flaw, indicating that you lack confidence in the client's position. You must be able to understand anger and manage it to implement your client's goals.

First, you must recognize that you are feeling angry and the reactive effect of this behavior. With this self-knowledge in hand, you can plan what you must do when the feeling of anger arises, including using role plays and developing habits to better control the anger. Some suggest that an effective way to manage anger is to develop a self-regulatory plan and implementation strategy. Just as a smoker who is trying to quit might plan what to do when he craves a smoke, so you might create a plan for when you start to feel angry. The more specific the plan, the better your chance of overcoming the feeling. For example, you might create the following plan:

1. When the opponent's lawyer accuses me of being unreasonable in my demand for damages, I will cite specific recent decisions and settlements of similar size.

2. I will repeat this little mantra to myself: "Do not get angry. Anger is not helpful, and it will harm the client."

3. If the opponent rejects those cases and refuses to discuss them because my client was negligent, recognize the tactic as a position bargaining tactic and not a personal affront. Plan, instead, to ask the opponent to place probabilities on the jury finding a fact in the opponent's favor, and if the opponent refuses, plan to write down your own probability to keep yourself more analytical and less emotional.

As with addiction management, anger management has steps. It involves recognizing the feeling and developing and using a mantra. It often gives you something physical to do, like writing down what you will do next, or writing what you will say before you say it, or playing with a piece of tape. In addition, it provides for a backup. In other words, when the feelings are very powerful, give yourself some place to go (take a break), or something else to talk about, or someone else to talk to or involve in the process.[3]

You can also plan what to do when you see your opponent getting angry. Naming it (saying that your opponent is angry) and taking a time out are common effective strategies. Examining your own behavior to determine whether you might have unfairly caused the anger and, if so, apologizing, is also a very good place to start.[4]

Experiences with adversarial bargaining have caused conflict resolution theorists to start devising a better model for conducting negotiations to resolve conflicts. And the problem-solver provides a way of turning a deadlock into a process.

A problem-solving model seeks to create a set of negotiating steps and procedures that will better control the biasing effects on client decision-making and better control the social and psychological forces that lead to deadlock. It also tries to provide a different, more creative strategy to devise more particularized creative solutions.

Problem-solving attempts to learn from psychiatry. Psychiatrists recommend that counselors, negotiators, and mediators listen—to understand—before trying to persuade to keep emotions from biasing the decision-making process. An important way to resist the adversarial role-playing involved in most position bargaining

---

3. Walter Mishel and Aaron L. DeSmet, *Self-Regulation in the Service of Conflict Resolution*, in MORTON DEUTSCH AND PETER T. COLEMAN, THE HANDBOOK OF CONFLICT RESOLUTION 269–270 (2000).
4. Keith G. Allred, *Anger and Retaliation in Conflict*, in MORTON DEUTSCH AND PETER T. COLEMAN, THE HANDBOOK OF CONFLICT RESOLUTION 246 (2000).

is for the problem-solver to instead initially take the role of "listener."[5] The need for true understanding is a threshold for any connectedness and necessary empathy, and is best described in the work of psychiatrist Tom Rusk, *The Power of Ethical Persuasion*. He writes:

> It's mysterious and ironic that after millions of years of evolution—and a hundred or so of modern psychological theorizing and research—we humans have not advanced very far in person-to-person communications. We can generally exchange thoughts and ideas pretty well, but nonetheless we often fail to understand each other. For the most part, what we fail to communicate clearly is our feelings, those nonverbal, deeply rooted energies that can lead us to act in contradiction to our will and our rational decisions. Between people, strong feelings can easily escalate a simple misunderstanding into a senseless battle of wills. Even wars between nations have begun that way.
>
> Modern psychology has done relatively little to help us comprehend our feelings, or learn to manage them in understanding, caring, and fairness in order to create happier, more fulfilling lives. Many successful books on communication strategies have sought to teach people how to expedite problem-solving or gain the upper hand in all kinds of negotiations. But these strategies almost always ignore the power of feelings in all kinds of relationships, and the need to uphold explicit social values in the conduct of human communication.
>
> As far as I'm concerned, there never was or will be a better basic communication strategy than the Golden Rule: Do unto others as you would have them do unto you. Ethical persuasion is a practical, strategic method of applying the Golden Rule to every kind of important communication—not as a means of merely doing a "good deed," but as a means of giving everyone a fair hearing, creating the optimal solutions for thorny problems, and fostering long-term, trusting relationships.

Rusk's listening techniques then correspond with the techniques that Mnookin describes in his book, *Beyond Winning: Negotiation to Create Value in Deals and Disputes*, and Fisher and Ury describe in their book, *Getting to Yes*. Rusk's ethical persuasion is the practical "how to" for the moral philosophy of persuasion. Rusk describes seven steps to good listening.

---

5. Professor Zwier was first introduced to the role of "listener" by Maude Pervere and Janeen Kerper at a planning conference held by the National Institute for Trial Advocacy for developing a new program for lawyers to reimagine the lawyer-client relationship. Pervere and Kerper then referred us to Tom Rusk's work, THE POWER OF ETHICAL PERSUASION, (1993). Rusk is a noted psychiatrist who has been instrumental in developing models for teaching community mediation.

Making the Other party feel understood ✱

1. Establish that your immediate goal is mutual understanding, not problem-solving.

2. Elicit the other person's thoughts, feelings, and desires about the subject at hand.

3. Ask for the other person's help in understanding him or her. Try not to defend or disagree.

4. Repeat the other person's position in your own words to show you understand.

5. Ask the other person to correct your understanding and keep restating his or her position.

6. Refer back to your position only to keep things going.

7. Repeat steps 1–6 until the other person unreservedly agrees that you understand his or her position.[6]

Listening, then, is a key to understanding, and understanding is key to solving problems within the moral orientation that takes feelings into account, but does not provide them with unfair or biased effects. You should listen first because it will help break you out of position-bargaining role playing. It establishes you in the learning mode first, as opposed to the doing mode. It subverts what you know to what the opponent knows and feels. In addition, to the extent that information is power, you have the advantage of knowing both sides (yours and the opponent's) before speaking. In addition, listening earns you the leverage of fairness. The more your opponent feels listened to and understood, the more the opponent will likely listen and seek to understand in return. Finally, these seven steps cultivate patience and openness, which are behaviors that evidence respect.[7]

Again, Rusk has some concrete practical advice for how to handle the third step, where you may express your position in the matter. Rusk's steps better ensure you are acting out of respect:[8]

1. Ask for a fair hearing in return.

2. Begin with an explanation of how the other person's thoughts and feelings affect you. Avoid blaming and self-defense as much as possible.

3. Carefully explain your thoughts, desires, and feelings as *your* truth, not *the* truth.

---

6. *Rusk, supra* note 3, at 7–8.
7. *Id.* at 69–70.
8. *Id.* at 89.

4. Ask for restatements of your position—and corrections of any factual inaccuracies—as necessary.

5. Review your respective positions.

The result is that the win-lose—"I'm right and you are wrong"—dichotomy may immediately be broken. The possible solutions that arise multiply greatly when the focus turns to what will create, maintain, or maximize the healthy relationships already present in the situation. Within a relationship of trust and respect, each negotiator will look for ways for each side to win. In fact, as we will explore in further chapters, this active listening and advanced empathy may be the negotiator bridge between position bargaining and problem-solving.

3.4 Social Psychology of Selected Tactics

Many standard negotiating techniques have psychological overtones. Several of the more common are worth addressing here.

3.4.1 *Timing Ploys*

A common negotiating technique is to set a deadline by which agreement must be met. This tactic often works. As time pressures increase, bargaining aspirations, demands, and the amount of bluffing tends to decrease.

3.4.2 *Overly Demanding and Other Biases*

Some research has shown that perceptions of one side being demanding, resisting, or unjust correlates with the other side raising intangible issues of honor, public image, face, and self-esteem. And it raises the broader question that challenges economic analysis of bargaining—why do the parties not act rationally and agree on questions of value?

Some have argued that position bargaining also fails to produce creative, particularized, and lasting solutions between the parties.[9] They argue that a different strategy for negotiation is needed—one that makes joint problem-solvers out of the negotiators, which allows the parties to better resolve their dispute.

Let's look more closely at the psychology of each party in the decision-making process to determine how to think differently and strategically about the case.

Cognitive psychologists, especially the *behaviorists*, caution that even professional decision-makers are not as rational as one might expect (especially as defined by optimal efficiency principals). The parties might value their cases differently because one is more naïve and intuitive or is susceptible to error or ideological bias. Or one side's client or lawyer is just simply not very skilled at case valuation or, in

---

9. Robert H. Mnookin, Beyond Winning: Negotiation to Create Value in Deals and Disputes, (2000); Fisher & Ury, Getting to Yes (1981).

the lawyer's case, counseling. They are stuck in the warrior mode and miss the keys to case valuation and settlement.

In a symposium presentation, Professor Lagevoort discusses cognitive psychological literature on decision-making biases and advises lawyers to take an interest in behavioral psychology because it affects decision-making and may inhibit optimal conflict resolution.[10] This literature suggests that nonrational biases come in seven forms.

3.4.2.1   Status Quo/Loss Aversion Biases and Framing Effects

This bias refers to a decision-maker's preference for risk aversion and a natural bias for the status quo.

3.4.2.2   Anchoring and Adjustment

This bias refers to the fact that people tend to "anchor" on some initial possibility in decision-making and fail to adjust carefully as new information becomes available.

3.4.2.3   Illusory Correlations and Causation Biases

Clients often find causal patterns and relationships in matters that are the product of random chance.

3.4.2.4   Biases in Risk Perception

Clients seem to ignore low risk factors that have not been made salient or seem to value uncertainty differently at the extremes. They tend to ignore risk differences in the 5–10 percent category and place more significance on removing the 5 percent and less risk of a bad thing happening.

3.4.2.5   The Hindsight Bias

People overestimate their fault when they could have predicted the outcome, didn't, and the outcome happens.

3.4.2.6   Context Bias

Relative preference between two possible outcomes may bias someone against a compromise as a third outcome.

3.4.2.7   Intertemporal Biases

Many people have a bias toward consumption and against deferred gratification.

---

10. DONALD C. LAGEVOORT, SYMPOSIUM: THE LEGAL IMPLICATIONS OF PSYCHOLOGY: HUMAN BEHAVIOR, BEHAVIORAL ECONOMICS, AND THE LAW: BEHAVIORAL THEORIES OF JUDGMENT AND DECISION MAKING IN LEGAL SCHOLARSHIP.

3.4.2.8 Egocentric Biases

Some people may construe events in a self-serving manner, explaining that successes are due to their efficiency and control whereas failures are merely a matter of bad luck, or other external circumstances that contributed to their gains.

Of course, not only are clients affected by these biases, but their lawyers are, too. Taking their client's lead, lawyers then tend to think of negotiation as an opportunity to not only persuade the opposing party about the predicted value of the cases as a matter of economics, but also to "bias" the decision in their favor by persuading the other side as a matter of psychology. Focus groups and mock trials can greatly aid in this process because they may provide the empirical correction necessary for the biasing effects on the various decision makers.

The problems with lawyers taking a solely economic valuation view of negotiation—discovering expected values at trial in the light of traditional court decisions—are twofold. First, doing so ignores the social psychology inherent in dispute resolution; and second, courts are most often stuck with a win-lose decision. One party wins and one loses. Seldom is the court able to customize a particularized solution to the parties' problem. Those solutions are left to the parties to arrive at both before and after the court reaches its decision, and it is very difficult for a litigator not to think in win-lose, "zero-sum game" terms.

PROBLEM 3.3

Green v. Hall and Rose

You are in negotiations with a real estate broker and her client concerning their refusal of your black client's offer to buy in favor of the offer of a white client. The seller says the white buyer's offer was higher and that she was under no obligation to accept the first bid. The black buyers say that their offer was turned down without their being given an opportunity to counteroffer. They say it is customary and common courtesy to give a buyer the opportunity to raise their offer.

The real estate broker has begun to take the steps necessary to promote better communication of offers between prospective buyers and sellers to ensure that racial discrimination does not take place. Your clients want to make sure that this does not happen again. In addition, your clients want the owner to pay an amount in retribution for the way they were treated.

- What overall strategy should you use in this negotiation?
- What style should you use?

In some circumstances, you must be careful not to come on "too strong," particularly where you expect those with whom you are negotiating to respond in a way that reflects their fear of losing status or control. Under these circumstances, the opposing negotiator may make a "strategic" decision that regardless of the ultimate outcome, she must make a public show of opposition that perception of status or control.

There are psychological issues at work between agent bargainers as well as between clients. To some, these psychological forces overwhelm the analytical ones and make conflict resolution a fundamentally nonrational, if not irrational process. They prefer position-bargaining strategies to deal with social psychological issues. Others would rather use cooperative strategies to provide each side with a better understanding of the other's point of view. They argue that the conflict resolution process depends instead on building trust, which in turn builds a relationship between the parties such that they choose to agree rather than fight.

Furthermore, the adversarial position-bargaining strategies used by lawyers can exacerbate feelings of mistrust and competition.

How this will play out depends on the specific circumstances. Using the *Green* problem above as an example, assume you are negotiating with the broker and use the owner's racist comments to ascribe intentional wrongdoing to the broker. If your only goal is to get the broker to do a better job of communicating with and on behalf of prospective buyers, attributing racist motives to the broker is likely to provoke a deadlock. The injustice of wrongly attributing motive can jeopardize the goal, and problem-solving will be at a premium.

Your client (in this case, the Greens), however, may have other goals in mind besides punishing the broker. They may just want to put the whole issue behind them. Conversely, if the client wants to expose a pattern of behavior, you might make public demands, even though you recognize that in the short term, doing so will make the broker more likely to resist. As with everything associated with negotiation, no one right way exists—there are only choices dictated by the circumstances of the particular negotiation. To add another twist, your history with the broker might be such that you know that regardless of which approach you take, the broker will react aggressively and that ultimately you will have "to go public" to put additional pressure on the broker. It all depends.

3.4.3   Deference toward Authority

In general human interaction, bargainers frequently display considerable deference toward high—or higher—status people by complying with their requests (or threats) or exhibiting other submissive behavior. For example, if you as a supervisor meet a subordinate in the cafeteria and say you would like to meet at 3:00 p.m., the employee likely will come to your office at 3:00 p.m. He will have deferred to a higher authority.

PROBLEM 3.4

In your position at work, what steps can you take to establish that you are the higher authority?

There are a number of things you can do to create the authority or impression of authority in response to Problem 3.4. As you look around your practice setting, what things indicate authority or lack thereof? Titles clearly create a sense of authority. Bankers have long recognized the importance of titles and use the title of vice president quite liberally to create the impression of authority. Are such titles present in your work environment? Compare the title of staff attorney against that of associate general counsel.

Physical environment can also create the impression of authority. Do you negotiate in a cubicle or in a formal conference room? Two very different impressions can result. Similarly, dress can help establish authority. Physicians wear white coats in the hospital even when not performing clinical roles to communicate status and authority.

Perhaps most importantly, what does your negotiating behavior say about your authority? Do you need a supervising attorney to approve every action? Has a supervisor re-evaluated an agreement you have reached, requiring you to seek changes?

3.4.4   Extreme Demands

In negotiations that reach agreement, bargainers generally attain higher and more satisfactory outcomes when they begin with extreme rather than more moderate demands. This makes sense when you recognize that one of the primary problems associated with negotiation is not having sufficient information to evaluate the strength of your position. When you buy a car, you usually do not have sufficient information to know whether your offer is too high or too low. Anyone who has bought a house knows the fear of the seller accepting your first offer and your own reaction or feeling that if they accepted the first offer it must have been too high. We will discuss in detail how to avoid this situation through a systematic approach to negotiation. You should always keep in mind that when in doubt, ask for more rather than less.

Of course, a risk is associated with extreme demands. While an extreme demand may result in more if you reach a settlement, an extreme demand may increase the other side's perception that you are not willing to negotiate seriously and therefore increase the risk of deadlock.

3.4.5   Allowing Yourself to Be Persuaded

Another important social/psychological factor at work in negotiations is that as a bargainer, you want to believe you are capable of shaping the other side's behavior—of causing the other side to choose as you do. Therefore, you might occasionally want to tell the person with whom you are negotiating that they have persuaded you on certain issues. This may create a more favorable relationship between the two of you.

3.4.6 *Promises and Threats*

If a bargainer believes she cannot successfully exert influence in other ways, she may revert to promises and threats. Threats result quite often from a negotiator's frustration and inability to develop more constructive approaches. If you supervise other people, think back to when you have had to threaten disciplinary action if the person did not change their behavior. Most likely, the threat came because you were frustrated by the fact that other, more constructive, actions failed. When you feel the pressure to threaten, or when you are threatened, your first thought should be that the threat is in reality a warning. The threat is a warning that you should redouble efforts to try to find more constructive actions.

The need to find alternative approaches in the face of threats is critical because the use of threats decreases the likelihood of a mutually favorable result. Once again, this is common sense. When you are threatened, what is your usual response? Are you more likely to give in or fight on regardless of the cost?

Merely acknowledging that these things occur is not enough. You must be prepared to identify how likely that are to occur in a particular negotiation and plan how to either use them to your advantage or minimize their impact. Take threats, for example. If you believe the person you will negotiate with will likely use threats and doing so will negatively impact the negotiation, prepare to respond accordingly. To craft an appropriate response, you must ask why people make threats. Typically, they make them because they have nothing else to use to get you to comply. Your first step may be to ensure that the negotiation takes a more principled approach, providing a more meaningful way of discussing problems. Your second step is to deal directly with the threat by figuring out those things that would make a threat effective and then diffusing them. How to do this is discussed in chapter seven, the Exchange.

3.5 Gender Differences

Women who negotiate on a regular basis often report that in negotiations, women are treated differently by men compared to the way their male counterparts are treated. Reports that women are subject to more attempts to intimidate are not uncommon. Women also report that they seem to approach the negotiation differently than men. Is there any truth to these anecdotal reports? Research indicates there may be some truth to these perceptions, though the data are mixed.

Professor Gerald Williams has reported that based on his empirical research, people do not change their approach to negotiation based on the sex of the opposing party.[11] Men who are cooperative in one setting typically are cooperative in all settings. This does not mean, however, that the perceptions reported by so many women are wrong. What this means, Williams theorizes, is that aggressive individuals are aggressive in all settings. Therefore, some men will make sexually demeaning statements to women, such as, "It's a tough world out there, honey, and you better catch up," as a means of intimidation. These are likely the same men who will make intimidating statements to other groups, saying, for example, "When you get a little more experience out here, son, you'll learn this is the way we do it."

On the issue of whether women behave differently in a negotiation, Williams points out that in hundreds of studies on the issue, the evidence is split equally between women behaving differently and women not behaving differently. Among those studies that indicate women behave differently, researchers came to the conclusion that females tend to be more cooperative than males. These same researchers have found that woman tend to be initially more trusting. Other researchers have also found that woman sit closer and generally show more cooperative nonverbal communication. Consistent with these findings is a study that shows that the more women act like stereotypical males, the more credibility they will have with men. Again, however, just as many studies indicate there is no difference.

---

11. GERALD R. WILLIAMS, A LAWYER'S HANDBOOK FOR EFFECTIVE NEGOTIATION AND SETTLEMENT (1981).

CHAPTER FOUR

PREPARING AND PLANNING FOR THE NEGOTIATION INVOLVING THE CLIENT

4.1 In General

Adequately preparing and planning for the negotiation are crucial to success. However, lawyers frequently fail to give preparation and planning adequate attention because of competing demands for their time. Good negotiating practice requires that you take whatever time is available to prepare for the negotiation, even if it is only ten minutes between meetings or ten seconds as you leave your office to talk to a disgruntled staff member.

Obviously, the more time you have, the more you can prepare. Because of discovery, you will frequently have access to a vast array of information about the parties, the events, and the alleged damages well before the face-to-face negotiation begins. In other circumstances, you may not even know the name of the person with whom you are negotiating before she walks in the office door, such as a prosecutor in a large metropolitan area prosecuting eighty shoplifters a day. Even under this latter set of circumstances, you can effectively prepare if you are aware of the stages you must complete in all negotiations.

There are three broad issues you must deal with in preparation and planning. First, you must identify what your client seeks to accomplish from the negotiation and what options are available to you to reach those goals. The adversarial negotiator converts those options into a position which she seeks to convince the other side to accept. For example, the client identifies, with his lawyer's help, the goal of having an income stream to allow the client to live comfortably despite permanent injuries received in an automobile accident. An infinite number of alternative positions ranging from zero to billions of dollars exist on the issue of enough money. The adversarial negotiator, working with the client, identifies the least advantageous alternative along this continuum that the client is willing to accept (e.g., the least she will accept). We typically call this the negotiator's bottom line or walk-away price. The adversarial negotiator will then identify an opening position along this continuum as an opening offer or demand.

A problem-solver is less likely to stake out either a bottom line or an opening position, but she must still identify the client's goals and any potential solutions that will allow these goals to be achieved. For example, a problem-solving lawyer, having identified an income stream as the goal, is likely to see a set amount of money in settlement as merely one possible solution. If providing a certain quality of life is the real goal, lump-sum payments are only one way to meet that goal. Other possibilities are structured settlements or the possibility of money plus training. Rather than immediately focusing on a limited number of positions, the problem-solver will begin thinking of a number of alternative ways to achieve the goal.

The second broad issue you must address in preparation and planning concerns analyzing information to determine not only what you believe to be the other side's goals, but also solutions you believe will meet those goals. The adversarial negotiator asks herself what is the likely position the other side will take and what is their probable bottom line. The problem-solver begins by asking what the other side likely wishes to achieve and what they will likely see as appropriate ways to achieve that goal. To accomplish this task, both types of negotiators must begin assessing the information presently available to them and begin thinking about the additional information they would like to have. To the extent this information is available from sources other than the person with whom you are negotiating, preparation requires obtaining this information.

The third broad task in preparation and planning is to begin deciding how you are going to achieve your goals in the negotiation. The list of decisions can be quite long. The overriding question, however, is quite simple: how can you maximize your success in this negotiation?

If you accept this book's premise—that a systematic approach based on a multi-stage process will allow you to achieve better results—the question then is, what do I do to make my approach effective? At this point, we have a bit of a chicken-and-egg problem because we have not fully identified the stages. It will come as no surprise given the above discussion that gathering information will be critical. We must ask, therefore, what steps do we take to maximize the process of acquiring information?

4.2 Determining Your Client's Needs, Interests, and Desires—The Necessity of Effective Client Counseling

Effective client counseling is critical to effective negotiation. For the adversarial negotiator to determine a bottom line or for the problem-solver to assess needs and to begin developing alternative solutions to the problem being negotiated presupposes: 1) that the client has effectively articulated those goals, and 2) with your help, the client has begun to identify acceptable solutions.

Pre-negotiation counseling typically focuses on a process that moves the client toward at least tentative decisions. Whether those decisions relate to the potential terms of a settlement in a personal injury lawsuit or the ultimate structure of a business arrangement in a transactional negotiation, you must have the client work through at least an elementary decision-making model.

Although there are certainly more sophisticated—or at least more complex—decision-making models, for our purposes a relatively simple model will suffice. Whether intuitively or systematically, what we typically do in working with clients who need to make a decision is to first identify their goal. What do they want to get out of the negotiation? Quite often the client has multiple goals, and he will need to decide which are critical and which he can live without. In *Potter v. Cal Ford* (*see* problem 1.1), for example, the plaintiff's goals may be to deter Ford from making a car that does not adequately protect passengers, to replace the financial support that Katherine provided him during his life, to help him transfer any responsibility he may feel for the accident on to Cal Ford, to get on with his life by being able to both honor the memory of Katherine, but also free him up to start a new relationship with his new-found friend Cheryl. If you represent the plaintiff, you must have Mr. Potter prioritize these goals. He must also consider whether the goals are mutually exclusive.

When helping clients identify the goals they seek to achieve, you must be careful to distinguish their goals from their position in the negotiation. Goals tend to be broader aspirations. For example, Mr. Potter may say his goal is to make Cal Ford and Ford Motor Co., et al, pay him a great deal of money. While this may indeed be a goal, it may also be only a reflection of a position designed to achieve a different, perhaps broader result. After careful discussion, you may find that what Mr. Potter really wants is for Ford Motor Co. to admit that their car was defective and be punished in a way that minimizes the likelihood the behavior (making a poorly made car) will occur again. Mr. Potter's desire for a large amount of money is merely one way of achieving the broader goal.

After goals have been clarified, you must next help the client identify possible solutions to achieve those goals. The range of possible solutions available to Mr. Potter are somewhat limited if the goal is to achieve a large cash settlement. He may have considerably more alternatives if punishment is the goal.

As just stated, after you have identified the broad goal, you next begin identifying options that will allow you to meet those goals. If you focus on a cash settlement, you can identify an infinite number of options ranging from zero to billions of dollars. You and your client will then look at these options in terms of positive and negative consequences.

Certainly one of the most significant types of consequences you can weigh will be the economic consequence of an alternative. Again, take the simple personal injury settlement example where the only issue is dollar amount. You and your client will consider the positive economic consequences of seeking a large settlement—acquiring a large amount of money will make life comfortable for as long as the client lives.

The negative economic consequence of seeking that large settlement may be that first, the demand is unlikely to be successful and second, opposing counsel may not take your position seriously, causing the negotiations to fail before they even get started.

You and your client will consider more than economic consequences, however. Remember our discussion of the social and psychological dynamic in the negotiation in chapter three? These social and psychological pressures affect our decision-making. Therefore, whether intuitively or systematically, you will factor social and psychological consequences into your assessment of the relative merits of options. A positive psychological benefit in seeking the large settlement might be that the client will feel that she is finally on the offense, standing tall, and "not taking it anymore." A negative psychological consequence may be that given the fact that the other side is unlikely to accept the offer, your client will continue to worry about the lawsuit and its related effects on her life. If your client is being pushed by a spouse (or partner), a positive social benefit of the alternative will be that the spouse is not angry with the client's position. On the other hand, a negative social consequence may be that the excessive demand may anger the spouse.

After balancing all the consequences—both positive and negative—you and the client will conclude that at some dollar amount, the negatives outweigh the positives. If you adopt an adversarial approach, your search for a bottom line or walk-away position ends when you find this point. In our example, it may be that the positive consequences of accepting $500,000 outweigh the negatives. At $499,999.99 the negatives may outweigh the positives and, therefore, be unacceptable.

The types of consequences affecting a particular negotiation will vary with the circumstances being negotiated. The economic consequences of a particular settlement will vary greatly. You can, however, identify a number of general categories. First is the direct economic payoff of the particular deal. Will the client be financially better off as a result of this agreement? If you are representing a company in the sale of a major asset, your client will consider such items as the cost of production, value of goods, how much the market will bear, desire to cultivate a relationship with the purchaser, availability of other suppliers, storage costs, and alternate dispositions of the asset.

You may also consider collateral economic factors, such as the cost of agreeing or not agreeing to the sale, or whether the result of this deal will affect your ability to get other deals. If you do agree to a certain economic solution, consider whether the result, if it becomes general knowledge, will cause the next person you negotiate with to expect the same treatment? How about lost work? Will the cost of getting a particular deal take more time than it is worth?

The social and psychological consequences also will vary from deal to deal, but there are some common types of social relationships that you should consider. Not surprisingly, these are similar to those discussed in chapter three.

For example, having to deal with a person on a social level may have an impact on your decision.

This process is as critical to an adversarial negotiator as it is to a problem-solving negotiator. While the problem-solver may not convert options into positions (over which debate proceeds during the negotiation), it is essential that you clarify goals, identify alternatives, and understand various consequences so you can develop creative problem-solving solutions.

In a particular negotiation, of course, your options may be more varied than accepting or rejecting a fungible item like money. Indeed, a problem-solver is likely to only tentatively fill out such a chart, because the problem-solver would expect that as the parties discuss the underlying needs, interests, and desires, they will identify additional options. Still, you may find it useful to begin clarifying the advantages and disadvantages of known options by listing them. Take a look at the example for the plaintiff in a sexual harassment case against a law firm. Assume the plaintiff's name is Newman and the law firm is Popchek, et. al.

Newman

Goals and Options

Goals

Be compensated for economic loss caused by loss of employment at Popchek, et. al., and punish the firm so that it will not happen again.

Option 1

Rehire Newman with credit toward partnership of time since termination, payment of back wages during time of termination, and apology for termination.

Advantages

- Economic damages covered.
- Apology acts as punishment

Disadvantages

- No guarantee that Newman won't be fired in the future or that partnership share will not be adversely affected.
- Apology is private, and there is no guarantee that corrective action will be taken.
- It will be an unpleasant place to spend professional career.

Option 2

Payment of lost wages from date of termination until new employment is found and payment of $100,000 in punitive damages.

Advantages

- Newman continues to receive money with which to carry on search for new meaningful employment.

- $100,000 will have a significant economic impact on firm, encouraging it to take corrective action; at the same time, Newman will have the satisfaction of a clear vindication.

Disadvantages

- Lost "equity" in credit toward partnership at a prestigious law firm.

- Vindication is essentially private, and money does not guarantee corrective action.

Of course, the foregoing is just the tip of the iceberg. In a complex "bet the company" case, you must think strategically about furthering the client's goals and implementing the client's objectives on a wide range of issues. Doing so not only requires that you understand the "end game" if other dispute resolution processes fail, but it also means that you must understand different dispute resolution methods and the strengths and weaknesses of each. For example, you must understand not only negotiation strategy, the ins and outs of mediation, and the pitfalls of arbitration, but also bankruptcy law, intellectual property law, antitrust law, and the companion procedural laws regarding removal, joinder, interpleader, multidistrict litigation, and class actions. Regardless of the process and substantive law setting in which you work, you must always see the process as a means to the client's objectives and be willing to consider switching, when possible, from one process and setting to another if doing so might work better to serve the client's goals. The key, then, is to inform, advise, and involve the client in a choice of dispute resolution processes. Their understanding of these choices will be vital to implementing their goals, as they will often be active players at various stages of each process.

Negotiation theory and practice—and the complementary field of conflict resolution—lay at the heart of each of these frameworks for dispute resolution. They are keys to your understanding of the strategies involved in different dispute resolution processes and settings. This chapter will focus on negotiation and conflict resolution theory, as it informs lawyer-client strategy in every step of the litigation process.

4.2.1 Strategic Perspectives

At the heart of dispute resolution is the management of information—what you give to the other parties and what you get from the other side. Information is the key to accurately evaluating the dispute as well as a vital element of predicting the likely outcome.[1] Understanding how information management affects outcomes will help you strategically plan for the conflict resolution that will best serve your client's goals.

In some ways, then, the litigation process itself (whether finally resolved by the parties themselves or with the help of a mediator or adjudicator) is one big negotiation/information exchange process. The litigation process is the default, and is itself designed so that the parties learn about each other's facts, values, perspectives on law, predictions of outcome; and if the parties do not resolve their dispute for themselves, the court learns about these same facts, values, perspectives on law, and predictions of outcomes and then reaches a decision. In litigation, each side discovers as best it can the other's view of the predicted value of the case in the eyes of the decision-maker, and if there is any overlap, the parties settle. It is a decision-making process that is based on economics, on rationality, and wealth maximization. Settlement is the outcome in more than 95 percent of cases, so the process seems to work pretty well most times. Sometimes parties complain about the expense of getting themselves in a position to determine the value of the case. But still, under the position bargaining model of negotiation, the process is designed to empower the parties to settle when they rationally should settle. Even where the parties resort to a court, the court's decision itself may not finally resolve the dispute, but instead provide the parties with further information and leverage to reach a different and even better settlement that better fits their needs.

It is important to recognize the values inherent in the adversary system. The traditional approach to litigation is premised on the model that better decisions are made if each side must test its information by evidence in front of an unbiased decision-maker. This process is based on the model of a fight, or competitive game, rather than on the basis of a cooperative model bent on getting at the truth. Embedded in the adversarial process is a *position bargaining* model of dispute resolution. The parties not only seek information that will allow them to value their cases, but also hide information of which the other side might take advantage. Each party then determines, from the information they are able to discover, whether there is any overlap between the parties' positions and seeks by threats and persuasion to move the other side closer and closer to its bottom line position, the position at which it would rather take a settlement than risk the uncertain outcome of a trial.

---

1. Gary Williams, Legal Negotiation and Settlement (1983); Bastrass & Harbaugh, Interviewing, Counseling, and Negotiation (1990); *see also* Steven J. Brams Joshua R. Mitts, *Law and Mechanism Design: Procedures to Induce Honest Bargaining*, 68 N.Y.U. Ann. Surv. Am. L. 729 (2013) (discussing asymmetric information).

The parties do not provide information to each other freely.[2] They seek to only inform the other side about those facts that they must turn over because of discovery rules. The adversarial nature of the process is inherent in the rules that dictate the parties' responsibilities in discovery. Information exchange in negotiation also seems to be driven by the assumption that you have uncertain information, at best, about your opponent's weaknesses, and if you settle out of court before putting people under oath at trial, you risk settling for too much (or too little). *Position bargaining* strategies best test what cards the other side actually holds. Your positions serve as bets in the gamble of litigation and *may* inform each side on what cards each holds. Position bargainers use their positions to get information and elicit a willingness to settle. While this exchange often occurs on the courthouse steps, it might also occur after jury selection, opening statements, after the jury has started to deliberate, or even on appeal.

A classic example of position bargaining occurs in a bazaar or market place. Imagine you are at an open-air market in Beijing. You stop at a table and pick up a shirt. The vendor says: "Do you like? For you, special price. One hundred yuan." You say, "Too much." The vendor says, "How much?" You say, "Thirty yuan." The vendor says, "No, how about two shirts for one hundred and fifty yuan." You say, "No, the most I pay is fifty yuan." They say no. You start to walk away. They say, "Fine," and throw the shirt at you. You pay fifty yuan.

Position bargainers use positions to get information about what the other side really thinks. They posture and bluff to try to force movement. They provide little information about why or how they determine the price. We don't know what the buyer wants the shirt for or how much the seller has in mark up or carrying costs. Reasons are not given. The parties think of the exchange as purely voluntary. Each may use psychology and threats and try to raise the sunk costs of each side by dragging out the time of bargaining. They may use the pressure of the public audience to shame the other into moving. But in the end, the process is governed by getting information by taking positions that test what each side thinks the transaction is worth.

4.3 Position Bargaining

4.3.1 An Analytical Economic Model

Assume, for a minute, however, that each side had perfect information about the other side's case. Assume that discovery has been completed and each side has all that it can legally expect to get. Position bargainers still must predict the outcome

---

2. Granted, the Federal Rules of Civil Procedure tries to change this by requiring information exchanges. Still, the risk of discovery is that the other side has not revealed everything, and so the court must test its evidence at trial.

at trial to determine the fair price of resolving the dispute. Every lawyer knows the dangers of prediction. Predicting victory can give the client false expectations, making her spend the money before she gets it. It also subjects the lawyer to the "But you said . . ." from the client when the prediction doesn't come true. Still, the client is entitled to make an informed decision when giving the lawyer settlement authority for negotiation purposes. And the question is whether economic models that use probabilities will provide the useful language of prediction the client needs to make informed decisions. In fact, the question of whether to use probabilities may be moot, because clients seem to be demanding as much. Certainly business clients and/or client insurers want a probability of success to set up reserves. And consumers demand it of their doctors, so why not of their lawyers?

To use economics and probabilities to provide the client with information about what their case is worth, you first need to be clear about what economic modeling and probabilities really provide. The beauty of economic analysis is that for every real world problem that makes prediction impossible, you simply make an assumption. And the result is a "mathematic-like" formula that gives the appearance of a scientific method, or certainty, and of objectivity. Perhaps it gives a false impression. In addition, a second dangerous assumption the economist makes is that jurors are rational. Economists also assume that the litigation process and trial will produce perfect information about a case. The question is whether these assumptions are so false and will so cloud any probabilities that the probabilities will become misleading rather that helpful.

On the other hand, you need to start someplace in communicating your legal assessment of the case, and with these two assumptions in mind, you can start to predict how jurors will likely calculate damages in a given case. Let's give it a try . . . because *analytically and strategically speaking*, we might be able to create a formula that will make us more precise in valuing our case and better able to inform the client about what to expect. The corollary benefits are also substantial. A by-product of making an economic calculation to place a value on the case is that doing so provides more information to the client so the client can truly control the outcome. A second by-product of using economic tools is that you will have more persuasive arguments in your negotiations about what the case is worth as well as the language to move your opponents off their position (provided our reasoning doesn't open up counter arguments to our disadvantage).

As we have said, before actually communicating with the client, you should look at the case from the perspective of the jury or other end-game perspective. First, in a typical tort situation (assuming the jurors have perfect information, as presented through the trial process), the jurors will need to determine the percentage of fault of each party. They then add up the fault attributed to the defendants (depending on joint and several liability rules) and subtract the amount of fault attributed to the plaintiff to come up with percentages of liability. Of course, in a jurisdiction that is not a "pure comparative" jurisdiction, this works. Jurors figuring close cases in "50-percent jurisdictions" (where the plaintiff is barred from recovery where the plaintiff's fault is equal to or greater than the defendants) may lean toward the plaintiff to make sure the plaintiff gets something—at least if they know about the results of finding 49 or 50 percent liability on the part of the plaintiff. Some jurisdictions don't tell the jury.

Second, if the jurors determine there is compensable liability, then they need to figure damages. Damages are made up of three types of damages: first, "hard damages," like 1) past medical expenses in personal injury cases and 2) past lost income figures (loss of business from product disparagement); then "softer damages," including 1) predictions on future medical expenses and 2) future loss of income; and finally, "softest damages," including 1) pain and suffering, or 2) humiliation and mental anguish, or 3) loss of consortium, or 4) loss of "hedonic" damages (e.g. the pleasure of playing the piano), or 5) loss to future trade, and/or 6) punitive damages, which send a message to the defendant and like defendants to deter future behavior.

Third, the jurors will need to multiply the percentage of fault by the total amount of damages found. Or depending on joint and several liability rules, they will simply take the total damages and subtract the percentage of fault attributed to the plaintiff to come up with a figure for damages.

Yet in predicting what the jurors will actually do in such a case, the lawyer knows that there are a lot of "nonrational" factors that the jurors may take into account. The particular judge may exercise a lot of subtle control over the process. Marginally relevant good or bad facts may significantly affect the outcome (like evidence that one of the parties is a saint or that one is not a nice person). The jurors may consciously or subconsciously take race into account—or age, or sex— or may be biased against corporations or angry at institutions and governments that make their lives difficult, especially where injury occurs to protected classes like the elderly, pregnant women, or children. The lawyer on the other side may be a particularly wonderful communicator, having demonstrated talent in bringing in spectacular verdicts for her clients. Finally, the make-up of the jury needs to be considered, as jury verdicts of city/minority jurors tend to give more to some plaintiffs whereas rural or suburban jurors and upper/middle class jurors may give less. Selecting potential jurors from driver's license registration versus voter registration can even make a large difference.

To try and factor these biases into any economic calculation, you may try to determine a multiplier—that amount by which you multiply the "hard" economic damages in the case—to come up with a prediction as to what the jury will do. (These multipliers may be less relevant in commercial litigation where the sympathy factors or the communities' views have less effect when the dispute is between two parties that can take care of themselves. Or maybe they still do play a role, especially depending on the good will that company may have built up because of its community involvement and corporate image.) And so certain jurisdictions try to keep tabs on how much juries give in relation to the "hard" damages in the case. Historically, Philadelphia or New York may have a multiplier of 4.5 to 5. Chesterfield, Virginia, may have a multiplier of 2 to 3. Of course, any given case can and should be distinguished from the average verdicts. And there are definitional problems with multipliers: for example, should future lost income be counted as hard damages in a particular case, or should pain and suffering be greater or lesser when death was imminent. Still, you can use the multiplier as a way of predicting how much over the hard damages the jury might pay in a given jurisdiction.

So, in a given case, you might value a personal injury case as follows:

$30,000 hospital

$60,000 future hospital (dis)*

$50,000 lost wages (+ int)

$500,000 future lost wages (dis)*

Total Special Damages	$640,000
Multiplier 4.5 =	**$2,880,000**

The difference is presumably made up in pain and suffering, emotional distress, and the like.

Further, you need to predict percentage of liability to plaintiff, say 30 percent.

30% of $2,880,000 =	$864,000
Net Damages	**$2,016,000**

Now, assuming that the probability figure is accurate, $2,016,000 is your prediction of the most likely jury damages award.

Or take, for instance, a client who wants to seek a preliminary injunction against product disparagement. Here, the prediction is about what the judge will likely do. The client may show a fall-off in business in the past three months that they can attribute to the alleged disparagement. They might project that if this disparagement continues, it could put them out of business. Assuming that they can show an income statement that shows net profits at $10 million a year, the losses they may show would amount to approximately $100 million over ten years. The chances that they might get an injunction might be 5 percent, but they might be willing to spend $500,000 in litigation costs even if it is only a 5 percent chance of winning.

In a jury case, some attorneys also find it helpful to know the latest percentages of plaintiff success once a case goes to a jury. For example, recent plaintiffs' lawyers quote a 70 percent win rate in front of Los Angeles County juries. Medical malpractice defense lawyers quote recent Center for State Courts statistics showing that doctors who are sued for malpractice win close to 60 percent of the time when the case goes to jury. (In fact, the center's statistics seemed to indicate that plaintiffs have a better chance to win if they try their case before only a judge.) Such percentages can again add information to your case evaluation as long as you realize the predictive nature of these figures and still assess the biasing factors of the individual case.

In a judge-decided case, a particular judge may be known by her track record of never issuing an injunction, and this information may be useful when framing the prediction for the client.

In negotiation, defendants' lawyers like to argue that economically speaking, the rational thing to do is weight each decision the jurors need to make by its probability of landing in plaintiff's favor. So weighing duty as well as weighing breach, proximate cause, and some damages would mathematically result in a better understanding of the probabilities involved. Instead of giving a probability to the chances of winning, they give a probability to each element of the cause of action and multiply them together. For example, if proving a duty existed was .9, breach was .5, proximate cause was .7, and proving some damage was .9, then the probability of plaintiff success would be .2835.

If we take the Popchek example, you would need to view the chance of getting a preliminary injunction in light of the court deciding Popchek's way on four different factors: the likelihood of success on the merits, the balance of harms, the adequate remedy at law, and on public policy issues (competition in the marketplace versus fair competition).

Yet probability weighting could be more sophisticated, but less complicated. In the garden-variety personal injury case, the plaintiff might argue that if breach is proven, then proximate cause and damages are virtual certainties. In the personal injury example above, the probability might be .45 (duty multiplied by breach). Plaintiffs would cite to attitudinal studies that seem to indicate that accountability for one's behavior is the number one value in the United States today (according to *Time Magazine* Poll, Spring, 2000). The thinking would be that the jury would focus in on one tough decision concerning who is responsible—the blameworthiness of the defendant—and then simply do what was required after they made that decision.

In *Jury Trials, The Psychology of Winning Strategy*, Donald Vinson[3] gives some support for plaintiffs' arguments that jurors think deductively from certain strongly held values. This would mean that giving a single probability on liability may be a more accurate predictor. For the purpose of early case evaluation, then, focus groups may provide a quick and most accurate prediction of what attitudes the jurors may have that are outcome determinative, and as a result, best help the lawyer and client assess the case's chance of success before a jury. To create a focus

---

3. Donald E. Vinson, Jury Trials, The Psychology of Winning Strategy, 1–46 (1986).

group, pay $15 an hour to twelve people that meet the demographics of your jury. Present opening statements on both sides, and for under $1,000 you can see where the jurors are likely to come out. Of course, when the focus group has questions and discovery and proof can be obtained, you might be able to refine your theories and themes in the process. In any event, for purposes of telling the client what the case is worth, the focus group could be a good predictor of how the jury might respond to your case. Of course, the credibility of the witness will not be tested, but you will be able to survey the attitudinal values of the likely jurors to determine what the likely result would be.

Similarly, current thinking about preliminary injunctions suggests that judges heavily weigh the balance of harms factor when determining whether to issue a preliminary injunction. Lawyer-conducted probability analysis in injunction cases that under-weighted this factor would not provide the client with an accurate understanding of whether the client should seek an injunction.

In addition, early involvement of damages experts is important for case evaluation. Used as a consulting expert rather than a testifying expert, such consultants can provide invaluable information to help your client value the case and subsequently make decisions.

Moreover, you (and the other side) may use focus group results to help value your case. Just as focus groups test markets and their reactions to products and the marketing of products, so focus groups can provide your client with better empirical evidence of what the case may be worth. If you fairly and objectively present information to the focus group, then it can give you not only insight into how to market your case and what themes will best resonate with jurors, but also information to help you persuade the other side that groups of likely jurors will place high (or low) values based on an "objective" presentation of the case.

Finally, for the purpose of developing settlement authority from the client, you need to calculate three additional economic forces: 1) the expense already incurred and the expense involved in further trial preparation, 2) the expense of the trial itself, and 3) a discount factor until trial. (I'm assuming you have already figured in the discount rate for determining the present value of future income streams. Of course, if your jurisdiction doesn't discount because it reasons that inflation and discount balance out, then don't discount.) With regard to the third point, in some jurisdictions, trial could still be a long way off—although if discovery is completed, as in the typical case, this is not likely a big factor. On the other hand, if payment is going to be made over a significant period of time, as with structure payments, then you need to be familiar with the present-value-of-money calculations to advise the client about settlement authority.

In sum, you would use the following to develop an economic value of a case, which would, in turn, lead to developing client settlement authority: total damages, minus plaintiff's fault; a weighing of this figure on percentage chance of

(handwritten margin note: Lawyer has to figure out prob. of amount per damages)

winning and proving damages as predicted; any discounting for present value; costs yet to be incurred in producing the result; and/or subtraction of contingency fees or other legal fees.

PDL (probability of defendant held liable) × TD (total expected damages) × P (probability of damages finding) – PPCN (probability of plaintiff's contributory negligence) – PPND (probability of plaintiff's damages associated with plaintiff's negligence) – D (discount to present value) – C (costs) – LF (lawyer fee) = Case Value

You can use this formula to help prepare for meetings with the client to discuss the legal and economic consequences of a decision—it will help you more precisely inform the client, and thus help you develop the proper settlement authority. It will also help prepare you to be more persuasive during settlement negotiations.

4.3.2   Client Role in Position Bargaining

In this regard, we must turn to how you will communicate this economic evaluation to your client. Of course, here is where you must be careful. When counseling a client who is the plaintiff, tell her how this figure depends on persuading the jurors (or other decision-maker) about a number of key elements of the case, including duty, breach, proximate cause, and damages. For example, you need to tell the plaintiff that the jurors may see future hospital bills as potentially curing the ailment; or that the chances of the jury attributing 30 percent to the plaintiff depends on the court excluding evidence of plaintiff's drinking because the breathalyzer indicated her BAC was under the legal limit. (Of course, if this fails, the lawyer will wish to keep people who are religiously opposed to drinking off the jury.)

An additional tip for communicating with clients that we'd like to pass on is that some lawyers like to summarize all the variables of prediction by giving a percentage chance of winning. This summary includes giving a best possible alternative, a most likely alternative, a likely alternative, and a worst possible alternative. In our example above, the lawyer might then add two figures in addition to the $2,880,000 best possible, $2,016,000 most likely, and say $100,000 as a likely alternative, as the figure that covers the plaintiff's out of pocket. And that may give something to cover plaintiff's attorney's fees, and $0 as the worst alternative. The plaintiff might even weight these outcomes by percentage.

Best possible	20%	$2,880,000
Most likely	50%	$2,016,000
Likely	30%	$100,000
Worst possible	20%	$0

In any event, your client is armed with substantially better information to make an informed decision, and you know more precisely what you think the case is worth and why. Chapter five discusses how you can use display technology to better explain how you have valued the case as well as help them understand how you view the case and what themes you will employ, but also how the other side views the case.

Moreover, the position bargainers argue that this kind of strategic process makes each side's thinking more objective and analytical. By knowing the limits of their authority and the steps they plan to take to arrive within a reasonable bottom line, the bargainers can better control their own behavior during the negotiation. In fact, at the end of the process, each side's figures should not be that far apart. Experienced, dispassionate business litigators often prepare a valuation from the perspective of the opponent, which allows them to anticipate the points of difference and prepare arguments to overcome those differences. This preparation process makes both lawyers better able to talk with each other and discover the strengths and weaknesses in each other's positions and reach a reasoned agreement. It is often the case that the lawyers work something out, even if on the courthouse steps, after jury voir dire, after opening statement, or after closing argument and before the jury reaches a verdict. Conversely, when the two lawyers fail to properly prepare and communication breaks down, the clients work something out. When this happens, the clients are guessing about outcomes and assessing risks in the light of their views of their business objectives.

Recognize, however, that the rationality of the probability-assigning process depends on the quality of the information each side has. Moreover, the assignment of probabilities is an inherently value-laden process. Creating probabilities depends on experience, but experience is always colored by that which went into developing it. So where a CEO experiences lawsuits by the government, with eyes that see the market as having been harmed by excessive government regulation, the CEO may place a probability figure on the chances of a win based on the CEO's chances at doing something about a broader societal issue. Or the plaintiff (and/or attorney) may demonize the opponent and place probabilities on the outcome at court based on these biasing beliefs. Building in a range of probabilities can at times still provide an analytical basis for reasoned agreement.

Yet position bargainers know that they must plan to conduct the negotiation itself to control the risks in any analytical approach to case valuation. They must test the other side's case to determine how good its information is and whether the values and perceptions of the opposing side so affect the valuation of the case that their client is risking an unfair, disadvantageous resolution. Position bargainers set up the negotiation in a way that helps maximize their advantages in information exchange, bargaining positions, and persuasion.

4.4 Planning for Position Bargaining

In light of the foregoing discussion, consider how you, as a strategic thinker, would plan your litigation with a negotiated settlement in mind, using strictly a position bargaining approach.

4.4.1 Information Exchange

The first step is to determine what style and strategies are most likely to produce the most information without revealing your own. Is it best to be friendly, creating a cooperative competition for information, or is it better to be aggressively adversarial, and control and test information? Your thinking on this issue will help you plan out whether and how to select the forum, conduct icebreaking, assert agenda control, employ appropriate questioning strategies, and prepare blocks that will help maximize an information exchange that will provide access to how the opposing side values their case, the opposing side's weaknesses, and any emotional or psychological factors that may affect case valuation.

4.4.2 Response to Opening Offer

Be careful not to "leak" too much information in a nonverbal manner when the opponent makes an offer. Just like in a game of poker, if you unintentionally reveal interest and acceptance, you tip off the other side to what cards you hold.

4.4.3 Opening Offer

Prepare an opening offer that balances your credibility as a speaker with your position-bargaining strategy of testing the other side's view of their and your case.

4.4.4 Persuasive Statements in Support of Your Positions

Prepare a detailed, multifaceted, appropriately passionate presentation to support your offer. (*Use display technology!*)

Have it build one argument on top of another, and prepare to deliver it with the right emotional fervor.

4.4.5 Plan Your Concessions

Prepare ahead of time the timing of, size of, and decision factors that will give rise to concessions. The most important of these is the size of the concession, because it can signal your bottom line. Make sure to accompany each concession with a reason for your concession. Don't concede twice without your opponent conceding in between—don't bargain against yourself. Note that you can initiate a second concession if your opponent reaches a condition that you have preset.

4.4.6   *Test Your Opponent's Bottom Line*

Know the ethical parameters of persuasion in the context of negotiations. Much has been written about the ethical issues you encounter when discussing a client's bottom line. Recognize that if you ask your opponent, "Do you have authority to move off your last position?" you are putting them in a professional and tactical dilemma. If they have room to move and say no, they risk deadlock and are in a conflict with the authority their client has given them. On the other hand, giving up client confidences about the client's communications to the lawyer about her bottom line is unethical.

4.4.6.1   **Ethical Parameters and Bottom Lines**

Some have argued that negotiators are free to lie if they are asked about their client's willingness to settle. Model Rule 3.4 and Comment 2 to Model Rule 4.1 seem to indicate as much. Take a close look at Model Rules 3.4, 4.1, and comment 2 to 4.1.

MR 3.4 Fairness to Opposing Party and Counsel

—A lawyer shall not: falsify evidence, counsel or assist a witness to testify falsely, or offer an inducement to a witness that is prohibited by law.

MR 4.1 Truthfulness in Statements to Others

—In the course of representing a client a lawyer shall not knowingly

   a) make a false statement of material fact or law to a third person; or

   b) fail to disclose a material fact to a person when disclosure is necessary to avoid assisting in a criminal or fraudulent act by a client, unless disclosure is prohibited by Rule 1.6.

Comment 2. Statements of Fact

—[2] Whether a particular statement should be regarded as one of fact can **depend on the circumstances**. Under the generally accepted conventions in negotiation, certain types of statements ordinarily are not taken as statements of material fact. **Estimates of price or value** placed on the subject of a transaction and a party's **intentions as to an acceptable settlement** of a claim are in this category . . . .

When you ask about your opponent's bottom line (or when they ask you about yours), you have created (or are facing) a dilemma. If you say you do not have authority to move, you may lock yourself in at the expense of settlement. Consider each of the following options:

• Based on what you have told me so far, I can't recommend to my client that she move off the earlier position. (*While you imply you could move, you make the question of whether you will move depend on your being persuaded to move.)*

- You first! Can you move any more off of your earlier position? (*Especially if you made the last concession, fairness seems to require a counteroffer, otherwise you would be "negotiating against yourself."*)

- I've been given broad discretion by my client, but I'm not willing to move based on what I've learned so far. (*Seems to imply that your opponent has not done a very good job persuading you or that you were not listening, so risks a heated response.*)

Others try to manipulate the client's "bottom line" during a negotiation. They may counsel their client to give them only limited authority during the early stages of negotiation, so that they can use their client to slow down the bargaining process and get client input as more is learned about the other side's position.

4.4.7   *Prepare for Deadlock*

One of the problems with deadlock is that you must take the steps to prepare for trial even as you know that there might be other grounds of fruitful discussion that may resolve the dispute. You should plan how to deal with deadlock. Will you walk out or will you stay and bargain hypothetically? With the latter, you and your opponent may brainstorm your way to a creative path to break the deadlock. Or you might take the opportunity presented by the deadlock to bargain like problem-solvers (see discussion below.)

4.4.8   *Wrap-Up*

Prepare to restate the terms of the agreement to be clear that you have a deal on each issue that is important to your client.

4.4.9   *Write-Up*

Plan ahead of time for who will write up the deal. If it's you, save some emotional energy for the write up. Parties can try to add or subtract from what has been agreed to during the write-up stage, so be careful here not to celebrate too early, leaving yourself no reservoir of energy, in case there are still problems with the deal.

4.5   Anticipating Other Side's Bargaining Range

Having identified your client's goals, you must next assess the other side's probable position. Here, as in other parts of the negotiation process, it is useful to place yourself in the position of the other side. If you have gone through a decision-making process described in the previous section, it is possible the other side has as well. With that in mind, assess the available information to judge the likely goals the other side may have as well as the options they are likely to have identified as meeting these goals. Then try to determine the likely positive and negative economic, social, and psychological consequences the other side will perceive.

After you have assessed the available information, the next logical step is to determine what additional information you need and how you can get it. A lot of information is, of course, available through formal and informal discovery. Where you can only get the information from the other side, you must decide how best to acquire that information (*see* chapter six on Information Bargaining).

An adversarial negotiator will find it useful to view the process of determining the other side's bottom line in light of our adversarial versus problem-solving approaches of negotiation. Take for example, the situation described in *Newman v. Popchek and Popchek, Blink & Denis*. The following diagram illustrates the plaintiff's negotiation plan.

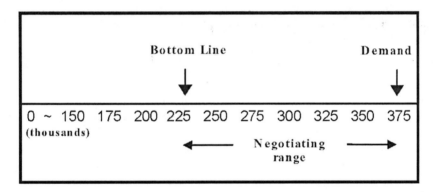

The next step for an adversarial negotiator is to begin gathering and assessing information to recreate the other side's bargaining range. In a perfect world, with perfect information and an idiot on the other side, adversarial negotiation is a process by which you seek information sufficient to judge the other side's bottom line and then offer it to them. Of course, in the real world there is not perfect information, and all other people are not idiots. In our example, you might assume that the opening position of the other side is that no payment will be made. What you are trying to assess is information that will let you decide how far up the scale the person is willing to go. Because you, as an adversarial negotiator, made your decision based on economic, social, and psychological consequences and their relative importance to you, you must seek the same type of information from the other side that will allow you to recreate their decision-making. Graphically, it might be presented as follows:

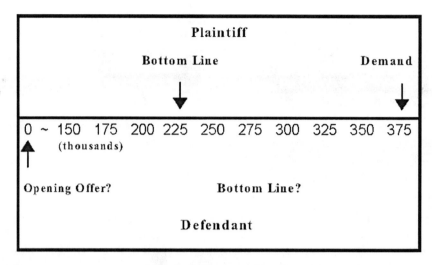

If you are acting as a problem-solver, you will seek and assess the same type of information. Rather than seeking the information to fathom a bottom line, however, you will want the information so you can determine the needs, interests, and desires that the other side needs to meet. If you can identify these needs, interests, and desires (economic, social, and psychological considerations), you can then begin considering and proposing alternative solutions that will satisfy both sides.

As a problem-solver, you will also seek to develop alternative perceptions of the problem so you can create additional proposals. In *Newman*, for example, you would recognize that the plaintiff's demand for $450,000 is merely their proposed solution to what the plaintiff sees as an underlying problem. To address this, you would try to determine the needs, interests, and desires that underlie the position and then engage the other side to jointly formulate a solution that meets those needs, interests, and desires. When, as a problem-solver, you propose a solution, you may well end up rejecting a narrow definition of the issue, such as how much money will be paid, and reformulate the issue to "How do we ensure Ms. Newman's uninterrupted professional development?" or "How do we insure that this doesn't happen to another women associate at the firm?"

As a problem-solver, you will use this approach in a wide variety of circumstances. Assume you are negotiating with a bank on behalf of a business client who is trying to avoid bankruptcy. The bank, quite predictably, may have expressed increasing discomfort with the loan. As a result of the bank's perceived (indeed very real) increased risk, the bank seeks to increase the rate on a line of credit. The adversarial negotiator from the bank will determine the level of risk the bank faces and equating rate with level of risk, determine the minimum rate acceptable to cover the risk while simultaneously trying to determine the maximum rate the customer is likely to pay. Acting as a problem-solver, you might try to recharacterize the negotiation and seek information about the bank's underlying concerns while trying to explain past failures on the part of the client.

In doing so, you might find that while your client's underlying business is quite good, she is unable to exercise competent fiscal management and has a lousy accounting system. You might also find out that these are the bank's expertise, so while the rate may go up, you might be able to minimize the rate increase by agreeing to "purchase" services from the bank that work toward solving the underlying business problem.

4.6   Negotiation Strategy and Client Counseling

Formulating and implementing a problem-solving negotiation strategy is integrally connected to client counseling. If you have chosen a problem-solving approach, you may find that education your client is a challenging process. For example, will Ms. Newman be open to accepting a personal apology in exchange for some amount of the money she would otherwise demand? Would Mr. Potter be willing to accept a contribution from Ford for a Chaired Professorship in Katherine Potter's honor? In a business dispute, would the client want to explore a business solution, such as some discount in the future or joint partnership on new deal? To be the most effective problem-solver, you need the client to buy into taking a more creative problem-solving approach to try to reach an early settlement. You will need a more detailed and complete understanding of the client's goals and values. The better you understand the client, the better you will be able to not only determine a value for the case and the bottom lines for both parties, but also create strategies for building trust and relationships between the parties. In addition, the better you understand the client's goals and values, the better you can discover a more particularized problem-solving solution.[4]

Still, in the real world of lawyer negotiation, no matter how carefully you prepare, the opposition may not want to play. The opposition lawyer may have her own needs for compensation that restrict the discussion of creative solutions that have an impact on her fee. Your opponent may have been directed by her client not to bargain in good faith. Your opponent may use the apparent cooperative setting to block giving truthful information, thus discovering the weaknesses in your case without trading any information and understanding of the weaknesses in her own case. Some even argue that as in the international political arena, it is ineffective if not unethical for a bargainer to worry about anything but her client's (nation's) own interests. Some assert that position-bargaining strategies are a matter of human nature (inherent selfishness)—that human nature requires the negotiator to be suspicious and mistrustful of her opponents and see any attempt to be open and cooperative as a manipulative strategy designed to give her opponent undue leverage in the resolution of the dispute.

---

4. ROBERT H. MNOOKIN, BEYOND WINNING, ch. 7 (2004).

In any event, you need to be cautious when implementing problem-solving models because your opponents may not be bargaining in good faith. It is important to realize, however, the advantages of cooperative problem-solving so you can advise your client about the potential use of a mediator. Moreover, you need to understand these two different strategies and approaches to negotiation—position bargaining and problem-solving—to plan and advise your client about the potential strategic uses of a mediator to help resolve the dispute (*see* chapter nine.)

4.7 Planning to Implement the Negotiation Process

Once you have assessed existing information about the other side's position, you must next address a third area of preparation and planning: what steps should you plan and take to maximize the success of the systematic framework we are trying to implement? Any number of process issues exist. How will you set the agenda? How will you ask questions? When will you make your first offer? Other questions arise that relate to specific stages in the process. Let's look at a few of these issues.

4.7.1 *Your Place or Theirs?*

Where should you conduct the negotiation? This question is instructive because it illustrates that a systematic approach may lead you to a conclusion that is contrary to popular wisdom. Many books on negotiation will tell you to always have the person come to your turf. It creates a psychological advantage for you—they have already made a concession and it puts you in the "power position." Such a rule is, however, inconsistent with the premise of this book—choice is critical.

While you may believe you get a psychological advantage by negotiating in your office, if you concentrate on the issue of information gathering, you will see that the answer is not so clear. Ask yourself: "If information is critical, where am I likely to get the most information—my office or theirs?" Looking at it simply as a question of where information is stored, you will likely get more information at their place. Viewing their surroundings will give you a great deal of information about the substance of the negotiation and the other side's personality. A visit to a potential business partner will give you information about that person or business just from the physical surroundings. For example, something as simple as seeing how busy the office is on a Friday afternoon or the condition of the furniture may give you a sense of the work ethic of the person.

If you want documentary information, going to opposing counsel's office may also make more sense, because he will have a harder time saying, "Gee, I don't have that with me," than if he were in your office. On perhaps a bit more sophisticated level, people are generally more comfortable on their own turf. As their comfort level goes up, people are generally more willing to talk. And because the more they talk, the more information you get, it once again may make sense to meet in their office.

You have to choose, given the particular negotiation, which place is better. In fact, you may decide a third location or via telephone is best. There may be considerations that lead you to negotiate by phone despite some of its obvious disadvantages, such as loss of nonverbal communication and access to other information. If, for example, you are intimidated by the other person, the telephone allows you to place distance between you and that person and to hide your own insecurity.

The above discussion assumes that you are able to control location. In certain circumstances, your only choice will be between doing the negotiation at one location or not negotiating. When your boss calls, you will probably meet wherever the boss wants to meet. Similarly, because of practical considerations of time and distance, you may find that your only choice is between a telephone negotiation and no negotiation at all.

Of course, you have many considerations even with an issue as straightforward as where the negotiation is to take place. Information, although important, is not everything, and you must consider other factors. Among other factors that make negotiating at your place an advantage are:

- your ultimate authority source may be easier to contact;

- you avoid the inconvenience of being removed from other obligations;

- you have the added psychological advantage that the other side came to you;

- you save money and travel time;

- you manage the atmosphere, including being able to control interruptions.

On the other hand, additional advantages of going to the other side's site include:

- you can concentrate fully on the interaction;

- the other side must deal with interruptions.

- it's easier for you to leave someone else's office, than it is to be forced to ask someone to leave yours;

- you can communicate a willingness to work with the individual by going to the trouble of visiting them.

4.7.2 *Determining a Purpose/Developing an Agenda*

How are you going to control the negotiation process? Beyond getting information, you need to ask how much and what kind of information you need? A particular meeting, for example, may simply be a get-acquainted session, where the emphasis will be on developing a relationship. In an international business setting, this may be particularly important (*see* chapter eleven). Acquiring information relevant to a particular agreement might be secondary. On the other hand, the meeting may be one in which you choose to seek as much information as possible about the other side so that you can prepare a detailed proposal to submit at a later time. What you expect to get should in part determine how you structure the negotiation session.

You can also plan how you are going to obtain the information. Are you going to use open-ended or narrow questions? Will you proceed to the point of asking for precise pieces of information or will you stick to generalities?

4.7.3 Determining Personal Attributes to Take into the Negotiation

You can (and should) plan your style for the negotiation. This isn't necessarily disingenuous—we change our personalities quite often in unconscious ways. We act differently at home and at work. Our personalities with a superior may be significantly different from that we display with a co-worker. In a negotiation, you can make these changes consciously to the extent that it fosters your goals. You can choose to be cooperative or adversarial, depending on what you are seeking. You can be open about your feelings or closed. You can communicate a structured approach to interviewing or an unstructured approach. The possibilities are limitless. Here, as with all aspects of the interpersonal process, the idea is to choose to act in a certain manner for a specific purpose.

Related to purposefully displaying certain personality traits is the idea that you are able to plan to play or not play certain roles. Society often defines certain roles for individuals, and you should decide whether playing that role is to your advantage. We know that a lawyer with a large firm in a major metropolitan area may project a public persona that is quite different from one a solo practitioner in a rural area would have. Whether these roles or stereotypes are accurate or not, you can decide whether to conform to that stereotype. A particular person you are negotiating with may react favorably to it, whereas a client may not.

4.7.4 Planning the Setting

The setting of the negotiation is often something that you can plan. We have already discussed location, but if the negotiation is going to take place at your location, you should think about the physical setting. As will be discussed in more detail in chapter six, nonverbal communication can impact the session. For example, how you arrange the furniture arrangement may facilitate or inhibit the exchange of information. Research suggests that in face-to-face meetings, people want some barrier, but not too great, between themselves and the person they are talking to.

If you are sitting behind your desk with the opposing lawyer sitting directly across, you may get less information than if both of you were sitting around a low coffee table. Some psychologists would also say that the absence of any barrier can inhibit communication. Without anything between you, the other person may feel you are invading her "space," increasing her anxiety level to a point where it inhibits communication.

If resources permit, plan the setting to meet some happy medium and have sufficient flexibility to allow for differing personalities you may encounter. The common setup of a sofa and chair at right angles allows the other negotiator to position herself at a comfortable distance. Something as simple as having chairs with wheels may give you the needed flexibility.

4.7.5 Choosing a Strategy

Another important planning decision is whether you are going to be an adversarial negotiator, a problem-solver, or some mix of the two? Will you be competitive, cooperative, or something in between? You should also begin to anticipate the other side's probable strategies. Are they likely to be adversarial negotiators or problem-solvers? Develop intermediate positions short of your bottom line and be able to justify each of those positions. In a non-litigation setting, if you are willing to offer a prospective associate an annual salary of $105,000, would you really prefer $90,000? If so, should you start by offering $75,000? Given what you know about this person, will offering less hurt the long-term relationship?

You should also investigate any controlling principles and determine whether they must or should be followed. Your ability to negotiate may be restricted by statutes, regulations, or rules of professional responsibility. Often you can question conventions that may apply. If you are selling a major asset, purchasers may expect you to set the price. A convention in most purchase and sale settings is that the seller sets the price. You might like to avoid doing this, at least early on, because price always depends on the other side's needs, and you might want more time to assess these needs.

PROBLEM 4.1

Assume you are hiring a new staff member to work in your law office.

- What conventions or controlling principles should you be aware of?

- How might you change these expected conventions?

In the above problem, a convention often at work in the employment setting is that, not surprisingly, the employer sets the salary. If you are hiring someone, you might want to reject this convention if you have insufficient information about the appropriate salary. You may already do this intuitively if you have ever asked someone what their salary needs are. Prospective employers also commonly ask for a salary history before the interview takes place. These are ways you can change a controlling convention that an employer makes the first offer on salary.

4.7.6 *Planning Use of Extra-Negotiation Factors*

Plan how you will use extra-negotiation factors. Can regulators, insurers, arbitrators, or mediators be helpful? For more details, see the discussion in chapter nine on alternate dispute resolution.

4.7.7 *Everything Else*

These implementation issues are examples of the many parts of a negotiation that you must plan. In the chapters that follow, we will identify what you need to do to implement the negotiation, while simultaneously identifying additional areas that require preparation and planning. It may be obvious, but it is still worth saying: if you have to do something in a negotiation, you have to plan how you are going to do it. Thorough preparation requires you to go through each stage of the negotiation and ask *what do I need to do, and how am I going to do it?*

Planning for Adversarial Bargaining	Planning for Problem-Solving
• Carefully determine the weaknesses of your own case and prepare blocking strategies • Gather all the information on not only your opponent's strengths and weaknesses, but "sunk costs" as well • Plan information exchange with pointed and insistent follow-up questions • If blocked, plan to identify block as evidence of weakness and expressly assume the information in your favor • Plan an opening offer that is high enough to risk little in the way of true assessment of your bottom line • Plan a multifaceted, detailed persuasive statement • Plan a dismissive reaction to opponent's opening offer, but probe it for leakage • Plan small concessions to signal little room to move • Plan to use time and deadlock to test opponent's real positions	• Carefully determine the good faith of opponent • Plan opening statement to persuade opponent to problem-solve • Plan to determine level of trust • Is it demonstrated by listening and nonverbal communication? • Has an early recognition of your legitimate claims taken place? • What risks are involved in revealing information too early? • Who will go first? • Revealing and persuading about legitimacy and fairness • Plan opening offers to include needs and goals • Plan questioning of opponents offer to determine underlying needs and goals • Plan processes for determining disputed facts and disputed values • Plan persuasion to brainstorm • Plan to let opponent suggest first alternatives

Planning for Adversarial Bargaining	Planning for Problem-Solving
• Plan to use threats, anger, and irrationality to force movement • Enlist client if producing "false authority"	• Plan objective analysis and perspective—neutral assessment? • Work on the same page • Plan a monitoring of proposed solution

Integrated Planning Approach
Assessment
Combined preparation and planning analysis (trust assessment)
Ice-breaking
Agenda control (assess trust and build it?)
Exchange and Assessment
Information exchange
Proposals offers, demands
Persuasion
Persuasion/justification (multifaceted including interests served)
Concessions/reformulations
Crisis: resolution deadlock (planning bridge to problem-solving)
If deadlock: suggesting objective processes, mediator, either evaluator or neutral
Closing or wrap-up
Memorialization and monitoring

CHAPTER FIVE

OPENING DISCUSSIONS: ICE-BREAKING AND SETTING THE AGENDA

5.1   Ice-Breaking

At the beginning of virtually any interpersonal communication, the participants engage in a process of ice-breaking, which typically involves small talk about non-threatening topics. Every good negotiation should allow appropriate time for this stage. Ice-breaking serves several important purposes. Primarily, it focuses on developing an appropriate relationship with the other side. Small talk at the beginning of the negotiation places the other person more at ease, and as the comfort level increases, the willingness to provide information should increase.

Ice-breaking also provides an opportunity for you to put yourself at ease. Your anxiety level may be higher than normal and talking about nonthreatening topics should help decrease your anxiety.

However, you should not overlook the opportunity to gather information during ice-breaking. The informal chat allows you to gather information that lets you evaluate the other side, view their personality traits, and decide how you can work with them. When you refer to a picture of children on the desk of the person with whom you are negotiating, and that person responds, "Yeah, they're cute kids, but then that's not why we're here," you have received important information about that person's future conduct and desire to set up a pattern of interaction.

And don't forget, the other side will be using the ice-breaking stage to evaluate you.

How much time is necessary for ice-breaking is a reflection of many things. Perhaps the most important of these factors are 1) prior relationship with the person, 2) the time available, and 3) the other person's inclination. Where the parties have had a long-term relationship, the ice-breaking at a particular meeting may be short or even nonexistent. This may merely be a reflection of the fact that ice-breaking has been going on for years and the goals associated with it have been met. In contrast, a new relationship will normally require more time to allow both you and the other person to meet the goals of ice-breaking.

Typically, people naturally fall into some type of ice-breaking or small talk. Too often, however, ice-breaking is ineffective in terms of our goals because it proceeds along the following lines:

Lawyer 1 (L1): Ms. Jones, thanks for coming in today. Did you have any trouble finding the office?

Lawyer 2 (L2): Oh, no, not at all.

L1: Good. I know parking can be kind of difficult around here, especially in the rain.

L2: Yes, I can't believe this weather.

L1: So, how can I help you?

Perhaps the biggest problem with this type of exchange is the topic. These topics are so obviously ice-breaking that the participants never get beyond a stilted "obligatory" exchange that merely provides a transition to the important part of the negotiation. It is the equivalent of the statement, "How are you doing?" as you pass a colleague in the hall. Each knows the other is not at that time really interested in a response to the substance of the question.

To effectively meet our goals for ice-breaking, the discussion must proceed more naturally, covering topics that do not invite a reaction indicating that the participants think it is a mere formality. You might ask what she thinks of a current event, be it sporting event, international incident, or local news story. Having this type of discussion is obviously easier with someone with whom you already have an established relationship. The relationship gives you a common background of information that allows you to pick a topic you can feel comfortable with and that will be both nonthreatening and interesting. A person who has a family can be asked, "How is John doing at college?" If you know someone has been sick, you might ask after that person's health.

In situations where you and other party do not have a preexisting relationship, your goal is to evaluate the information available, however limited, to see if you can find a nonthreatening topic to discuss. When visiting a person's place of business, this is much easier because your presence at the location will give you information. A set of golf clubs or picture of a sailboat on the wall provide ample opening for a discussion related to those activities.

Even the person that comes to your office has provided at least some information from which you can glean a topic. If the person is from a supply company, you might simply state: "I was interested when I heard that you were connected with the XYZ firm. I've always had an interest in ____." Even a person without an appointment brings the fact that they are unannounced, and a good-humored opening might be: "This is what I like about the job—tell me, how did you decide on me?" Or you might choose to be more competitive and put the person on the defensive by saying something like, "I suppose I can make some time available now."

Ice-breaking also provides an opportunity to gather important information in its own right. In other words, an appropriate topic for ice-breaking can also produce important information. For example, a general question of "How's business?", if answered, may give you important information about time, importance of the subject of negotiation, etc.

And finally, if we view the negotiation as a series of interrelated steps, we can determine how ice-breaking facilitates any of the other steps.

PROBLEM 5.1

Assume Lawyer 1 is negotiating with a lawyer who has flown in from a distant city. They have scheduled an early morning meeting, and the following occurs:

L1:   Hello, Mr./Ms. _____. Nice to meet you. How was the flight over?

L2:   Fine.

L1:   Did you just get in?

L2:   Yes.

L1:   Did you have time to check into the hotel yet?

L2:   No.

L1:   Would you like my secretary to call and confirm for you?

L2:   No, not really. Actually I was hoping to wrap this up and get on the road to catch a flight.

L1:   Great. When does your flight leave?

L2:   In about two hours.

What are the advantages of such an exchange?

In Problem 5.1, the Lawyer 1 picked a topic that is appropriate for developing rapport with the person. Asking after their comfort communicates concern for them as individuals and allows them to talk, helping put them at ease. The topic also provides important information that there is a time constraint and that the other lawyer is confident that a resolution will be reached in fairly short order.

This example also illustrates how the approach must be flexible. Having struck on an important point—the time constraint—you might alter the framework, jumping to information bargaining to follow up on this topic. You would continue to ask questions, making sure you understood the extent of the time constraint. But be sure to remember to return and complete the ice-breaking and agenda setting.

In addition to gathering information, ice-breaking provides an opportunity to begin setting the overall strategy and style of the negotiation. In the above example, the lawyer is clearly setting up a cooperative style. A competitive style could as easily be initiated by cutting ice-breaking short or showing a lack of interest in the other person as an individual. As you begin to set your style, you can evaluate the style of the other side during ice-breaking.

Problem 5.1 also gives you a sense of what more you can learn from the evaluation process. Even from the bare transcript, it appears that Lawyer 2 may not be responsive to extended ice-breaking. The short, "yes"/"no" answers may signal her impatience with a process that is not "all business." Or it may communicate that Lawyer 2 may have a "greater need" to use time according to an unspoken set of values, whether it is because they have a child who is sick and they need to attend to, or another case that is pressing, or some other distraction at work that keeps them from being more sociable.

5.2 Agenda Control: What and How You Will Negotiate

At some point, the parties should agree on an agenda for the negotiation. Absent a surprise visit or telephone call, part of the agenda is typically set before the interpersonal contact takes place. In other words, the parties are almost always aware of what they are going to negotiate. The parties may have previously set the agenda by phone, mail, the complaint, indictment, or the like. Even so, someone has to lead the transition from ice-breaking, perhaps by saying, "Well, I guess we're here to discuss the accident (or the merger/the contract/or the like)," and begin discussing the items on the agenda.

In some cases, you may want to amend the agenda based on new information you have acquired: "Thanks for sending me that information. I know we set this meeting up to talk about _____, but as I went through the information, it looked like maybe we should talk a bit about _____. Given what I've seen here, it may help us save some money and give you a better position."

And in certain circumstances, you may be negotiating the terms of a broader negotiation. At the international political level, this can be seen before summit meetings, where countries conduct preliminary negotiations to decide the topics the leaders will actually discuss at the summit. This also occurs in legal contexts—in a merger or acquisition negotiation, the parties may disagree about whether a basic issue is even negotiable. Where the parties sit down to discuss merging personnel policies, the acquiring business may be in such a strong position that it insists that whether the acquired business changes its policy is not a negotiable issue, but only when it will do so. Likewise in many plea negotiations, a guilty plea on at least some criminal charge is a given.

Agreeing how you are to negotiate the issues is as important as agreeing on what to negotiate. Research indicates a correlation between success and ability to control how the negotiation proceeds. This makes sense if you accept the fact that a systematic approach to negotiation results in better settlements. If, as we will discuss, information bargaining must precede making an offer, then the party who ensures that it can information bargain before being forced to make a proposal will likely do better.

Saying you need to control the agenda is one thing, but how do you do it? Perhaps the most obvious way to try to gain control is to simply begin the negotiation the way you want to and assert control. Using the eleven-step process, start ice-breaking, state your agenda, and then start information bargaining, as in the following example:

L1:   That sounds like a great vacation. You must have had fun.

L2:   We sure did.

L1:   Well, we better get down to business. I know you are busy, so I don't want to take up any more time than necessary. I have found that the best way to proceed is if we first make sure we're here to talk about the same thing—the possibility of my client exchanging his testimony against Smith in exchange for a deal on the liquor store charge.

L2:   That's right.

L1:   Good. Then let's do this. I'd like to ask you some questions. Find out a bit about your perspective. After I have had a chance to do that, you can ask me some questions. After I've had a chance to get to know your needs better, then I'll be in a position to see if there is anything we can work out.

Note in this example, defense counsel has basically said that she is 1) going to set the agenda; 2) going to information bargain; and 3) only then going to consider whether a proposal is appropriate. This approach helps you deal with the person who attempts to get you to commit to an offer before you have had a chance to discover important information.

You can use the same approach to decide which issues to negotiate. You might approach an angry lawyer as follows:

L1:   Mr. Smith, Carol tells me there is a problem. Please come to my office.

L2:   I can't believe it!

L1:   Can I get you some coffee?

L2:   No. You can tell me why my client's got ten years' seniority and ends up getting fired while on vacation. This is unacceptable!

L1:   I see you are quite angry. Let's talk about it. Tell me what you believe has happened and let's see if we can figure out a way to get your client to understand what has happened and why.

In this example, the lawyer attempted through ice-breaking to set a more reasonable tone as well as suggest that a problem-solving procedure is appropriate. At the same time, the lawyer has suggested that the issue to be negotiated is how to explain to opposing counsel's client what has happened and why. What the lawyer is trying to keep off the agenda is the employment decision itself.

Controlling the agenda, however, is more than trying to ensure that the process goes through these steps. If you want to be a problem-solver, it means setting the style and keeping it set.

L1:   Charlie, our clients have been working together a long time. And I hear your client wants to reconsider their arrangement, deviate from the terms of the contract. Let's do this. You tell me where your client sees itself in the next few years—what its goals, plans, and desires are. Then let's see how we might meet those needs.

Or in the case of *Newman v. Popchek*, the firm's lawyer might try to cast herself as a mediator:

It's clear that Ms. Newman and Mr. Popchek have had a dispute. It seems that to work out an agreeable compromise we need to design a process to make sure all are treated fairly. That process must sort out what truly happened between the two; what level of intent, negligence, or innocence was involved; and then what each side fairly needs to justly resolve things between them. Why don't we exchange views of what each says happened, and then each can describe what are fair needs that must be dealt with; and finally, let's brainstorm some solutions that might help satisfy as many shared, conflicting, and independent needs that we identify as we can?

Controlling the agenda also involves ensuring that where multiple issues are to be discussed, you control the order in which you discuss the issues. For example, you may want to start with a minor issue. You might concede the issue and then set up a fairness doctrine, that it is now the other person's turn to give something. Negotiating the minor issue might also allow you to 1) establish competence to negotiate, 2) test the other side's preparation, or 3) develop a pattern and practice of agreement.

Controlling the agenda also means recognizing that you can characterize or quantify an issue in a number of ways; then you try to get the other side to accept the favorable characterization. Take as an example the sale of a large asset. In a negotiation with a potential buyer, the actual price can be set using a number of values: depreciation, appreciation, return of investment, need to get rid of the asset, need of the customer to have the asset, appraised value, or some combination of these. Effective agenda control means getting the discussion to proceed using the valuation method most favorable to you—or at least getting the most using the valuation system the other side prefers. To be effective, you must be prepared to argue the appropriateness of each such characterization. You may even be able to show how several of these methods arrive at the same favorable result.

Preliminaries to a negotiation are frequently lost opportunities to lay the groundwork for a successful setting. The above discussion has shown how you can use even the small talk at the start of a negotiation to your advantage as well as how to set and control the agenda. We will next turn to the important information-gathering phase of a negotiation.

Adversarial Approach to Ice-Breaking and Agenda Setting	Problem-Solver Approach to Ice-Breaking and Agenda Setting
• Feigned cooperation and interest to get information about opponent's vulnerabilities	• Genuine interest to develop understanding and a threshold of ethical persuasion
• How's business? (pressure if bad, largess if good)	• Upfront expressions of respect, acknowledgement, and openness to do what is objectively right and fair for everyone
• How's the practice?	
• Going on vacation? (personal deadlines)	• Explanation of benefits of trust, cooperation, and processes of fair, open exchange
• When is your flight?	
• Time constraints?	• Make an early significant concession to demonstrate good faith and demonstrate trust
• Suggest agenda that maximizes control of information exchange one way	
• Block exchange or vulnerabilities by using agenda control techniques	• Design agenda to build trust, use language of needs and goals, and engender creative problem-solving

---

Integrated Approach to Ice-Breaking and Agenda Control

- Cooperative style
- Active listening
- "Strategic ice-breakers" designed to test trust
- Genuine ice-breakers designed to build trust
- Suggestions of problem-solving processes, but agenda control designed to test trust and good faith
- In areas of information risk, suggest agenda of process of verification
- Prepare to shift out of problem-solving to adversarial or vice versa, depending on trust assessment

---

CHAPTER SIX

INFORMATION BARGAINING

Once you have established the agenda, the negotiation typically moves into an exchange of information stage. This stage of the negotiation requires you to ask yourself 1) what information do you need to seek; 2) what information do you want to disclose; and 3) what information do you want to hide? Your decisions on these three questions will have a significant impact the negotiation's outcome.

PROBLEM 6.1

Given what you know about the distinction between problem-solving and adversarial negotiation, can you think of any general distinctions between the two approaches when it comes to deciding what to seek, reveal, or hide?

We will not discuss Problem 6.1 at this point. As you read through this chapter, however, see what distinctions there are.

6.1   What Information Do You Want to Seek?

The adversarial negotiator wants to obtain information that will allow her to determine the other side's bottom line. As we discussed in preparation and planning, the adversarial negotiator seeks to identify information that will allow her to make a reasonable estimate of the other side's bottom line.

The problem-solver wants to have information that will allow him to determine the needs, interests, and desires that he needs to meet. If he can identify these needs, interests, and desires, the problem-solver is in a position to begin considering and proposing alternative solutions that satisfy both sides.

The range of useful information, of course, depends on the issues being negotiated, though they tend to fall into economic, social, and psychological considerations. Of course, use the Internet to see what you can discover about both the opposing client and the lawyer who you will face in the negotiation. Are either on social media, including Facebook, LinkedIn, or Twitter? Have they posted or appeared in any YouTube videos? Do they regularly contribute to special-interest forums?

Up front, it may be important to clear up issues of representation. In *Potter v. Cal Ford*, for example, does counsel for Cal Ford also represent Ford Motor Co.? If Ford Motor Co. is at the table, there might be more resources for settlement, but there may also be more restrictions on the settlement because of how it might attract or impact existing or future litigation. Where discovery is ongoing in a case in federal court (your opponent has complied with obligations to turn over mandatory discovery), it also might be useful to check to ensure you have information about any insurance policies and policy limits that might cover the behavior of the parties.[1]

Other economic factors that might have an impact on settlement include any continuing factors from the incident that may affect employment, whether the person has a new job or is considering a new job offer. For example, in *Newman v. Popchek, Blink & Denis*, the defendants would like to know what the job market is like for someone with Newman's qualifications, whether Newman is able to sustain herself during protracted litigation, and what her long-range plans are. Other factors might include how will she be able to manage her health care in the time between employment. In the areas of social and psychological considerations, there are a number of participant-related factors based on the social psychology of the negotiation process as discussed in chapter three. Among these factors are discussed below.

---

1. Rule 26. Duty to Disclose; General Provisions Governing Discovery

   (a)   Required Disclosures.

      (1) *Initial Disclosure.*

         (A) *In General.* Except as exempted by Rule 26(a)(1)(B) or as otherwise stipulated or ordered by the court, a party must, without awaiting a discovery request, provide to the other parties:

            (i)   the name and, if known, the address and telephone number of each individual likely to have discoverable information—along with the subjects of that information—that the disclosing party may use to support its claims or defenses, unless the use would be solely for impeachment;

            (ii) a copy—or a description by category and location—of all documents, electronically stored information, and tangible things that the disclosing party has in its possession, custody, or control and may use to support its claims or defenses, unless the use would be solely for impeachment;

            (iii) a computation of each category of damages claimed by the disclosing party—who must also make available for inspection and copying as under Rule 34 the documents or other evidentiary material, unless privileged or protected from disclosure, on which each computation is based, including materials bearing on the nature and extent of injuries suffered; and

            (iv) for inspection and copying as under Rule 34, any insurance agreement under which an insurance business may be liable to satisfy all or part of a possible judgment in the action or to indemnify or reimburse for payments made to satisfy the judgment.

6.1.1 Negotiator Experience

Although statistical evidence shows that experience alone does not make one a good negotiator, lack of experience may contribute to deficiencies that the other side can exploit, such as lack of confidence or lack of understanding the value of a particular negotiating chip being discussed.

Your own common experience will confirm this. People new to a job are generally less confident. Statements made to this person, such as, "Well, the way we usually handle this is . . ." can increase this discomfort. When you were new to your job, you may have felt that way. Less experienced people you deal with probably feel that way as well.

PROBLEM 6.2

Assume you are a prosecutor getting ready to meet with a public defender who has just passed the bar. You are going to discuss the possibility of the public defender's client pleading guilty.

- How might an adversarial negotiator use the inexperience of the person with whom they are negotiating to their advantage?

- How might an adversarial negotiator treat this inexperience differently?

- Is there a risk to negotiating with an inexperienced negotiator?

- If you are the inexperienced one, what might you do when dealing with an experienced negotiator?

Looking at the questions raised in Problem 6.2, an adversarial negotiator might decide to exploit the possible inexperience by highlighting her own experience. Occasional use of phrases such as, "Your predecessor always did this," or "As you get more experience, you will see that we usually do it this way," may increase the less experienced lawyer's insecurity. This insecurity may in turn create a willingness to concede when in doubt.

The problem-solver, on the other hand, might view inexperience as an opportunity to educate the other person, persuading them that there is a better approach than staking out positions. Statements such as, "I've found the best way to approach these negotiations is to _____," may be effective.

One of the risk posed by having an inexperienced negotiator on the other side is that insecurity does not equal trust, and trust is what is ultimately required. At some point, the adversarial negotiator is going to offer her bottom line, and she will want the other person to believe it is true. If the negotiator is not at her bottom line, then she may have to make further concessions because she was not believed. Even worse, if the negotiator is at her bottom line, there may be no agreement because the other person thinks she has more to concede.

Lack of trust is a risk for the problem-solver as well. The problem-solver will need to persuade the other side that problem-solving is appropriate and that ultimately a given proposal is the best for everyone concerned.

Another risk is that the inexperienced negotiator will have precisely the opposite reaction to that anticipated. That is to say, her reaction may be: "I'm new to this, and I'd better show I'm tough." Indeed, the social-psychological pressures discussed in chapter three may very well force the inexperienced person to protect herself by being less accommodating.

If you are the inexperienced negotiator, you have to communicate that an attempt to use your inexperience against you will not be effective—just as you would with any other tactic. This might mean you respond to statements like, "This is the way it is usually done," by simply saying, "I'll check that out when I get back to the office." When dealing with particularly heavy handed attempts by your opponent to play-up his experience, you may choose to confront the problem directly: "Let's get serious Charlie, I know you have more experience, but that's not going to get you any place."

6.1.2 Time Constraints

Research indicates that time pressure tends to increase the likelihood of agreement because bargainers reduce their aspirations, demands, and bluffs. This suggests that when you believe the other side is making excessive demands or is inappropriately trying to bluff you, you might try setting a time limit. When dealing with such a person, simply limiting the time you give them can often be effective: "Charlie, I'm glad we were able to meet. Unfortunately, I'm pressed today, and I've got to be at another meeting in thirty minutes."

6.1.3 Authority to Settle

Does the other negotiator have the authority to settle and what are the limits of that authority? When you make a proposal, you need to persuade the other side. But who must you persuade—the person you are dealing with or someone else? If it is someone else, then you need to know who the true decision-maker is so you can find out what is important to her.

Anyone who has bought a car knows how effective it can be to separate the negotiator from the person with the real authority. Any time the salesperson is confronted with an offer from you, they take the offer to the sales manager. Not surprisingly, the salesperson usually comes back saying the sales manager said "no." You ask why, and you get a very ambiguous, "It's just not good enough." You then ask to talk to the sales manager, and the salesperson says that is not possible. If this happens, you should probably walk out. How can you effectively negotiate if you cannot find out what the real decision-maker values?

PROBLEM 6.3

It is easy to overestimate the value of separating yourself from the ultimate authority. While there may be advantages to having the ability to make statements such as, "I'll have to check on that with my people," what are the disadvantages?

The biggest disadvantage in separating yourself from your authority is illustrated by your reaction when the tactic is used against you. Your normal reaction would be: "Why aren't you negotiating with the person with authority?" Or worse, you might see it as a bald attempt to manipulate you.

And remember, if you use such tactics, you can seriously affect your credibility. If you constantly refer to a higher authority, your own similar statements may be less credible: "Why should I believe you now, when on other important issues you said you had to check with your boss?" Likewise, repeated references to a need to check with someone else will often result in the other side stepped up its pressure to speak directly to that authority.

6.1.4 *Work Load of Other Side*

Is the other negotiator so overworked that he has an incentive to resolve the matter quickly?

6.1.5 *Who and How Paid*

Does the other negotiator get a direct reward for this negotiation, and if so, how is it determined? Is the attorney on the staff of the entity or person he represents, or has he been hired on an hourly basis? Is he motivated to resolve the matter quickly to avoid additional expense?

In a nonlegal matter, are you negotiating with a salesperson? If so, is she on commission? Can you find out whether the commission is based strictly on individual sales or does the commission depend on when the sale takes place? For example, salespeople sometimes earn a higher commission for a certain level of total sales within a period, such as a quarter. Would your particular sale move the salesperson up to a higher commission?

6.1.5.1 Motivation or Desire to Be a Problem-Solver or an Adversarial Bargainer

We have discussed how the strategy the parties choose can affect the nature of the negotiation. Which strategy is the other negotiator likely to take: adversarial, problem-solving, or some combination of the two?

6.2 Where to Get Information

Now that you have decided what information you want, the question then becomes how do you gather that information. First, remember that because of the information's critical role, you should obtain it from anywhere, at any time, from any source. One value of viewing the negotiation process as a series of interrelated stages is that although doing so emphasizing that certain things are done at certain points in the negotiation, it also suggests that fruitful opportunities to meet the goals of one stage may present themselves in other stages. Ice-breaking is a perfect example of a stage in which you can facilitate information bargaining. Topics that might be appropriate to discuss during ice-breaking may well be inappropriate at a later time.

Imagine that you have to schedule a negotiation session. It is summer time, and you either call the person or see him at some social function. You might take the opportunity to not only work on the relationship, but also gather some important information. The conversation might go like this:

> L1:   Charlie, it's good to see you. I'm sorry I haven't gotten back to you. Your call came in while I was on vacation.

> Charlie: Did you have a good time?

> L1:   Great time. Went to the beach. Back now and ready to go. How about you? Any vacation plans?

> Charlie: Yes. We're taking the family to the beach ourselves.

> L1:   Great. Where do you go?

> Charlie: Got a place down on Long Beach. Spend a couple weeks each year down there. Sort of a family tradition. My folks come down. We have a real good time.

> L1:   Sounds like fun. When you heading out?

> Charlie: Week from Friday.

In this brief interchange, the lawyer has discovered information that he can use to facilitate the negotiation. The adversarial negotiator might use this information to schedule the negotiation just before the planned vacation, on the theory that Charlie would probably want this resolved before he leaves so it does not worry him during vacation. The problem-solver, however, might use this information to set the appropriate relationship and to develop trust by saying, "Well, let's not let our business interfere with your trip. What would be best for you, meeting before or after your vacation?"

In addition to deciding where to get information, you should consider the wide array of sources of information. Sources of information can be categorized as indirect or direct and as discussed in section 6.9 as verbal or nonverbal.

6.2.1 Indirect

An indirect source is any source other than the person with whom you are negotiating. A wide range of possible sources exist, depending on the particular negotiation. If you visit the opposing counsel's office indirectly, i.e., on some errand that does not involve your opponent directly, you can gain valuable information just by viewing the office. In *Newman v. Popchek*, the plaintiff's lawyer may be able to find out how highly Popchek, Blink & Denis values its reputation by asking other lawyers or law firms. If a site visit isn't practical, periodicals as common as the daily newspaper may contain financial information about the firm.

Certain information must, of necessity, be obtained indirectly. Take the purchase of a car. Perhaps the most important piece of information that you as a car purchaser can have is the car's actual cost to the dealer. Once you know this, you are in a much stronger position to make an offer. You will probably not get this information directly from the car dealer, but you can obtain it from an indirect source such as one of the many consumer-oriented magazines or books, bank "blue books," (resources that tell banks about car values so they can make loans), or Internet resources like CarFax.com.

6.2.2 Direct

Direct methods involve gathering information directly from the person with whom you are negotiating. The most obvious direct source are the statements made by the person with whom you are negotiating. Documentary material, of course, can be just as critical in many negotiation situations.

6.3 How to Get Information in General

In the context of the give and take of negotiation, you cannot underestimate the importance of gathering information face-to-face. The most common way to get the information is to ask for it. The techniques you use to ask for information during a negotiation are fundamentally the same as those you use whenever your goal is to acquire information.

6.4 Types of Questions

As with negotiation in general, information bargaining can be more effective if you approach it systematically. To develop a systematic approach to asking appropriate questions in a negotiation, you must understand the various types of questions.

One way to categorize questions is by who selects the topic of the question—the questioner or the questioned. In general, questions categorized in this way are of four types: open-ended, narrow, "yes"/"no," and leading. Which type of question you ask should result in different amounts of information being given, both in terms of quantity and quality of information. As with most aspects of interpersonal skills, there is no one correct type of question to ask. Each type of question has its own advantages and disadvantages. By looking at these various advantages and disadvantages, however, you can derive some general principles or suggestions for appropriate questioning.

6.4.1 Open-Ended Questions

An open-ended question allows the person questioned to select the topic and to discuss what she believes is important about that topic. A classic open-ended question would be, "Tell me, what's on your mind?" or "Can you tell me about your plans?" or "What are your client's goals in this deal (or litigation)?"

Open-ended questions have several advantages. First, and perhaps most importantly, open-ended questions normally get you the most information. Open-ended questions invite the person questioned to talk about whatever is of concern, without restrictions on the topic or limitations on length of response. When combined with good active-listening skills (discussed below), the open-ended question maximizes your acquisition of information.

Because the person is encouraged to talk, open-ended questions also will normally increase the likelihood that the negotiators will develop a good rapport. The fact that you are willing to listen should communicate your interest and your understanding, thus allowing you to more effectively develop a good working relationship with the other person.

Another major advantage of open-ended questions is that they encourage the other person to identify the important agenda items. Whenever you are negotiating with someone, you will usually have a list of topics that you feel are important and need to be explored. If you use an open-ended question before you turn to your own topics, you will increase the possibility that you will find out what is important to the other person. You can then compare what is important to you and what is important to the other person and structure further questions accordingly.

Getting the other person to raise topics can be particularly helpful if you need to explore sensitive items. For example, if you are trying to negotiate the agreement to merge two companies, the scenario might work out as follows:

L1:   Let's talk about your needs.

L2:   Well, they haven't changed much since we last talked. Independence is still critical. The support you folks can provide our company doesn't outweigh the inconvenience of an extra administrative layer we don't want. Central administrations can be lousy in the best of circumstances.

L1:   Anything else?

L2:   Well, to be honest, we need to protect the senior management.

L1:   What else?

The other person has raised the issue that senior staff may be a problem, thus making it easier for you at some later point to come back and say, "You mentioned the senior staff. Tell me more."

PROBLEM 6.4

Imagine you are going to interview a person to find out as much about their employment as possible.

Imagine you are limited to asking questions that can be answered "yes" or "no." What questions would you ask? What difficulties would you anticipate for this task?

Now imagine you can ask any questions you like. What questions would you ask?

Problem 6.4 provides a useful exercise that illustrates the importance of open-ended questions. Take sixty seconds and interview someone about their employment using only questions that can be answered "yes" or "no." The exchange might go something like this:

Q: Do you fix things?

A: No.

Q: Do you make things?

A: No.

Q: Do you provide a service?

A: Yes.

Q: Are you a doctor?

A: No.

Q: Are you a banker?

A: No.

Q: Are you a dentist?

A: No.

Q: Are you a lawyer?

A: Yes.

Q: Do you do criminal work?

A: No.

Q: Do you do civil litigation?

A: No.

Q: Do you do transactional work?

A: No.

The questioning could go on forever, and you still might not get the information you need. "Yes" or "no" questions require you to think of every possible piece of information that may be important—a task that is impossible for most people. In this interview example, you need to be able to conceive of every possible variation on employment to be sure that you have all the information. Even when you get a "yes" for an answer, the task simply presents an infinite number of new questions:

Q: Are you employed?

A: Yes.

Q: Have you been employed for more than a year?

A: Yes.

Q: Have you been employed for more than two years in your current job?

A: Yes.

The logical approach, of course, is to ask an open-ended question. Not only will you get more information, you may get information you would never have thought to ask about. Ask your partner open-ended questions, and what is likely to happen?

Q: Tell me about your job, would you?

A: Well, I'm a law professor at Emory University School of Law, and I have been in law teaching for the past thirty-five years.

Q: Tell me more.

Nonetheless, open-ended questions also present several disadvantages. Because the person is free to discuss anything, you may get a large amount of irrelevant information. The amount of irrelevant information may be particularly large if the person has brought any psychological needs, such as venting anger. The irrelevant information may also be so great that the person's response becomes unduly long and diffuse. On the other hand, the time and effort you put into open-ended questioning may pay off in the form of a better rapport. Further, it should be obvious that you only know information is irrelevant after hearing it. In the midst of a great deal of irrelevant information, you may also find one important piece of information.

A final disadvantage to open-ended questioning is that because it is general in nature, it allows the person answering more flexibility to avoid questions. As a result, you may need to follow up with more direct questions.

6.4.2   Narrow Questions

A narrow question is one in which the questioner selects not only the general subject matter, but also which aspect of the subject matter will be discussed. In our interview example in Problem 6.4, a narrow question would be: "What courses do you teach?" The biggest advantage of this type of question is that because it is more specifically focused, it increases the likelihood that the questioner will only receive relevant information. Assuming the person questioned is cooperative and not seeking to avoid giving information, a narrow question elicits a higher percentage of relevant information in response.

The disadvantage of a narrow question, however, is that the total amount of information received will be less than with an open-ended question. Narrow questions provide much less opportunity for the other person to raise topics, and thus, if you does not question on a particular topic, that topic may not get raised. All you are likely to receive in response to the previous question is information about the other courses taught, whereas in our open-ended question we may get additional information. Further, for you to gather complete information using narrow questions, you must have sufficient knowledge of all relevant areas of inquiry.

In terms of developing a rapport with the other person, a narrow question may work either as an advantage or a disadvantage. To the person seeking a sympathetic ear, the narrow question provides less opportunity to meet his psychological needs. To lawyers in a hurry, however, the narrow question may be a more efficient use of limited time.

6.4.3   "Yes" or "No" and Leading Questions

Questions that can be answered "yes" or "no" have the advantage of producing high-quality, accurate information (assuming the person questioned is truthful). However, as pointed out with open-ended questions, this accuracy comes at the expense of reducing the quantity of information.

> "Yes" or "no" questions can also be characterized as being direct and consequently are usually more threatening than more open-ended questions. To certain people, this will harm rapport development, increasing anxiety or communicating a perceived lack of "personal interest" on the part of the person asking the questions.

Finally, leading questions are an extreme form of "yes" or "no" questions that suggest the answer to the question. The questioner asks, for example, "You're looking for a settlement structure that provides Ms. Newman with a stream of income until she can get a new job, right?" As with "yes" or "no" questions, assuming the person questioned is truthful, the quality of information is quite high. Leading questions have, however, all of the disadvantages of "yes" or "no" questions with the additional problem that they make it easier for you to be misled. To the extent that you indicate to the person what an appropriate response would be, the quality of information you receive may actually decrease because you are hearing what the person believes you want to hear, not necessarily the truth as seen by that person.

6.5   The Funnel Approach to Questioning

The four types of questions discussed above form a continuum, going from open ended to narrow. If we view the advantages of each of the question types, we see that certain questions are appropriate for different circumstances. The good questioner uses each type of question when it is appropriate, given the particular advantages of the individual question type. Indeed, it is possible to view fact-gathering as starting at either end of a continuum, running from open-ended questions and working toward leading questions.

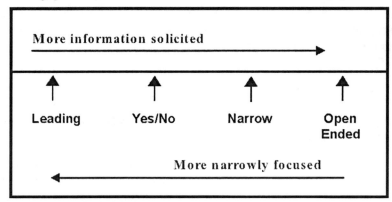

Moving either from leading to open-ended or open-ended to leading questions, the questioner uses all four types, thus taking advantage of each type of question.

Going from open-ended to leading questions is referred to as a funnel approach. As a general rule, most experts recommend using the funnel approach when you want to systematically gather as much information as possible.

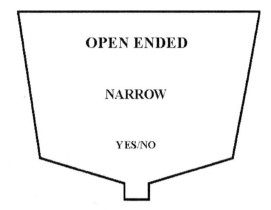

Because open-ended, general questions help develop rapport, and a good relationship is something that you usually want to have throughout the negotiation, the funnel approach seems most appropriate. If you want to systematically approach information gathering, you need to identify the important topics early in the process. Open-ended questions help you do that. Remember narrower, more specific questions burden the questioner with be forced to think of the general topic in the first place. If you want to encourage the other person to suggest information that you might not cover, the time to do so is at the beginning of the negotiation in response to open-ended questions.

The advantage of starting with open-ended questions is apparent in light of the risks of narrow questions. If you first cover all the topics you think are important, turning to the other person and asking, "Can you think of anything else?" may be futile. Changing to open-ended questions at the end may not work for two reasons. First, because you have already extensively discussed various topics, the other person may not be motivated to suggest additional topics.

A second and related problem is that questioners "train" people to respond appropriately. If you start out asking "yes" or "no" question, you subtly tell the person answering that her appropriate role is to provide brief, concise answers. When you later ask an open-ended question, the person answering, having played this role throughout the exchange, is unlikely to respond openly. On the other hand, a person you have "trained" to respond to open-ended questions is more likely to keep providing lots of information throughout the exchange.

Also remember that narrower, more specific questions, such as "Is Ms. Newman looking for work?" or "Why hasn't she found a new job?" are more threatening, and if you ask these type of questions too soon, you may hurt the rapport that you, as a cooperative negotiator, are seeking to achieve. Also, on a practical level, if you remember the specific question early in the interview, you likely will remember it at the end of the interview as well, so you lose little by putting the question off and you gain much by having patience.

Typical open-ended questioning, starting a funnel approach, might be as follows. The questioning lawyer (L1) represents Popchek, Blink & Denis:

L1: Will you bring me up to date about Ms. Newman?

L2: Well, she's not happy.

L1: Why don't you tell me about it?

L2: I don't see the necessity, you've gotten discovery.

L1: I'd certainly like to find out where she is today, tell me what you think I need to know to get this thing settled.

L2: It's what we've been talking about all along. Her reputation is damaged, she's lost income, her future earning power has been impaired, she's very angry, and—justifiably—she's hurt.

L1: Anything else?

L2: Yes. She wants PB&D punished.

L1: Good. I'd like to talk to you about each of those. I, of course, have some questions myself for you and Ms. Newman.

Ms. Newman's representative's reaction to the open-ended question, "Will you bring me up to date about Ms. Newman?" is "She's not happy," which is a great example of a type of block called "over-answering" the question. It provides so much information that it doesn't reveal anything that can be used as leverage.[2] The good negotiator, however, will attempt to keep the questioning open-ended and try a different, though still open-ended question: "Why don't you tell me about it?" Here, Ms. Newman's representative opens up, and gives what we see as the common response of people to open-ended questions—lists. With a few questions, the lawyer has elicited a "gush" from the person that contains what appear to be the most important topics they will need to discuss.

The lawyer is now in a position to evaluate what the person has told her. Perhaps more importantly in light of the topics mentioned, the lawyer can begin to systematically explore not only the topics she has brought to the negotiation, but the new topics introduced by the other side. She can now better decide which topics are important to discuss, how to discuss them, and in what order.

Having done so in your own negotiation, you now can now choose whether to first discuss items mentioned by the other person, items on your own agenda, or items that appear important to both sides. If developing a rapport remains a primary consideration, you may, for example, prefer to benefit the other side by meeting his needs first. You can then exhaust each topic, in turn, using the funnel technique.

---

2. We will discuss more blocking techniques in section 6.6.

Once you decide which topics to discuss, you should next narrow the inquiry by going to that topic and asking narrower, though still quite open-ended, questions. In reality, then, our funnel analogy is really more accurately described as funnels within funnels. Each new topic creates the beginning of a new funnel of inquiry.

OPEN ENDED QUESTION

To illustrate this further, assume you are meeting with the lawyer of a company that is interested in purchasing a business owned by your client. The purchasing company is new to you, and you feel you need to get a great deal of detailed information before your client is prepared to even consider doing business with them. The meeting might proceed as follows:

Q: Good afternoon. I'd like to talk to you about doing business. I, of course, have some questions about you and your company. Would you tell me about the company?

A: Well, we are just expanding into this state. We've seen steady growth over the past few years and find ourselves well positioned to expand.

Q: Tell me more.

A: We're family owned. Mr. Duffy's father started the company back in 1950. Duffy senior died about ten years ago, and the son took over.

Q: What else?

A: I'm not sure what you mean?

Q: Tell me some more about the company.

Note here that the lawyer is trying to keep the questions open-ended as long as feasible. At some point, the person questioned may balk at the approach and the lawyer might need to begin narrowing the questions.

A: Not much else to say.

Q: Tell me about its size, level of sales, that type of thing.

A: As I said, we're growing. We sell to about 50 percent of the hospitals in the tri-state area. Mostly private hospitals.

Once the person no longer gushes, the lawyer might narrow the questions by raising additional topics in question form:

Q: What type of products?

Q: Service support?

Q: How about inventory?

Q: Tell me about yourself.

These questions are really just topics the lawyer feels are important, but were not raised by the potential purchaser's lawyer in the gush. Again, however, you should try to keep it as open ended as possible. If your goal is to acquire as much information as possible, the next step is to pick one of these topics and ask about it in an open-ended way.

Q: Awhile back, you mentioned you sell to about 50 percent of the hospitals in the tri-state area. Tell me more about that.

Here, the lawyer has picked a topic and has begun discussion with a good open-ended question that should maximize information he gets. Additional topics should present themselves, and the lawyer can choose which are most important to follow up, seeking more and more specific information, or which can be set aside for later discussion. Indeed, the lawyer may choose to address an entirely new topic, feeling that he needs a more general overview, and later return to this topic to "complete the funnel."

To complete your systematic exploration of this topic, or any other topic, you will need to pose progressively narrower questions. Continuing our example, here is a series of questions that might follow the earlier questions:

Q: You've mentioned inventory—tell me about your suppliers.

Q: Who are they?

Q: Tell me about your relationship with them.

Q: Tell me about the financial arrangements.

Q: What are the regular trade terms offered to the company?

Q: Are there any special terms involved?

Q: Are discounts taken?

Q: Are payments prompt?

Q: Are any items in dispute?

Q: Are contracts or franchises involved?

Q: Tell me about those.

Q: When does it (the contract or franchise) expire?

When you have fully explored the topic—or again choose to hold off on this level of detail at this time—you choose a new topic and work the funnel:

Q: You mentioned the manufacturing and retail sides; why don't you tell me something about the company's plant and equipment?

Necessary follow-up questions (in order of progressing narrowness) may include:

Q: Are the facilities owned or leased?

Q: Who owns the leases?

Q: What are the lease terms?

Q: Any options?

Q: Where is the facility located?

Q: Single purpose or multi-use?

Q: Tell me about its operating capacity.

Q: Is the capacity sufficient for future needs?

Q: Anything else you can tell me about the facility?

Now that you have gone through the information in considerable detail, the next stage is to view the information you have gathered and seek precise details that may not have been mentioned. At this stage, various pre-printed forms are particularly valuable. Also, direct questions, such as those involving costs or discounts that are perhaps too threatening at the beginning of the negotiation, are less likely to adversely affect the interview.

Using the techniques discussed here during a negotiation raise a number of complicating factors. Most obviously, the person on the other side may not be as cooperative as you would like. You might ask the perfect open-ended question, and he may give you short answers. Also, your attempt to get the gush may get you only one topic before you are asked to answer a question. The fact that both sides are seeking information is, of course, why we call it information bargaining. What you must keep in mind, however, is that although the gush may take multiple questions and trickle out in what is difficult to see as a gush, you should make every attempt to keep the inquiry as open-ended as possible until you are comfortable that all the important topics are on the table. Spending time eliciting the gush, even when it comes out in a trickle and requires a number of questions and is interrupted by your having to answer the other side's questions, is nonetheless critical.

One of the other main difficulties with open-ended questions is that they can be time consuming, and in the real world you may not have the luxury of a complete funnel approach. Your initial open-ended questions, however, remain critical. The gush sets up the solution to the problem that it takes too much time. Where time is limited, the gush is critical because it provides you with the list of topics on which to spend your limited time.

PROBLEM 6.5

Refer to the example of the acquisition of a new business deal with a series of related, though separate topics (e.g., management, inventory, etc.). Quite often, the circumstances surrounding your negotiation involve some prior transaction or occurrence. Rather than a series of topics, you need to explore the chronological event. For example, your client may be having difficulty getting a subcontractor to comply with a contractual obligation or the contractor may be trying to renegotiate the completion of the contractual obligation.

What is the funnel approach equivalent when dealing with a chronological problem?

An open-ended question that might be appropriate for a chronologically based negotiation is illustrated by the following example:

Q: I understand you are having some recent difficulties. Why don't you start at the beginning and take me step-by-step through the problem?

A: I'm not sure what you mean.

Q: Well, why don't you start at the point when you began the project and take me step-by-step through what happened?

During this stage, if you want the person to proceed with a chronology, the next appropriate question may simply be, "Then what happened?" Each event mentioned is the equivalent of the funnel within the funnel. You can begin exploring individual parts of the chronology with such questions as: "You mentioned that on September 5 you talked to the bank. Will you tell me about that?"

Many lawyers have gone to negotiations to resolve litigation that has been going on for years, with massive discovery, and asked only specific questions, only to find out later that the other party had undergone financial setbacks and was on the brink of bankruptcy. Never assume that facts have not changed. A good open-ended question such as, "Bring me up to date," may save you frustration and embarrassment later.

6.6   Information You Do Not Want to Reveal

If you are asked a question during negotiation that you would prefer not answering, you have three choices: tell the truth, avoid the question, or lie. Regardless of other considerations, whichever you choose to do, do it affirmatively. Few people will debate that it is inappropriate to lie in a negotiation. While there may be short-term benefits given the importance of information, lying can ruin your reputation, hurt your credibility, and destroy any long-term relationship you hope to have (not to mention that you may have committed fraud).

Revealing the information may be the best course. If you choose to do so, do not hesitate. Do it affirmatively. If you are going to be honest about telling the truth, you might as well get the full benefit from it.

Assume PB&D's lawyer initiated the following exchange:

Q: Does Ms. Newman intend to continue the practice of law?

A: Well, uh . . . she has a number of options.

Q: But are there other specific possibilities that she is looking into?

A: Well, she's considering the AG's office.

Here, Ms. Newman's representative ultimately reveals the information without much struggle, but it appears grudging. The truth comes out, but the lawyer loses credibility because it appears he tried to avoid giving the information. If the information is going to come out, get the benefit of communicating your honesty and forthrightness by stating it affirmatively and then putting the proper spin on the information. For example:

Q: Does Ms. Newman intend to continue the practice of law?

A: Her reputation has been so damaged by your clients that her ability to obtain comparable employment in the practice of law is severely limited. She is therefore considering mitigating the damage by going into the public sector.

Short of lying, you may choose to avoid revealing the information by blocking or fending off the question. There are standard blocks used to fend off questions.

Take the question from a prospective employee: "What's your standard salary package for new staff?" One type of block is to leave the questioner with the assumption that the question was answered:

> A: We've never had an arrangement quite like this. You can't really say we have a standard package.

A second type of block is to narrow the focus of the question, in this instance perhaps focusing on the word "standard."

> A: We really don't have a standard package because each staff member is treated as an individual. That's the kind of hospital we pride ourselves on being. Now, I guess what I'd like to hear from you is . . . .

A third type of block is to restate the question to your liking.

> A: You mean is there a salary package that we always provide no matter who the staff member is and what the relationship is like? We don't have one. Now, I guess what I'd like to hear from you is . . . .

A fourth block is to destroy the desire for follow-up questions:

> A: You mean is there a package we always establish no matter who the staff member is and what the relationship is like? Of course not. For example, let's take a person with ten years' experience with a major metropolitan hospital, already living in the area, with the ability to start immediately. That person is quite different from the person with limited experience and the need to provide strong supervision and advanced training. Now, I guess what I'd like to hear from you is . . . .

A fifth block we've already mentioned—over-answering the question:

> A: Our standard package is to treat each individually as fairly as possible in light of their particular circumstances.

A final common block is simply to answer the question that was asked, thereby "under-answering" the broader question implicit in the question asked. Too often the question is imprecise, not really asking for the information intended. Nevertheless, the person being questioned hears the question, realizes the intent behind it, and usually answers what was intended, rather than what was actually asked. In our example, the person asked what the employer offered as a standard package for new staff. The prospective employee probably intended to ask something like, "Given what you already know about me and my experience, what are you prepared to offer me in terms of a specific package?" That is a tough question to avoid. However, what the prospective employee actually asked was, what is the standard package? An effective block to this imprecise question may be simply to answer the question asked, not the question that was intended to be asked: "We don't have a standard one."

To be effective, you must affirmatively state the block and then follow up with a question of your own. This way, you shift the initiative from the questioner and avoid his follow-up questions.

The real risk of blocks is that if the questioner perceives it as a block, you have effectively communicated that you are hiding harmful information. While the questioner may not have the specific information, the person will realize that you would have revealed it if it helped you. Added to this, the questioner may begin to question your credibility. Use blocks carefully.

As with all aspects of negotiation, you must view the use of blocks not only from your perspective, but also from the perspective of the other person. In other words, whether or not you use blocks, the other person might, and you should be aware of them. You must train yourself not only to listen for the substance of the answer to your question, but also to determine whether or not the answer is responsive. If the answer is not responsive, it may be a block.

If we look at the standard types of blocks in the *Newman* negotiation, you might ask: "Does Newman intend to continue to practice law?" The range of blocks might include:

A: She does not have any current employment.

A: She's keeping her options open to all possibilities.

A: You mean has she given up on the idea that she should be employed in a major law firm with the potential for a salary in the high six figures?

A: Any decision Ms. Newman makes will depend on a number of considerations.

How you handle people who fail to reveal information varies depending on the circumstances. In certain circumstances, doing nothing is appropriate. Simply remember that their refusal to disclose has its own meaning and use that information as you would any other. For example, any of the blocks just covered clearly indicate the person is uncomfortable making the first offer. This suggests she is unsure what the value of her side should be, and you should encourage her to expect a lower value.

In some circumstances, you may have made the block easy, and you should rephrase your question. Here, you might rephrase the question as, "Is Ms. Newman looking for work other than the private practice of law?" Even with good questions, variations can get you information that was previously blocked. For example, "Where has Ms. Newman applied for work?"

In certain circumstances where you have a sufficiently strong relationship that will withstand the tension it creates, confrontation might be the appropriate response: "Boy, Charlie, I haven't heard such bologna since the presidential debates. Give me an answer." Where the relationship with the person is no longer important, the confrontation may also rise to a personal challenge and the anxiety may result in information: "You didn't really answer the question; let me rephrase it . . . ."

One way of looking at this specific area of inquiry is to see that it asks after Ms. Newman's intent with regard to settlement. We will discuss how inquiries of this type raise difficult ethical and strategic considerations in chapter twelve. The way the question is phrased may give you opponent an excuse to say, "I don't know how she feels about that" (unstated, "in the light of what I have learned so far from you during this negotiation").

Where the other party uses the "There are too many variables to answer that question" block, your best response is probably to take each variable and ask how it affects the answer. "It would depend on the amount of the offer, the situation at home, the chances to return to private practice should the need arise, the nature of the work involved," should be followed up on to learn if she has a specific offer and the terms of the offer.

6.7 Impediments to Questioning

Do not assume that what appears to be a lack of cooperation by someone with whom you are negotiating is always motivated by an attempt to manipulate you. Questioning in a negotiation will not always proceed smoothly. The other person may be nonresponsive or talk about tangential points. Their need for information may be so strong that it runs directly contrary to your attempt to systematically gather information.

Psychologists have identified a series of reasons why people being questioned do not provide clear, accurate, and organized information. While this book is certainly not a treatise on psychology, it *will* help you to understand the negotiation dynamic if you know some of the more common inhibitors. Only after identifying what is inhibiting the communication process are you able to identify a solution (and perhaps better avoid the pitfalls to the negotiation process that may arise by attributing to your opponents nefarious motives when there are none).

6.7.1   Ego Threat

Self-esteem is a critical factor in most people's psychological make-up. People will often avoid providing information that they believe will present a negative image and hurt their ego. For example, a person who has had a series of financial reversals may be unwilling to provide accurate information for fear you will view her as incompetent or foolish.

6.7.2   Result Threat

People refuse to give information because they fear it will hurt their attempt to get the result they want. Take, for example, a merger and acquisition negotiation. Revealing business reversals may pose a personal threat to a party, because she fears that the acquiring business will refuse to offer her favorable terms as a result of the information.

6.7.3   Role Expectation

Society puts individuals into certain roles, and others expect that people will act according to these roles. In a legal negotiation, this is most apparent in how the respective lawyers view their roles. The lawyer who believes—or has a client who believes—that lawyers are supposed to be tough, aggressive negotiators may simply not realize that an alternative exists. The problem goes beyond mere intimidation. If one lawyer views negotiation as a debate over positions, he may be unwilling to give the opposing counsel a correct statement of underlying needs because he expects the opponent to use it against him. Indeed, if you perceive your role as a cooperative problem-solver, this misperception can sometimes lead to deadlock, because your attempts to get opposing counsel to open up and talk freely may be met with one- or two-word answers.

Perceived inequality of status can likewise affect your negotiations. If you are negotiating with an older lawyer, you may have to fight the reluctance to defer to the person merely because of status. Similarly, you must not let the person's status intimidate you to the point you do not ask the questions you need to ask or allow the other lawyer to avoid answering the questions you have asked.

6.7.4   Perceived Irrelevancy

If one of your goals is to obtain accurate, relevant, and reliable information, problems can result from the other person having a different view of what is relevant information. A person may simply not mention information because they think it is irrelevant. Further, if you seek what the person perceives as irrelevant information, they may react negatively, hurting rapport and inhibiting your attempts to acquire information.

6.7.5   Greater Need

The other person's goals for the negotiation often are such that you can do little to simultaneously meet your goals and his. Imagine a situation where you are talking to a lawyer for the company your client would like to acquire. You may be asking for a great deal of specific information that you can then use to justify a specific proposal—yet in what is clearly intended to be a cooperative, problem-solving negotiation, your opponent avoids talking about what the name of the merged company will be. It may be that this lawyer's client has a need that is greater than the money part of the deal, such as a desire to have his name memorialized in the new business.

In *Newman*, when the firm tries to pin down the financial needs of Ms. Newman, but her attorney keeps talking about vindication, this becomes a pretty clear indication that Newman has a higher need. Two things therefore follow. First, if you are to avoid deadlock, you may have to temporarily give up what you are trying to do to allow you to address this greater need. Second, if you recognize the problem as the opponent having a greater need, you may take advantage of this, especially if your opponent's need is unimportant to you. For example, if Ms. Newman has a greater need for vindication than money, this indicates she might settle for less money in exchange for a public apology. If it turns out that the apology is not an issue for your client, you can trade your meaningless bargaining chip (an apology) for a blue chip (less money).

6.7.6　Forgetting

Human beings forget. Related to forgetting, the person being questioned may be confused or have incomplete memory. Memory is made up of several factors, including not only the original perception at the time, but that perception modified over time by external factors. For example, a client's relationship with her lawyer may be influenced not simply by their own personal contacts, but by the statements made to her by other people who have dealt with the lawyer in the past.

6.7.7　Time and Money

Time is a significant factor in most business relationships. A busy person may give less information to avoid the added cost of a longer negotiation. The person may feel time spent with you is time more profitably spent elsewhere. Trying to negotiate a small claim, for example, may be complicated by the fact that opposing counsel believes she is too busy to discuss such mundane issues as your "little accident." Your task will be to recognize this as a problem and conduct the discussions in a way to minimize the effect of this attitude.

6.8　Techniques to Motivate

You can deal with problems that inhibit your information gathering in several ways. While none of these are foolproof, they do provide a range of techniques you can use to encourage the other side to provide information.

6.8.1　Education

One of the most effective, and perhaps least used, techniques to get someone to provide information is to educate the person. Quite often, problems that inhibit the questioning result from the person not having a systematic view of the process and not knowing that anything is wrong. By educating the person, you can often reap immediate rewards.

The person giving short answers to open-ended questions or the person who jumps from one topic to the next might benefit from a simple explanation of the process you would like to follow:

> I realize we have a limited amount of time to spend today, so I thought we might proceed as follows. I am feeling a bit overwhelmed by all that I don't know about this deal and worry that I won't be able to recommend a specific deal if I don't get caught up. I've found that I can most efficiently use your time if I start off with some general questions and have you tell me as much about each topic as you can. I can then go back and ask you for any additional specific information I need. Then we can answer any questions you may have.

6.8.2   Cost-Benefit Analysis

You can also use education to provide a cost-benefit analysis to help with problems caused by the other party's ego being threatened by a bad loan or other business issues. For example:

> It must be difficult talking about these business reversals. As difficult as it is, we need this information. In fact, having it is less harmful than not having it, because we can't resolve this outstanding problem without some very specific information.

6.8.3   Empathetic Understanding, Recognition, and Catharsis

Sometimes people come to a negotiation with psychological needs requiring empathy, sympathy, catharsis, or recognition. Often the best technique to get beyond these needs is to provide the empathetic or sympathetic ear or to create a chance for the person to have the catharsis. For example, providing Ms. Newman a forum to vent past grievances may be extremely helpful to your position if you represent the firm. By sitting back and listening, you may be able to convince her that things have changed. Further, you can provide recognition by statements such as, "This is important information," or "You're providing me with a good background here."

6.8.4   Active Listening

By applying active and passive listening techniques, you can not only foster the giving of information by the person, but also help maintain an appropriate rapport. Listening techniques range from neutral or passive to directive or active. Passive or neutral responses to a person's statement convey little information to the person and are designed to simply indicate that you are still listening and the person should continue talking. Active or directive responses communicate information—your interpretation of the person's response—and therefore may direct the person toward new topics or indicate to the person that they need to clarify information they have already provided. The following are common listening techniques you may find helpful.

6.8.4.1   Silence

Silence can be one of the most effective neutral probes for information. People are socialized to abhor silence. We turn on radios without really listening to them; we hum; we have music in elevators. Given silence, most people will seek to fill it with noise. This is as true in negotiations as it is in life in general. If you do not speak, chances are that the other person will. Simply waiting as little as a second after the person drops her voice indicating she has finished may be enough to encourage her to continue. This technique is particularly helpful following an open-ended question.

6.8.4.2   "Mm-hm"

Utterances such as "Mm-hm," "yes," or "I see" are neutral probes and communicate that you are listening intently to what is being said. When followed by silence, the statements encourage the listener to keep talking.

6.8.4.3   Restatement

A slightly more directive listening technique is restating what the person says. Restatement shows the person that you are listening; in fact, it indicates that you are listening so intently you are able to repeat the person's exact words. For example:

> L1: So after the last staff meeting, they decided to seriously discuss this attempt to control emergency room activity.

> L2: The decision to seriously discuss the attempt to control emergency room activity came after the last staff meeting?

Restatement is more directive than "Mm-hm" because it communicates your greater interest and therefore indicates to the person that you need more information on this topic. It is particularly effective in bridging combative and competitive exchanges to a more empathetic and problem-solving approach. If you can demonstrate empathy and understanding by accurately summarizing the opposition's positions and demands, then the opposition may feel that they can trust you, listen more completely to your side of the case, and work together to devise a win-win strategy for resolution.

6.8.4.4 Clarification

Asking for a clarification is more directive than restatement.

L1:   So after the last staff meeting, we decided to seriously discuss this attempt to control the emergency room.

L2:   The decision came after the staff meeting. I'm not sure I understand. Was there a connection between the meeting and the decision to change procedure?

6.8.4.5 Reflection

Reflection can also help. With reflection, you add an interpretation to the person's statement. Because the interpretation contains information about your perceptions, the statement may be quite directive.

L1:   So after the last staff meeting, we decided to seriously discuss this attempt to control the emergency room.

L2:   The decision came after the staff apparently expressed concern over the current condition of the emergency room.

You can reflect feelings as well as facts.

L1:   So after the last staff meeting, we decided to seriously discuss this attempt to control the emergency room.

L2:   It sounds like there is some anger about the control.

Reflection can also be a key bridge to problem-solving. If catharsis is to be gained, the person with the emotion needs to feel listened to. By then reflecting, you may lead the other party to be able to feel more able to put the emotion aside and deal more objectively with the situation. (Of course, others may worry that encouraging the expression of strong emotion will only make a party more wedded to his position. The usefulness of reflection is very context- and party-specific and is, therefore, a more risky active listening technique than the others listed above.)

6.9 Nonverbal Communication

In addition to verbal communication, you should be as aware of nonverbal communication in a negotiation as you are in an interview. Nonverbal information is often more valuable, because the other side often does not intended to communicate it, and therefore it is more reliable. Indeed, professional negotiators refer to such unintentional communication (whether verbal or nonverbal) as "leakage."

A complete review of nonverbal communication is beyond the scope of this work. A brief review, however, should emphasize its importance. Nonverbal communication can be divided into four types: chronemics, kinesics, proxemics, and paralinguistics. With regard to each of these, experts have drawn various conclusions, but four generalities particularly apply in legal negotiation and deserve special mention.

First, many experts believe that the effectiveness and usefulness of words tend to be overestimated. Some experts estimate that as much as 60 percent of all important messages are passed nonverbally. An awareness of nonverbal communication is therefore critical for interpersonal communication. Second, not only is a great deal of information passed nonverbally, certain types of gestural language cannot be communicated by words.

A third important point is that some nonverbal information is a physiological response to stress and therefore may be a more accurate indication of information. Blushing, for example, may be a more accurate indication of embarrassment than any spoken words. Finally, many psychologists believe that there is always what they refer to as message redundancy. In other words, people communicate the same information in multiple ways. A person who is uncomfortable in a particular situation may both wrap his arms around himself and blush. Given that nonverbal communication is subject to interpretation (persons wrapping their arms around themselves may simply be cold), message redundancy allows us to search for a confirming interpretation of a message we think we are receiving nonverbally.

6.9.1   Leakage

Almost anything the other side does may leak information. For example, when the other party is coming in from out of town, has arrived the night before, and shows up at your office with a suit bag, she "leaks" information that she has checked out of the hotel. This gives you information that as the negotiations take longer and longer, the other side may need to quickly resolve the negotiation or change their travel plans. The additional trouble may not make a critical difference, but it may put additional pressure on the other side.

Like any information, you can actively seek leakage. Take our previous example, where the lawyer has to sell a large asset. During the ice-breaking stage, you may bring up the question of whether the out-of-town buyer needs hotel accommodations to see if the buyer will leak whether he has plans to stay overnight. You may then determine the time frame with which you have to work.

Two types of leakage merit special mention because of their reoccurrence in negotiation after negotiation. First, there is the leakage resulting from waffle words. These are words that communicate a lack of a firm position. How many times have you or the person you are negotiating with said something like, "We are looking for something between ten and fifteen?" You usually cannot ask for a range in a negotiation. If you hear this range, you should assume that either ten or fifteen is acceptable, depending on which is more favorable to you. On the other side of the coin, the only time you should speak of ranges is when you attach conditions to explain the range, such as, "We want ten to fifteen, depending on whether . . . ." Also, when using the term "looking for," you leak the fact that you will take less. If, for example, ten were your real bottom line, you likely would have been more affirmative and emphatic, saying, "We want ten."

A concession pattern can also leak information. As many negotiators approach their bottom line or commitment point, concessions tend to get smaller and smaller and faster and faster. If you listen and keep track of the size and speed of concessions, you may get a sense of whether the latest concession is truly the bottom line.

6.9.2   Chronemics

Chronemics, or the use of time to communicate, can take many forms. A lawyer can communicate a great deal about the importance of the negotiation based on his use of time. If he squeezes the negotiation in between two other meetings, he obviously does not highly value the negotiation. Similarly, a lawyer who is chronically late communicates information about his perception of the relationship.

6.9.3   Kinesics

Kinesics is study of how the body communicates information. Interestingly enough, researchers indicate that most people focus on the face of the other person in an interview. Most people also believe the face reveals the most accurate information. Research also indicates, however, that a listener tends to watch the speaker's eyes more closely than a speaker watches the listener's. The lesson from the research seems clear. We should continue to be aware of the face as a primary source of information, but be aware that some nonverbal information may be missed when we fail to watch the entire body.

Examples of kinesics are familiar to most people. With respect to body posture, slouching may connote lack of concern or defeat. Foot movements or tapping or swaying of legs and feet may show nervousness. Hand movements, such as placing the hand over the mouth when talking, may show the speaker is unsure about the statement being made. Facial expressions can communicate a wide range of information including disgust, anger, sadness, and joy. Eye movements are also significant—rolling eyes may show disbelief, while darting eyes may show anxiety.

6.9.4   Proxemics

Proxemics is using the environment to communicate. We have already discussed a major environmental control in the negotiation when we discussed not only where the negotiation should take place, but also arranging furniture and controlling control intrusions into one's space.

Psychologists also tell us that objects such as flower vases and abstract sculpture in a negotiation setting tend to facilitate informality and cooperative behavior. Books in a negotiation setting tend to inhibit informality and cooperative behavior. Round tables increase informality and feelings of closeness.

Proxemics is at play in other contexts as well. As with all nonverbal communication, proxemics is subject to interpretation, and you need to confirm that information. For example, when you are greeted at the door (or when you greet someone) and that person moves toward you, is she indicating that she is pushy, aggressive, assertive, or is she showing that she's merely anxious to get to know you? If she takes a step back, is she indicating that she is welcoming or is she leaking that she is passive or easily manipulated?

As mentioned before, how you place furniture within a room can either facilitate or inhibit communication. As a general rule, placing large objects between people decreases communication. If you wish to develop a cooperative, caring relationship, it makes sense not to interview the person from behind a large desk. Sitting side by side is perhaps best. On the other hand, in many cultures being physically close can inhibit communication. As with most interpersonal skills, flexibility in proxemics is an advantage. Arranging the furniture in a way that lets you choose how close to sit can facilitate communication. In addition, the type of furniture can have an on impact the flow of communication. Chairs with wheels can help communication, as can chair and loveseat arrangements. With a chair and small couch arrangement, you can sit in the chair and the other person can adjust her proximity by choosing where to sit on the couch.

6.9.5   Paralinguistics

Paralinguistics is using the voice itself to communicate meaning. For example, voice quality—whether it is tense or breathy—will communicate very different messages. The pitch, pace, tone, and volume of the voice all work together to communicate different messages. You can communicate a deliberative mood, for example, by slowing the rate of your speech. High pitch, fast pace, or high volume may communicate lack of time or patience.

By choosing which word to stress in a sentence, you can greatly affect that sentence's meaning. The simple sentence "I did not call Alice a crook" takes on a variety of meanings based on which word you emphasize. The variety is almost limitless, but can range anywhere from having said nothing negative about anyone; to having called someone other than Alice a crook; to having called Alice a name, but not the name "crook."

6.9.6   Combinations

Not all nonverbal communication fits nicely into only one of these categories. Perhaps one of the most common examples of proxemics and kinesics combined in an interview is when the speaker moves toward or away from you during the interview. This changing of the environment by leaning the body can communicate a great deal about the interest or lack of interest the person has. It can also indicate the degree of comfort the person feels toward you.

Finally, it is not important what label we apply to the behavior as long as we are aware not only of the messages we receive, but also of the messages we are sending.

6.10 Recap

As you can see from the above, information bargaining is an important phase of any negotiation. The saying "knowledge is power" certainly applies to the negotiation setting. Your quest for information about the other side will pervade much of the process, and you should never let an opportunity slip by to add to your information about their position.

Adversarial Information Exchange	Problem-Solvers Information Exchange
• Ask open-ended questions designed to get the opponent to reveal • Ask precise follow-up questions designed to pin down and discover the extent of the opponent's vulnerabilities • Recognize blocking strategies that limit exchange of vulnerable information • Use agenda control • Answer a question with a question • Over-answer a question • Under-answer a question • Answer a related question • Use a provocative non sequitur • Exchange vulnerabilities, but make opponent go first • Rule a question out of bounds	• Let opponent go first • Use restatement and reflection till opponent agrees you understand their point of view • Recognize and concede valid points made by opponent • Share your perspective, but only as how "you see it," not as the truth • Ask your opponent to restate your side and demonstrate understanding of your position

Integrated Approach to Information Exchange
• Start as a cooperative adversarial until opponent demonstrates good faith
• If not, stay adversarial till deadlock on key information
• Teach or persuade opponent to use problem-solving information exchange
• If agrees and you trust opponent—then try problem-solver techniques listed above

Next, we will address the actual give and take of a negotiation—the exchange.

CHAPTER SEVEN

EXCHANGE

7.1 The Offer

Eventually, one of the negotiators will suggest a solution to the issue being negotiated. No matter whether the solution is presented as an offer, a demand, or a proposal, an effective solution has a number of common elements. If you ask yourself what you are trying to accomplish with your proposal, it becomes clear that on a broad level there are two goals. First, you want the proposal to be perceived as fair, just, and equitable, and one that meets everyone's needs to the extent possible. Common sense tells you that if the parties do not believe the proposal meets these criteria, it is unlikely to be accepted.

However, another equally important goal exists. You must also persuade the other side that you have nothing else to offer. Whether phrased in the harsh language of a competitive adversarial negotiator that "The offer is fair and you won't get a dime more!" or in the terms of a problem-solver that "It's fair, and I can't think of a better solution," you will not reach an agreement if the other side believes that despite the offer's fairness, more favorable terms are available.

The difficulty with this second goal is that you must persuade the other side that you will offer nothing else, knowing that down the road you may very well give some more. You must make the proposal in a manner that is persuasive and does not undercut your credibility when later it turns out that (as an adversarial) you make a concession or (as a problem-solver) reformulate your proposed solution.

7.2 Justification and Persuasion

7.2.1 Reasons for Everything

Providing reasons for your position is an essential element of any attempt to negotiate systematically. To give your proposal credibility, you must show why it is fair, just, and equitable, as well why you will not give more. An unsupported proposal does little to persuade the other side of anything other than that you picked a particular number or other solution out of the air. If you will pick one number out of the air, why won't you pick another number more favorable to the other side? Reasons help you persuade the other side that the proposal is fair, just, and equitable and that you are not prepared to offer more.

7.2.2   Objective Criteria Arguably Beyond Your Control

Perhaps the most important component to persuasion in negotiation is the ability to use objective criteria that are arguably beyond your control. Objective criteria are more persuasive than subjective. When the defense lawyer is negotiating with plaintiff's counsel and says, "We won't pay more than $70,000 because it is fair," the statement is unpersuasive. Fair to whom? Based on what criteria? Wouldn't $75,000 be fairer? Saying "$75,000 is all I can offer because of restrictions by the insurance company," is marginally more persuasive. A semi-objective reason—they won't let me do it—supports this statement, but the reason is not beyond the control of the lawyer's client.

Saying "$75,000 is our offer—it makes sense given that we settled a similar claim for $75,000 last week," is much more persuasive. Here, the statement is supported by an objective indicator of the "market" price, which is arguably beyond defense counsel's control because it is either set by the nebulous concept of "the market" or by other plaintiffs' attorneys.

Even proposals involving something less quantifiable than money, such as work schedules, are more persuasive when they are objective. A labor lawyer might say:

> The schedule is simply not fair. Look at the schedules over the past three months. During that time union employees have consistently been denied overtime on weekends. Here, let me show you . . . .

Anybody with an adjustable rate mortgage, home equity line, or credit card has experienced discomfort over the bank's ability to control interest rates. This discomfort is in part related to this issue of objective criteria. Customers frequently reject pricing on such adjustable rate loans if based on prime plus some percentage point. One possible reason for this rejection is that while prime is objective, the customer may not perceive it as beyond the bank's control. The offer does not sound fair, just, and equitable because the customer has an underlying fear that the bank will arbitrarily increase prime. Basing the rate on something like the cost of funds to the bank (such as United States Treasury Bills), however, may sound more persuasive because whether correct or not, customers perceive it as less subject to the bank's control. The fact that the bank's prime is driven by cost of funds and that all pricing—whether based on prime or cost of funds—is ultimately controlled by market forces is irrelevant to this customer. A rate based on the cost of funds is more attractive because it appears beyond the control of the bank.

Often, the most difficult part of making a persuasive statement is identifying the objective criteria that can be used to justify a subjective issue. Imagine you are setting up a health maintenance organization or managed care facility. You must negotiate with various private physician groups to get them to join the new organization. You might have problems persuading a potential group practice that the proposed business relationship actually will provide a better level of service for the group's patients. If you are representing the promoters of the new business entity, you must identify objective measures of patient satisfaction and quality of service to support the proposal. Here, statistics on patient turnover, new business, or the like might be persuasive.

In a merger or acquisition negotiation, there might be an issue of distrust between two previously competing businesses. Identifying a way to quantify trust can be quite challenging, but you may find it helpful to point to specific trust-building measures in other acquisitions. For example, the acquiring company can make an objective and persuasive showing that it has a good record for employee retention following an acquisition. Also, making a specific commitment public by way of a press release may make the commitment seem beyond the control of the negotiator and therefore more permanent and consequently more persuasive.

The connection between effective client counseling and the ability to develop objective criteria should be apparent. Having the client identify what he would like to accomplish is clearly an essential step. Getting the client to help you identify the potential rationales for why that result is appropriate is equally important.

PROBLEM 7.1

In *Newman v. Popchek*, Ms. Newman has indicated that her primary goal is to get as much money from Popchek, and Popchek, Blink & Denis, as possible. What objective criteria, arguably beyond your control, can be used to justify a particular high settlement?

Assume instead that Ms. Newman has indicated that money is not nearly as important as getting a new job, having sufficient cash flow during the job search, getting health insurance to cover her pregnancy, and get an apology. What objective criteria, arguably beyond your control, can be used to justify a particular high settlement?

Identifying objective criteria, of course, depends on the particular facts associated with a negotiation. However, the criteria must be something valued by the person with whom you are negotiating. For example, in the above problem, a reasonably safe working premise (that we will of course check out during information bargaining) would be that Popchek, Blink & Denis value money and reputation. To maximize the amount of money Ms. Newman can demand, a number of criteria suggest themselves. Clearly, jury verdict research is an important criterion. Past jury verdicts are both objective and arguably beyond the control of the parties, and the more similar the case, the more persuasive the analogy. A typical persuasive statement based on jury verdicts might go:

Our client has authorized me to accept lower figures to settle this case. Let me explain how we have arrived at this figure. We have done extensive research on verdicts in these types of cases. Independent of our own research, we have consulted with Jury Verdict Research, Inc. I have its report here, as well as a listing of similar cases involving sexual harassment against professional women. You will see that the verdicts range between $375,000 and $1.3 million. Given the public nature of this dispute and the fact that Ms. Newman is in the higher income bracket among the plaintiffs in these cases (the $1.3 million was a physician, we have a $450,000 verdict for an associate), at least a $450,000 verdict is likely. We recognize, of course, that between trial and appeals we are looking at four years to recover that amount. So we are willing to reduce it to its present value. Our accountant tells us that the present value of $450,000 in four years is $375,000. We estimate that we will also save $45,000 in litigation expenses. Subtract that and you get $330,000.

Jury verdicts are not the only objective criteria. Experts in an appropriate field often provide value data on which you can base offers and persuasive statements. Indeed, choosing different criteria can result in vastly different offers.

7.2.3 Argumentation

One of the best analyses of what makes arguments persuasive comes from the field of rhetoric. We add to and modernize the description of these classical rhetorical elements as follows.

7.2.3.1   Be Detailed

The more detail you provide to support your position, the more persuasive it will usually be. The statement, "The schedule is fair because it is consistent with what is happening at other comparable businesses," is objective and arguably beyond management's control. Compare it, however, to the following statement:

Before we made the schedule, I checked around. I checked the other comparable employers. At Metropolitan, the average amount of overtime for workers is forty hours for the last six months. During that same period the average has been thirty-five hours for City as well as University hospital. Here we see that each union member in this department has averaged thirty-six hours during the last six months. Here, let me show you our schedule . . . .

The second statement has the same rationale as the previous example, but it is more persuasive because it contains detailed information about not only how the schedule was created, but how it compares to others.

Detail often requires proof. For example, when we justified $330,000 on jury verdict research in the previous scenario, the statement was quite detailed and the lawyer was prepared to provide documentary proof that she had not just pulled the figures out of the air. Providing copies of the economist's report (as well as his curriculum vitae) might be helpful.

7.2.3.2 Apply Multidimensional Reasoning

As a general rule, more supporting reasons make your position more persuasive. If you can show the other party that no matter which way you both look at a problem, the solution always seems to be the same, the other party will more likely perceive the solution as fair, just, and equitable. A simple car negotiation involving the purchase of a used car illustrates the point.

Buyer: I'll give you $15,000 for your car.

Seller: Too low, the ad says $16,000, and I'm not going any lower.

Buyer: But, wait, look at this. I checked the Blue Book value on this car. Here, see for yourself. The wholesale price listed is $16,500, the retail price is $17,000. But you need to, according to the book, subtract $750 for high mileage. That makes the price $15,750. Then you have to figure the tires need to be replaced—that's another $150 apiece, so we're at $15,150. Bottom line is I'm also going to have to have the engine looked into, and you have said yourself there hasn't been any brake work. That's bound to be needed, so $15,000 is right.

Seller: I don't know . . . .

Buyer: $15,000 also makes sense from what I see in the market. Look at these other advertisements. Here's the same make and model, a year newer, for $17,000. Here's the same make and model, but a year older for $14,500. Also, you are the one who told me the dealer wouldn't give you what you thought the car was worth in trade-in. You'll do better with my $15,000 than with the dealer's trade-in value. Don't forget that if you take it today, you can cancel the insurance right away—that will save you a couple of bucks, and you avoid the hassle and expense of trying to find someone else.

Here, the persuasive statement points out five reasons why $15,000 is the correct price: 1) Blue Book value; 2) market price based on other advertisements; 3) can't get a better price at dealer; 4) time savings; and 5) money savings. Individually, each of the arguments have a different persuasive force. The Blue Book argument is objective and beyond the control of the parties. It is also highly detailed. The Blue Book argument, however, has a major flaw in that the buyer does not explain picking the wholesale price as a starting point—that is not really beyond the control of the party. The other advertisement argument is objective, but lacks detail. The final three arguments are beyond the buyer's control, but lack detail and objectivity. Taken together, however, they are more persuasive than taken alone and create a more compelling rationale.

The same affect can be used in a number of situations. For example, assume the lawyer's client is seeking to sell a multimillion dollar item:

> Buyer (B): You're the seller. What's the bottom line?
>
> Lawyer (L): Two million dollars.
>
> B: How did you arrive at that figure?
>
> L: It seemed a fair price in light of existing circumstances. We know replacement cost is $2.30. Original cost was $1.75. The price should be somewhere in between.
>
> B: What about depreciation?
>
> L: I look at depreciation this way. This is more like a vintage car than a Chevy. Initially, there is going to be some depreciation, but with rising costs, its value has got to increase. Its value won't catch up to a new unit, but kept in condition, it could well never go below its original cost and may increase in value as well.
>
> B: But what's magic about $2.0 million?
>
> L: It's not magic. Look at it from my perspective. This unit is an investment. A reasonable return on an investment like this would be 10 percent a year, and that's $250,000 for the past two years. Do the math—without compounding, $1.75 million plus $250,000 is $2 million. Two million is also consistent with the recent appraisal we had on the unit.

Here the lawyer has used replacement costs, appreciation based on original cost, return on investment, and an appraisal to support his position. Each is objective and arguably beyond the control of the lawyer. For example, she did not create the concept of appreciation—it exists in the real world. Clearly, some of the rationales are more beyond the control of the lawyer than others. The lawyer did, after all, pick the appreciation value and probably also selected who was going to be the appraiser. Taken as a whole, however, the arguments taken together are more persuasive than when taken individually.

7.2.3.3   Make Balanced Arguments

Proposals have to be fair, just, and equitable to both sides. Any rationale that merely focuses on one side is inherently less persuasive. No matter how objective, detailed, and multidimensional you make the argument, if you focus solely on the needs, interests, and desires of your client, the other person will react with something along the lines of: "What's in it for me? This deal needs to meet my needs as well." The argument requires, therefore, a balanced rationale that shows how it meets both sides' needs, interests, and desires.

However, the argument cannot focus solely on the other side's goals. A persuasive statement that never shows what you get out of the proposal may cause the other person to question your credibility. The negotiation involves meeting both sides' goals. If you fail to articulate the reasons the proposal meets your needs, the person with whom you are negotiating may think you have hidden something and are afraid to reveal some benefit you seek.

7.2.3.4   Be Emphatic and Emotional

If you do not believe in your position, why should anyone else? You must communicate conviction by being appropriately emotional and emphatic. While this does not mean tears, it does mean being affirmative and not equivocating. Compare the following statements.

Wrong

> The most we are willing to offer is in the neighborhood of $300,000.
>
> We're looking at $300,000, and the client does not want to make an apology.

Correct

> The client will pay only $300,000, the terms must be confidential, and there certainly won't be an apology.

Wrong

> I don't know—it's unlikely I could get approval for that offer.

Correct

> That offer is unacceptable.

7.2.3.5   Make Sure Certain Arguments Are Subtle

Despite the fact that most arguments are persuasive when they are detailed, some arguments are actually made less effective with detail. Take a variation on a merger and acquisition negotiation:

L1: You're buying, what's the bottom line?

L2: Six million dollars.

L1: How did you arrive at that figure?

L2: It seemed fair in light of existing circumstances. We know book value is $6.85 million. Our start-up costs would be $3 million. And we value the goodwill at $1 million. That's $4 million. The price should be somewhere in between.

L1: What about my client's experience?

L2: That's a separate issue. We will agree to continue his employment at $100,000. And besides, let's face it—your client needs to sell. From what I can tell, you don't have much choice. From what you've told me, there's no other purchaser available and he doesn't have the resources to compete.

Put yourself in the position of the client who is to be acquired. How would you feel if you were in the position and this argument were made to you? Would there be a chance that you would react negatively on a basic personal level and decide, no matter how badly you wanted to sell the business, you would not be so blatantly pushed around?

Certain arguments simply cause people to act in a nonrational manner. They force people to take action, as discussed in chapter three, not because the action takes them toward their rationally determined goal, but because of some social-psychological reason. The threat to the seller's ego by such a direct, personal challenge might force the seller to walk out. When it is likely that an argument will precipitate nonrational behavior and you are confident the other person will make a detailed argument to himself, the argument should be subtle. Change the last paragraph in our previous example to:

Let me tell you, we appreciate your willingness to talk to us and have no intention of taking advantage of today's tight market conditions.

You can be assured the other party will fill in the details of that tight market, including the fact that no alternative purchaser exists. In fact, you could probably be even more subtle and not mention the tight market at all. If the seller's need and limitation of options has already been mentioned as part of the information bargaining, you can be confident that the tight market argument will be made in the seller's own mind regardless of what you say or do not say.

7.2.4   The Role of Threats

Threats are among the most overused tactics in negotiation. Just as we did with the use of subtlety, ask yourself how you feel when threatened? The fact is, threats increase the likelihood that a person will respond irrationally. And using threats decreases the likelihood that the type of relationship necessary for effective problem-solving and long-term trust will develop. In fact, social-psychology research indicates that by using threats, you actually decrease the chance that you will achieve a mutually acceptable result.

While threats are often inappropriately used, research indicates that they can be effective. Whether you choose to use a threat or need to respond to a threat, your first step is to determine what makes a threat effective.

To be effective, a threat must meet a number of elements. First, the threat must be heard. If the threatened party cannot hear the threat, the threat will be ineffective. This suggests that one appropriate response to a threat is simply to ignore it—pretend you did not hear it, that it simply was not made. Another effective tactic is to call a halt, or recess, to the negotiation, if it appears that the other side is about to issue a threat.

Second, to be effective, a threat must be understood as a threat. For example, a common threat is that the other party will tell other people in the community how uncooperative, demanding, or unreasonable you are. Treating this as a nonthreat can be effective.

> L1: I don't think the clients of Popchek, Blank & Denis will be happy when they find out about the behavior of senior partners.

> L2: I think our clients will be pleased to know we don't cave in to unsubstantiated charges. We have a reputation for aggressive litigation, and our clients would expect us to act in a manner consistent with that reputation.

Third, an effective threat must involve an issue that the person being threatened values.

> L1: I don't think the clients of Popchek, Blank & Denis will be happy when they find out about the behavior of senior partners.

> L2: I think Newman should know from working at the firm that Popchek, Blink & Denis doesn't care what other firms think. It has a reputation for aggressive behavior that might offend people. The fact that there are these unsupported charges won't make people think any less of the firm.

Fourth, to be effective, the threat must be believed. An effective way to counter the threat may be rejecting the possibility that the threat will be carried out. This may actually simply require you to ignore the threat. If you are negotiating with a lawyer who threatens to sue if your client does not comply with some demand, you can usually safely ignore the threat if you know from advance preparation that this particular lawyer has not filed a lawsuit in recent history.

Fifth, to be effective, a threat must be prospective.

L1:   When other staff hear this, you will . . . .

L2:   I already have the reputation of being . . . .

Finally, a threat must be proportionate or rational. If it is neither, ignore it.

Problem-solvers have a much different approach to dealing with threats, focusing on why people make threats. Social psychologists tell us that people often make threats when they have no other tactic to use. If this is the case, the appropriate response to a threat is to provide the negotiator with an alternative approach. Take, for example, the situation where you offer a proposal and the other person responds with, "Well, we're just going to have to sue." An appropriate response might be to get the person to focus on the more principled, systematic approach and invite them to participate:

> That is one alternative, of course. Before you do that, let me ask you to share with me why you think my position is so unreasonable?

You might even go so far as to suggest the other side criticize your detailed persuasive statement.

> That is one alternative, of course. Before you do that, let me ask you to share with me why you think my position is so unreasonable. For example, how else can we value the loss you allege your client has suffered?

7.3   Concessions, Reformulations, and Counterproposals

The difficult part of making a concession is doing it while maintaining your credibility. If after making a persuasive argument you make a subsequent concession, you run the risk of losing credibility. After all, when you made your previous proposal, you said that you are not going to give one more dime, and now you are reaching into your pocket for another dime. After your last offer you said there was no more to give, and that was not true. Why should your opponent believe this time that more concessions will not be coming?

So how do you maintain your credibility in the face of the concession? How do you communicate that your last offer was not pulled out of the air? Because if the other negotiator believes that the first offer was pulled out of the air, she may believe that the new offer was also pulled out of the air and therefore wait for yet another concession. This is a particularly significant problem if you are already at your bottom line, and she does not believe that you are. Deadlock is the likely result.

The principal way to make a concession while maintaining your credibility is to only make a concession that is in some way related to your prior proposal's justification. Usually, this means being sure that the other side sees that you are conceding because you have been persuaded that there is something about your original justification that requires the concession.

7.3.1 Splitting the Difference

The problem of "splitting the difference" illustrates the point. Assume you developed your objective, detailed rationale previously.

> Our client has authorized me to accept $330,000 to settle this case. Let me explain how we have arrived at this figure. We have done extensive research on verdicts in these types of cases. Independent of our own research we have consulted with Jury Verdict Research, Inc. I have their report here, as well as a listing of similar cases involving sexual harassment and defamation against professional women. You will see that the verdicts range between $375,000 and $1.3 million. Given the public nature of this dispute and the fact that Ms. Newman is in the associate income bracket among the plaintiff's in these cases (the $1.3 million was a physician—we have a $450,000 verdict for an associate), at least a $450,000 verdict is likely. We recognize, of course, that between trial and appeals we are looking at four years to recover that amount. So we are willing to reduce it to its present value. Our accountant tells us that the present value of $450,000 in four years is $375,000. We estimate that we will also save $45,000 in litigation expenses. Subtract that and you get $330,000.

Assume the other lawyer has countered with $200,000, and after a number of hours without movement the other lawyer says, "Why don't we just split the difference —we'll give you $265,000."

If you split this difference, what does it communicate about your original rationale? Logic would indicate that if you are now willing to move $65,000 for no reason other than it is the midpoint between two positions, the original, detailed, objective rationale was a pretext. You may not care about maintaining credibility at this point. However, if you need to be concerned about this because you, or your client, expects to deal with the other side in the future, you need to find a rationale for the move. You can move from $330,000 to $265,000 and maintain credibility if the move is either explicitly or implicitly tied to one of your original reasons.

> L1: I have checked around, and the $330,000 makes sense based on an expected verdict of $375,000. You are asking us to essentially discount about 20 percent. Based on what—risk at trial?
>
> L2: Yes. Juries are unpredictable.
>
> L1: Well, I'll take that back to my client.

Here, the lawyer has moved, but in a way that does not indicate the previous offer was a lie. The lawyer moves in a way that communicates the new figure is rationally based and unlikely to change.

If you follow this approach, you may find yourself in the position of wanting to concede, but being unable to because the other side cannot think of a way to convince you. You may have to help the other person, as the lawyer for Newman did in the previous example by suggesting a reason for the $65,000 concession.

Finally, even if settlement does not come immediately after an offer to split the difference, do not forget that the lawyer who made the suggestion has already indicated that the midpoint is acceptable. The practical result is that you should usually read the offer to split the difference as a unilateral concession of the suggested amount.

7.3.2 Note for Problem-Solvers

Problem-solvers should follow the same general approach as adversarial negotiators do. You should note a couple of differences, however. First, because problem-solvers are trying to develop a joint solution to the problem, they typically do not refer to offers and demands. They prefer to use words and phrases such as proposal, solution, proposed solution, or "an idea to throw out on the table." Second, problem-solvers often invite the other side to critically analyze their proposal as a way of generating suggestions for improving it. Third, because the problem-solver is seeking a creative solution, they are normally less committed to a specific proposal—that is, they are more willing to reformulate an idea and have less pride of authorship. Fourth, a problem-solver will avoid using terms such as concession and compromise, because the words denote positional bargaining. Rather, problem-solvers will "take a suggestion and reformulate a proposal."

7.4 Forgiveness and Apologies

Forgiveness—whether of a loan, debt, or of someone's behavior—is an option that often sits next to, if not on, the negotiation table. Where the parties are "stuck" with each other because they have no choice—an estranged couple have to work together to raise the kids, two entities have to share investment risks even though a party is unable to live up to its earlier promises, or two peoples have to live together despite a past conflict filled with atrocities—one option is for one of the parties to treat the other as if the past did not happen. They may view a fresh start as a better alternative than continued fighting and litigation. Whether it is in South Africa, where the parties chose to use a Truth and Reconciliation Commission rather than continue apartheid policies;[1] or a lender like the World Bank, who chooses loan forgiveness over requiring crippling payments that bleed valuable resources away from a country's fight with Ebola; or a domestic dispute, where one of the parties chooses reconciliation for the sake of the children over a protracted and messy divorce, an alternative in the negotiation may be forgiveness rather than continuing the conflict.

---

1. Truth and Reconciliation Commissions have been used with varying success in Liberia, Kenya, and Rwanda. For examination of the use of TRCs on an international stage, *see* PAUL J. ZWIER, PRINCIPLED NEGOTIATION AND MEDIATION IN THE INTERNATIONAL ARENA: TALKING WITH EVIL (2013).

In *Newman v. Popchek*, for example, one or more of the parties may want to explore the issue of whether an apology, either private or public, might help solve the dispute. If, for example, Mr. Popchek is willing to make a private apology, how might that impact Ms. Newman's willingness to settle, the amount of the settlement, and the wording of the apology? Would Ms. Newman be able to set Mr. Popchek's behavior aside and continue to work at the firm? If the firm were big enough, there might be a way to ensure she did not have to work with Mr. Popchek. Would the partners be able to "forgive" being sued and treat Ms. Newman as if she were a lateral hire?

Of course, one block to a discussion of such a solution is whether the lawyer each of the parties has discussed apologies with the client. If not, the lawyer for Ms. Newman could simply say that he has no authority to discuss an apology and so does not know how Ms. Newman would value it for settlement purposes. The same could be the case with the defendant law firm.

Sometimes, one of the parties wants to explore the possibility of reconciliation, but the lawyer for the opposition blocks the discussion of the possibility. For example, if the lawyer for Ms. Newman never communicates the offer to apologize to his client, then the topic never gets on the table. Ms. Newman's lawyer's conflict of interest (the lawyer's contingency fee is reduced if the settlement value of the case is reduced by an apology) may hinder discussion of an apology. One of the reasons for a defendant like Mr. Popchek—were he willing to discuss an apology—to consider mediation is to cut through this block by counsel to give his desire to try and apology a chance to work.

When counseling Ms. Newman, Ms. Newman's lawyer might feel that the possibility of her considering an apology in lieu of some of the money she is seeking might be a good solution. After all, 1.2 of the Model Rules does require the lawyer to consult with the client about the means used to pursue the client's goals.[2] Consequences that the lawyer should discuss with the client include the social, moral, and psychological consequences of any decision. What should Ms. Newman's lawyer discuss when he raises the

---

2. But see, Comment 5 to Model Rule 1.4, recognizing some practical limitations to how much detail the lawyer might discuss with the client about negotiation strategy.

> [5] The client should have sufficient information to participate intelligently in decisions concerning the objectives of the representation and the means by which they are to be pursued, to the extent the client is willing and able to do so. Adequacy of communication depends in part on the kind of advice or assistance that is involved. For example, when there is time to explain a proposal made in a negotiation, the lawyer should review all important provisions with the client before proceeding to an agreement. In litigation a lawyer should explain the general strategy and prospects of success and ordinarily should consult the client on tactics that are likely to result in significant expense or to injure or coerce others. On the other hand, a lawyer ordinarily will not be expected to describe trial or negotiation strategy in detail. The guiding principle is that the lawyer should fulfill reasonable client expectations for information consistent with the duty to act in the client's best interests, and the client's overall requirements as to the character of representation. In certain circumstances, such as when a lawyer asks a client to consent to a representation affected by a conflict of interest, the client must give informed consent, as defined in Rule 1.0(e).

possibility of Ms. Newman accepting some sort of apology or granting "forgiveness" for what was done to her?

- For forgiveness to be meaningful, there should be some confession of what was done and why.

- Forgiveness does not require forgetting.

- Forgiveness needs to be completely voluntary and is not required by law; that where Ms. Newman chooses to forgive, she may be forgoing significant damages that she would otherwise be entitled to under the law

- While most psychologists think of forgiveness outside of the "Exchange" of the law, the lawyer might use counseling as a way to get Ms. Newman to explore the value she might place on the apology. The lawyer might point out her right to judge the sincerity of the apology as a way to determine whether Mr. Popchek's behavior will likely continue with other female asociates.

- If the apology is sincere—and he admits that he was angry and frustrated at the loss of their relationship—how much less would Ms. Newman be willing to take in money to settle the case? $10K, $50K, $100K? Would she accept a letter of recommendation that indicated her leaving was not her fault?

- What if Mr. Popchek had sexually harassed other female associates before? How does that affect the need for deterrence, the amount the firm should pay, and what policies and procedures they need to put in place going forward?

- The lawyer might explore with Ms. Newman the complexity—both at trial and in life—of understanding and explaining why Mr. Popchek may have said what he said to Ms. Newman. This discussion might go beyond evaluating the claim's success at trial to discussing how easy it may be to demonize Mr. Popchek; this, in turn, may lead to an opening for a discussion of whether Ms. Newman might be willing to go back to work for the firm or to pursue an apology from Mr. Popchek. In addition to forgoing litigation expenses, Ms. Newman might also explore how her anger at Mr. Popchek and the firm might be alleviated by a reconciliation process. A consequence may be that it "frees" her to think about and work toward the future, less constrained by the past.

- Of course, there are risks of moving too quickly to reconciliation that need to be discussed. He may have simply objectified her and saw her as someone he wanted to have sex with. Still, it is more likely that his motivations were more complex than that. He may have been afraid of getting older, flattered by her attention, honestly misled about her feeling towards him. None of this would minimize the hurt he caused by how he treated her or the misuse of his power to impose himself into the work relationship in such a way that had to have caused intimidation. Understanding the complexity of his motivation may open up the space, assuming the apology might be fulsome and sincere, for some forgiveness.

At the very least, an apology may be an option worth discussing. It also is a very useful exercise for the lawyer in a number of ways. It will help him articulate his client's demands ("We want an apology, a letter of recommendation, a sexual harassment policy with teeth, and $350K"); give him potential concessions (valuing each option); and give him an important information gathering strategy to help him not only determine Mr. Popchek's level of contrition, embarrassment, or guilt for what he did, but also the firm's true feelings about Mr. Popchek's behavior toward female associates.

7.5 Typical Exchange Tactics and a Systematic Approach

You will find in today's literature on negotiation a wide variety of stand-alone negotiating tactics. Some of these tactics we have already discussed in the context of a systematic approach to negotiation. The purpose of this text is to suggest that a systematic, principled approach will be more effective than a series of "tricks of the trade." However, many of these stand-alone tactics fit well within the systematic approach presented here as examples of specific phases. Also, having analyzed how these tactics fit within the systematic approach will help you decide how to counter such a tactic when it is used against you.

While a complete review of all these suggested tactics is beyond the scope of this work, we offer a review of some of the more common suggestions to support what was said earlier. There are no rules—there are only choices to make. Using any specific tactic makes sense only if it fosters the systematic approach you have chosen and is appropriate in your specific negotiation at that specific time.

7.5.1 *Anger*

Negotiators sometimes resort to feigned anger as a means of trying to convince an opponent that they are serious about their position. They also use it to intimidate. However, real anger is the result of frustration or anxiety, and it is often not consciously intended to do anything. If you feign anger, be careful. That feigned anger may induce the other person to become frustrated or anxious, which, in turn, could cause the other person to walk out.

Real anger can be quite dangerous. When you lose control because of frustration and anxiety, you run the risk of communicating more than you wish. Your mere display of anger may divulge important information to the other side, namely, that something has made you frustrated and anxious. On top of that, the substance of an outburst may inadvertently reveal information. For example, a lawyer on the other side of a negotiation over the merger of two corporations blurts out, at the prospect of deadlock, "Your arrogance is overwhelming . . . ." Assuming the anger is not feigned, the outburst gives you important information about how that lawyer perceives you. You can choose either to foster that anger or, if you believe it is counterproductive, take steps to diffuse the anger. The outburst, for example, may reflect that the deadlock is not over the substance of the negotiation, but because of a clash of personalities. You can then make the informed choice to try to break the deadlock by diffusing the personality clash rather than trying to make a substantive concession, such as offering more money.

One way to defuse the situation is to be prepared to use reflective listening probes. But before you can do that, you have to be able to recognize whether your opponent is actually angry. In addition to indicators such as voice tone, pace, and volume, the changing content of their arguments can show anger is taking hold. Typically, your opponent gets angry when he feels you are not understanding the dilemma he is facing or the significance of what he has said before. Your opponent may say things that are not productive to good communication or problem-solving. He may overstate, exaggerate, or misstate the facts as a way of communicating how strongly he is threatened, afraid, or hurt by the situation. Your natural response maybe to respond by calling him out on their exaggeration or to exaggerate, threaten, or misstate back to show that you too can get angry and that you will not be bullied.

As a result, managing your own response to anger is vital to your ability to make sure the negotiation doesn't become too personal, give rise to misstatements on your part, or deteriorate into an unproductive and unhelpful debate. One way to deal with your own rising anger is to name it, engage in active listening, restate and reflect what has been said, describe the facts as you see them, and then open the discussion to a topic of whether the two sides might be able to merge their different perspectives into productive problem-solving.[3] You might say:

> In response to what you have just said, I can feel myself getting angry. I know that when I get angry, I have a tendency to say things that are not helpful to the negotiation. Can I make a suggestion? You obviously are feeling strongly about your position, and I need to listen carefully to it, because I need to better understand how you feel about it. Please, what am I missing?

> * * *

> So let me see if I understand better your position. [*Fairly restate their position, being careful to reflect the feelings they have expressed as well as the content of what they have said*]. Have I captured the way you see the

---

3. TOM RUSK, THE POWER OF ETHICAL PERSUASION: WINNING THROUGH UNDERSTANDING AT WORK AND AT HOME (1993).

situation? [*Expect some refinement and perhaps some de-escalation of feelings at this point.*]

Keep this up until they tell you that you understand their point of view. Then say:

Great. Now I want to tell you how my client sees things and then make a suggestion about how we might merge these different perspectives.

When anger is used against you, you may be able to take advantage of it. Listen carefully to the outburst's substance. You might try showing that you are personally hurt by the outburst. Making the other person feel guilty may help you control his anger by simply embarrassing him. In any event, make sure your response is temperate. Think twice before you respond in kind. Escalation might result in the breakdown of the negotiation and seriously interfere with the ability to start discussions later.[4]

7.5.2 Aggression

Aggressive behavior, like anger, is designed to intimidate. As with anger, a more temperate response is usually appropriate. You might try to control the behavior by conducting the negotiation in a way that minimizes its impact. Similarly, it is harder to be aggressive with other people present, so negotiating in a team might be helpful. Likewise, a telephone negotiation make it is harder for a party to be aggressive and, of course, easier for you to terminate the meeting. Another tactic you may employ if you are negotiating with an aggressive lawyer is to meet at his office. It's a lot easier for you to terminate the session by walking out if the aggression becomes intolerable.

7.5.3 Boulwareism

Boulwareism is a tactic named after a former vice president of General Electric. The tactic involves making one offer, demand, or proposal, and then never making a concession. It is really a take-it-or-leave-it tactic. The theory is that you will have gained sufficient information before making the proposal that you can communicate your best offer up front.

Looking at this tactic in light of our systematic approach, it may take considerable education on your part to convince the person you are serious. You will need to persuade the other person not only that the first offer is fair, just, and equitable, but that there is indeed no more. Most people think that a controlling principle of negotiations is that first offers are always negotiable, and you may have difficulty persuading someone that this convention does not apply.

---

4. Douglas Stone, Bruce Patton & Sheila Heen, Difficult Conversations: How to Discuss What Matters Most (1999).

A very real problem with this tactic is formulating an appropriate take-it-or-leave-it offer. Negotiation is a fluid process. As you gather information—not just in formal information bargaining, but through making offers and counteroffers as well as persuasive statements—you eventually gain the confidence to know what is truly the best proposal for you.

And finally, if you choose to use Boulwareism, you must also be prepared to stick to it. If you ever make a concession, your credibility is seriously impaired.

7.5.4 *Balance or Slightly Outnumber the Other Side*

It is often suggested that you will gain an advantage in the negotiation by balancing your side's negotiators or outnumbering the other side. This may be useful. Again, going back to the systematic approach, we can see that there may be advantages. As we pointed out in chapter three, you cannot ignore the social-psychological dynamic of the negotiation process. Having an equal number of negotiators may make you less intimidated and therefore more effective. Likewise, outnumbering the other side may increase their anxiety.

As we have seen before, however, increasing the other side's anxiety can carry a downside. If your goal is to be a cooperative problem-solver, such a tactic could destroy the relationship you are trying to achieve. Given that, multiple negotiators may be useful for other purposes. As seen from the above discussion, many competing demands are placed on a negotiator—listening, asking questions, responding to questions, and formulating proposals. Sharing these responsibilities can be a great help. For example, assigning a secondary negotiator the task of simply listening is useful. Periodic caucuses in which the negotiators compare notes on what has been said may give the principal negotiator a better perspective on the changing dynamic of the negotiation itself.

On the other hand, having a single negotiator has a number of advantages. The presence of just one negotiator prevents the other side from taking advantage of potential divisions among multiple negotiators, such as differences of opinion. With a single negotiator, complete responsibility rests on one person and thus minimizes the missteps of one negotiator interfering with the actions of a partner. A single negotiator may also find it easier to take advantage of unexpected opportunities.

A variation on the multiple negotiator is often called Mutt and Jeff or Good Cop/Bad Cop. In this situation, one negotiator appears reasonable and sympathetic while the other is demanding and aggressive. The demanding, aggressive person quickly rejects proposals while the other attempts to reach an agreement. The sympathetic negotiator then suggests concessions that might bridge the gap between his own partner and the person with whom they are negotiating. The tactic, which appears so blatantly manipulative on paper, can be used with incredible success by many negotiators and is quite popular.

7.5.5   *False Demands*

Demanding something the person doesn't really want is another common tactic. By communicating the false demand along with the real demands, the negotiator establishes a bargaining chip to be later traded away. Viewed in our systematic approach, one risk this tactic entails is that if you are not as persuasive with this demand as all your other demands, the other side will clearly see that it is false. In turn, you must not give it up without good reason. Finally, be prepared to face the fact that if you ask for it, you might get it.

7.5.6   *First Offer*

It is often said that you should never make the first offer in negotiation. As with most rules, there is an element of truth to this rule, but it is also terribly misleading. Quite often, you have no choice but to make the first offer. If, for example, you are selling something, you will normally be expected to set the asking price. While it may not be impossible to get the buyer to make the first offer, it is unusual.

Understanding why a rule such as this developed will help you decide its utility. In other words, what is the risk of making the first offer? Typically, the risk is that you will underestimate your position and ask for too little. The great fear in buying a house, for example, is that the seller will take your first offer and you will feel you offered too much.

Thinking once again in terms of our systematic approach, the risk in making the first offer is that you might make it before you have sufficient information to assess the relative positions of the negotiators. The risk is not in making the first offer, but in making the first offer with insufficient information. In other words, the advantage of getting the other side to make the first offer is that they may prematurely move from the information bargaining stage into proposal stage.

As you gain information, the risk of making the first offer decreases. If you are in a situation where it appears inevitable that you will have to make the first offer, it merely emphasizes the importance of approaching the negotiation systematically—that is, to be sure to engage in adequate information bargaining before making the proposal.

You commonly encounter this difficulty when the other quickly brushes off ice-breaking and says, "That's great, but let's get to the point." This is, in our framework, an attempt to get you to skip information bargaining. If you make an offer now, there is a high risk that you will offer more than is required. You must control the agenda to move the process back and complete the information bargaining. For example, you might say:

> Well, I'm certainly here to see if we can do business. The fact is, though,
> I'll need a lot of information before I can make a judgment about whether
> that's even possible. Why don't we do this—you've sent me some helpful

information, but let me ask you some questions to clarify some things and find some new pieces. Then I'll be in a better position to see what we can do. For example, tell me something about . . . .

7.5.7   *Never Negotiate against Yourself*

You negotiate against yourself when, having made an offer that has been rejected, you make a concession before the other side makes a counteroffer. Again, the rule that you should never do this has a legitimate basis under our systematic approach. You should never concede without having been persuaded that something about your initial justification may have been wrong. Making a concession for no reason other than the fact that the other side rejected your previous proposal seriously affects the credibility of the original and all subsequent offers.

7.5.8   *Telephone Negotiations*

The reality is that much negotiation takes place on the telephone. Economic necessity mandates that person-to-person meetings cannot always be held. Telephone conversations are inherently less personal, and therefore the other negotiator will be less likely to treat you as another human being and perhaps more likely to be adversarial, competitive, and even deceptive. Nonverbal communication becomes even more important, and you must pay careful attention to the pitch, pace, tone, and volume of the other person's voice.

If you initiate a telephone negotiation, you must be as prepared as you would be negotiating face-to-face. If you receive an unexpected telephone call and the other side wishes to negotiate, you should feel little obligation to engage in meaningful discussion if you are unprepared.

7.5.9   *Time Pressure*

Setting an artificial time frame can be a useful tactic. Remember from chapter three that time pressures tend to decrease people's aspirations, demands, and bluffing. Where someone is very interested in making a deal, the deadline's pressure might result in their making concessions that otherwise would not occur.

On the other hand, if you can possibly avoid it, do not try not to communicate if you have time pressures that the other person does not share. Also, where you are given an artificial time pressure—accept by today or we withdraw the offer—ask yourself how credible the limitation is. Finally, do not reveal to the other side any time deadlines you may be under to wrap up a deal because they may seek to use the deadline to their advantage.

The above discussion should place the exchange phase of the negotiation, and what occurs therein, in context.

Adversarial Approach to Exchange	Problem-Solving Approach to Exchange
• Extreme offers with limited reasons • Threats • Closely guarded reactions to offers • Limited forced concessions • Moving only for a reason • Leaving no dollars on the table • Using escalation • Walking out • Coming in with limited authority • Using irrationality of client as leverage • Making non-negotiable demands	• Brainstorming solutions • Sharing information on probabilities and consequences • Examining the problem from opponent's perspective • Taking a broader approach • Considering perspectives of parties not at the table but in significant relationship with the parties • Exploring alternative ways to meet legitimate demands • Using time extensions to break impasses

An Integrated Approach to Exchange
• Making offers that fit needs and goals of opponents • Exploring opponents offers for needs and goals • Making concessions based on having been persuaded • Using probabilities of proof to make concessions

The next chapter will address the final phase of the negotiation.

CHAPTER EIGHT

CRISIS AND OUTCOME

8.1 Crisis

Crisis is the point in the negotiation at which the parties either agree or deadlock. Aside from making concessions, which might destroy the value of an agreement for your side, there is no sure way to avoid deadlock. In the real world, not all deals are meant to happen. In adversarial negotiating terms, the parties' bargaining ranges simply may not overlap. In problem-solving negotiation terms, the parties may simply be unable to come up with a solution acceptable to all.

However, when deadlock appears imminent, do not simply give up. As with any problem in negotiation, think about what is causing the problem? Here again, the systematic approach helps.

8.1.1 Check Whether There Has Been a Failure of Process

Many negotiations deadlock because a failure has occurred in one stage or another in the negotiation process. Examine each stage to see where the problem may have arisen. Have tensions resulted in a relationship among the negotiators that prevents agreement? Has animosity grown to the point that there will be no agreement because people do not like each other? If you believe the parties have failed to develop the appropriate relationship, you could suggest that time might be well spent trying to foster that relationship. Consider taking a break, and then coming back for a fresh start. One technique is to have each side summarize the other side's case and last offers. That way each side is forced to listen and to empathize with the other side's case, at least to the point of accurately stating it as a condition of going forward.

A failure may have occurred in the information bargaining stage. If the parties, for example, cannot agree on the actual market value of an item, there may be no chance of reaching agreement. Is there a neutral way of determining market rate? Perhaps you have not been persuasive. Have you or your opponent made irrational concessions, attempted to split the difference perhaps and therefore been unable to persuade each other that you are indeed at your bottom line?

Stopping to assess the negotiation in terms of the stages may help you respond to the impending deadlock or prevent it entirely.

8.1.2   Consider Changing Strategy

If you are an adversarial negotiator, you should probably consider a fundamental change in strategy as deadlock approaches. Remember from chapter one that what makes problem-solving particularly effective is trust or little risk. Has trust developed, or is there no risk, so that you can move to problem-solving? Or, if deadlock is near and you really need to reach an agreement, ask yourself if you will lose anything by abandoning your position, expressing your needs, interests, and desires, and seeking a problem-solving solution. Of course, you will not always overcome the deadlock, but you have little to lose at this point by focusing the discussion on underlying needs.

8.1.3   Third-Party Intervention: Alternate Dispute Resolution

Where the negotiation involves a dispute between the parties, and negotiation does not appear to be able to settle the dispute, you might consider some form of alternate dispute resolution, such as involving a mediator as a third party. Alternate dispute resolution may be particularly appropriate where the dispute can escalate into an expensive, time-consuming, emotionally draining lawsuit.

A complete discussion of the various forms of alternate dispute resolution is beyond the scope of this book. However, you may find it helpful to have a basic understanding of the various options available. Typically, privately arranged alternate dispute resolution includes negotiation as well as:

- arbitration, both binding and nonbinding;
- mediation;
- third-party evaluator or appraiser;
- summary jury trials/mini-trials;
- a combination of some or all of the above.

These types of third-party intervention may be effective because each helps to:

- reduce irrationality;
- reduce impact of social-psychological influences;
- explore alternative solutions;
- provide opportunities for graceful retreat; and
- facilitate communication.

8.1.3.1   Arbitration

Arbitration is typically viewed as an alternative to litigation. In essence, arbitration is a private form of litigation in which the parties choose the person who, after hearing some form of presentation from each side of the dispute, renders a decision much as a judge would. The theory is that a neutral third party in a private setting has several advantages, including:

- the parties can select an arbitrator who has particular experience with the type of issues raised in the dispute;

- the dispute can be resolved privately, thus avoiding much of the adverse publicity associated with a public lawsuit;

- arbitration tends to be more informal, and it is even possible for the parties to represent themselves rather than hire an attorney;

- arbitration can be completed more quickly than a lawsuit;

- arbitration may save money.

Arbitration is based on an agreement of the parties. As such, the parties can tailor the arbitration to meet the particular needs of the dispute. A primary point of agreement will have to be whether the arbitration will be binding or nonbinding. The parties can agree that the arbitrator's decision is binding and thus enforceable against the losing party. On the other hand, they can agree that the result is nonbinding. If the decision is nonbinding, the result is in effect advisory and may suggest to the losing party that they should not pursue the matter through litigation because they will probably lose.

8.1.3.2   Mediation

Mediation is the process by which a neutral third party helps the parties to the dispute resolve the matter. A mediator has no authority to impose a solution and often does not even propose solutions, but rather helps the parties to come to their own agreement. Because the parties normally must agree to mediation, you can tailor the precise role of the mediator to a specific problem. More will be said about how to think strategically about using a mediator in chapter nine.

8.1.3.3   Neutral Expert Evaluator/Appraiser

Often the parties look to the mediator to provide some valuation expertise, but this is not necessarily her role. The mediator might see doing so as being inconsistent with her need to stay neutral. Or she may believe she does not have the proper expertise. Sometimes the parties may agree that some part of the dispute—the value of a closely held business in a contested divorce or of an asset in a division of an estate—might benefit from a neutral appraiser. The parties' lawyers can suggest a process that can help select the appraiser through which trust can be built in the eventual outcome.

8.1.3.4   Summary Jury Trials/Mini-Trials

As a variation of arbitration, trials by private judges are becoming more popular. The precise name given to these private trials varies depending on the particular ground rules established, but in general, each method relies on a private judge to conduct a form of trial. The trial is often an abbreviated version of what would happen in court—presenting testimony in summary form or limiting the time available to each side to present evidence. A particularly creative variation is to conduct such a mini-trial and, rather than having the judge make a decision, the disputants return to the negotiation table to see if they can settle the dispute with their new awareness of how the trial might go.

8.2   The Outcome

Every negotiation is unique when it comes to the specifics of what constitutes a good outcome. There are, however, a number of general considerations to keep in mind. The outcome should, in no particular order,

- reflect the parties' goals and authority;

- minimize new problems;

- be efficient; both low cost and relatively simple to execute

- be achievable;

- be enforceable;

- be implementable;

- be fair, just, and equitable;

- have the desired level of specificity/ambiguity;

- be comprehensive;

- anticipate contingencies.

8.3   Wrap-Up

The negotiation as a whole, and individual sessions of a negotiation, must end as they began. Parties often forget that ending a negotiation entails a number of concerns. First, just as you want to start the negotiation setting the proper tone, you want to end it with the appropriate tone. People tend to remember most what they hear first and last, so the ending should involve rapport building (or perhaps rebuilding).

On a substantive level, the wrap-up should include a summary of the work completed to that point. If you have completed the negotiation is complete, completely restate the agreement you have reached. If additional negotiation is required, you should summarize progress to date so that there will be less chance of misinterpretation at the next session.

At the end of each session, each party should have a clear understanding of what its next step will be and when the next meeting (or how it will be determined) will take place. If the other person has indicated during the negotiation that she will provide you with certain financial information, for example, you must reiterate that promise and establish a specific time frame. If you have promised to do something, restate that commitment and give a time frame for its delivery.

8.4   Memorialization

In today's world, almost any negotiation—especially one involving lawyers—will end with some form of writing, whether styled as a contract or summary of the negotiation. Given the free-flowing nature of negotiation and the limitations of the human mind, when you sit down to summarize the agreement, you will often find that certain issues remain unresolved—or at least their resolution is ambiguous. Given this fact, it makes sense that you should do the summary yourself, if possible. This allows you the first opportunity to resolve these issues or ambiguities. Presenting your resolution to the other side is, in a sense, establishing the agenda for resolution of these hopefully minor issues.

Sometimes the final write-up can lead to an unwinding of the deal. When faced with such a situation, you can again learn from the international political arena. President Jimmy Carter, for example, believes the parties should be always looking to draft one agreement. The international mediator can present a single document back and forth between the parties until the parties have agreed in writing on the terms of the deal. The lesson for you may be for you and the other side to have a mediator draft and present the write-up of the agreement.

Adversarial Approach to Deadlock	Problem-Solver Approach to Deadlock
• Appear to make best final offer • Use escalation • Walk out	• Verify deadlock and restate last positions • Examine positions for psychological biases

Adversarial Approach to Deadlock	Problem-Solver Approach to Deadlock
• Refuse further discussion and make it difficult to communicate	• Bargain hypothetically, without any commitments • Propose discussion of ways to persuade opponent's client to move • Propose discussion of ways to persuade your client to move • Brainstorm what might make a difference • Try to get on the same board or page • Raise alternative means to verify, evaluate, and develop processes of trust • Consolidate gains and reduce differences • Use ethical understanding to defuse anger • Revisit underlying needs and goals • Suggest arbitration or mediation

Integrated Approach
• Moves from adversarial to problem-solving depending on trust and ripeness

CHAPTER NINE

NEGOTIATORS AND MEDIATORS

One of the most important lessons that negotiation theory and practice teach today's lawyers is how to think strategically about mediation. That is because mediators fall into two different types. Most are retired judges who are using their credibility gained in helping resolve other cases in court to aid the parties' valuation of their cases. In this type of mediation, the mediators are willing to provide an objective perspective to help the parties evaluate their strengths and weaknesses. Others see themselves as neutrals. They eschew giving opinions regarding a case's value, believing that to do is unethical. They merely seek to facilitate communication, understanding, and empathy between the disputants and then help them generate creative options for a solution. These mediators help the parties predict consequences and set up monitoring devices to ensure the solutions are carried out.

For example, lawyers can learn lessons from former Egyptian president Anwar Sadat's insertion of "mediator" President Jimmy Carter to help Egypt make peace with Israel. Sadat initiated conversations with Carter, pledged his cooperation, and enlisted his support in picking the timing, place, and parties. Note that President Carter, with an understanding that he did not want the UN Security Council members—including Russia and China—to be at the table, invited only representatives from Israel and Egypt to Camp David. Would the Egyptians (and President Carter) eventually sell out the Palestinians to secure peace with Israel? That is a question for history. Our point here is that a mediator can have his own agenda, interest, and priorities. And if a mediator weighs in with his own values, he can shape the outcome in significant ways.

There are as many different premediation processes and mediation stages as there are mediators. Some mediators are very informal and demand very little in the way of a premediation discovery and production of documents. Others are more formal and demand that the parties sign a premediation agreement in which the parties agree to mediate in good faith, provide full and complete answers to the mediator about the strengths and weaknesses in their cases, and agree to fully disclose material facts that relate to the fair resolution of the dispute. Some insist on an understanding that the mediator will use certain principles throughout the mediation. For example, the mediator may insist that the parties be respectful to each other during the mediation. Or that the mediator will help the parties evaluate their options in the light of how well they options protect human rights, rights of women and children, or prevent the problem of impunity for past wrongdoing. Others are more practical, using principles that help the parties evaluate their options under principles of how quickly the fighting or dispute will end, how easy the terms of the salutation are to execute, how to keep the dispute resolution at low cost, and how the parties can avoid publicity.[1]

One of the most important factors in choosing a mediator is the mediator's reputation of being prepared and invested in the process. Over and over again at the Camp David Twenty-Fifth Anniversary Forum, the parties involved commented that President Carter's level of detailed preparation was key to the success of the negotiations. President Carter reportedly had briefing books that included minute details so that he even knew what time of day was best to approach each party with proposals, based on an investigation of the parties' personal work habits. Such detailed preparation allowed him to adapt strategy and tactics and to go from group meetings, to caucuses, to taking breaks, to taking walks, to shuttling back and forth with proposals and suggestions, which kept the negotiation alive, even when the outlook was bleak.

As to the stages of mediation, some follow the stages of a hearing—the parties give their opening statements, then each take turns asking questions. The mediator then conducts her fact investigation. There are some extreme types of position-bargaining mediation in which the mediator does away with opening statements. Worrying that opening statements just make parties more wed to their side of the case, these mediators prefer to demand the parties to start by making opening offers and then concessions to move the parties to a solution. Using "split the difference" strategies, probabilities, risk analysis, discounting to present value concepts, and economic analysis, these mediators try to bring the parties into agreement about the dollar value of their case.

Some mediators will make extensive use of caucuses between the mediator and each side—some with only lawyers present, some with lawyers and clients present, and some with just clients present. During these caucuses, the mediator may ensure each side that she will hold the party's information in confidence, thus gaining an understanding of how far apart each side is. If there are significant differences in how each side sees the case, the mediator will explain to the parties the points on which they are being unrealistic and try to persuade them to rethink their positions. Some mediators then will engage in "shuttle" diplomacy between the parties until the matter is resolved.

Some mediators eschew caucusing, feeling that private conversations only contribute to mistrust and fears that the mediator is picking sides. These mediators will at least initially insist that the parties stay together to hear how each side sees the situation. They don't fear that emotional presentations will make the parties hold

---

1. Paul J. Zwier, Principled Negotiation and Mediation in the International Arena: Talking with Evil (2013).

too dearly to their grievances, believing that catharsis is more easily achieved where each side feels it has been heard.

Other mediators also resist valuing the case. If the parties deadlock, these mediators prefer to bring them together to facilitate the exchange of creative problem-solving solutions through brainstorming and careful examination and exploration of each side's underlying goals and needs.

9.1 An Integrated Approach to Preparing for Mediation

You prepare for mediation in same way as you would any negotiation, considering the following issues.

9.1.1 Assessment

Your preparation and planning for the assessment stage will look familiar.

9.1.1.1 Style and Strategy

You must decide what role you will adopt—will you be a competitive adversarial, a cooperative adversarial, a cooperative problem-solver, or a cooperative adversarial?

9.1.1.2 Ice-Breaking

How will you approach ice-breaking? Will you be friendly and engage in rapport building with the mediator, the opposing lawyer, or the opposing client? What information will you try to get during this informal session? If appropriate, should you offer an apology or express empathy expressed to set the right tone?)

9.1.1.3 Agenda Control

Previously, we discussed the importance of controlling the agenda. Will you suggest an agenda to the mediator during the opening or during the first caucus? Will you suggest a process for information exchange to the mediator that she could take to the opposing party(ies)? Will you suggest a problem-solving process for the mediation, in which you and the other side seek to identify shared needs, independent needs, and needs in conflict and then engage in a suggestion of creative win-win solutions for resolving the dispute?

9.1.2 Exchange and Assessment

9.1.2.1 Information Bargaining

What questions do you need answered before you are willing to trust the other side with vital information? Will you block information exchange until you are satisfied that the other side is bargaining in good faith? How will you answer the mediator's attempts to determine your bottom line? When you engage your client in premediation counseling, will you instruct your client to reveal the client's authority in stages, based on what you learn for the opposition? How will you prepare you client to answer a question like: "What is the most (least) you are willing to give to the other side?"

9.1.2.2   Proposals, Offers, and Demands

What will be your opening offer? What persuasive reasons will you give to justify your position?

9.1.2.3   Persuasion/Justification

Will you prepare your opening or closing statement with all the care you would if you were giving it to a jury? Will you use exhibits and display technology to show the mediator and opponent what the fact-finder will see at trial? Even in cases where the mediator has done away with opening statements, will you give a digital or hard copy of exhibits or other written statement of your case to the mediator and opponent?)

9.1.3   Assessment, Exchange, and Persuasion

9.1.3.1   Concessions/Reformulation

What concessions will you make and when will you make them? Will you be prepared to give reasons for your concessions, or will you credit the opponent for having persuaded you to make the concession? Will you be cooperative or competitive during the concession phase?

9.1.3.2   Crisis: Resolution or Deadlock

Will you walk away? Engage in brainstorming? Propose creative solutions? Agree to a process for future mediation?

9.1.3.3   Closing or Wrap-Up

Will you take the initiative to restate the proposed elements of the resolution before the parties finalize the agreement?

9.1.3.4   Memorialization or Write-Up

What enforceability concerns does the solution raise? What contingencies do you need to put in place to verify what you and the other side have both stated and exchanged? What guarantees do you need to ensure that the parties implement the agreement as intended? Will you suggest that the mediator do the wrap-up and control the write up?

9.2 Particular Position-Bargaining Considerations for Mediation

Mediators provide a number of useful purposes when seen in light of a position-bargaining strategy.

- The mediator can lend credibility to your client's valuation of the case.

- The mediator can help the parties get information about the opponent's bottom line, strengths, and weaknesses.

- If so inclined, the mediator can act as an expert evaluator of the case, relying not only on her experience in judging responsibility or evaluating credibility and persuasiveness of stories, but also on her substantive or technical expertise.

- The mediator can use position-bargaining strategies to move the parties to a reasoned settlement.

- The mediator can suggest deadlines to move the parties to a quicker resolution.

Mediators can also help you in a number of different ways:

- probe positions and test them for evidence;

- use contracts and processes for exchange of information;

- use confidentiality and caucuses to "leak" information to each side;

- use persuasion;

- trade concessions of equal value;

- split the difference.

9.3 Particular Problem-Solving Considerations for Mediation

As we have discussed, some mediators who think of themselves as neutrals or facilitators, eschew valuation and position-bargaining strategies when they conduct mediations. Facilitative mediators are particularly good when you want to implement a problem-solving strategy to resolve the dispute. If the mediator will use techniques to maintain neutrality, refuse case evaluation, facilitate communication, and use brainstorming and other counseling techniques to create win-win solutions, then the mediator can be vital to implementing a problem-solving strategy.

The problem-solving mediator can:

- suggest problem-solving processes;

- overcome opponent resistance to problem-solving strategies by making suggestions from the position of neutrality—because a distrustful party might reject these same solutions as tricks or manipulations if they were suggested by an opposing lawyer negotiator, when offered by a neutral they will more likely be adopted;

- facilitate discussion of underlying goals and values;

- create fair processes for providing information and valuation;

- facilitate generating multiple alternative solutions that create win-win outcomes;

- suggest creative valuation methods so parties can turn values into positions;

- create implementation processes that build in fairness, predictability, and trust.

Notice how differently you should prepare for a problem-solving mediation.

- The audience of your persuasion is the opposing side, not the mediator.

- Your language is that of a problem-solver. You talk of goals and needs, not positions or interest.

But beware—if your opponent employs a classic position-bargaining strategy, it is unlikely that she will think to come armed with the information she needs to engage in broader problem-solving. Even if the parties tried to implement a problem-solving strategy in the negotiation, without buy-in up front, the early sessions are likely to be unproductive until the bargainer has a broader understanding of the client's goals—or in the worst case, until the bargainer feigns interest in problem-solving, only to discover weaknesses in your case.

When you suggest the parties use a facilitative mediator, however, you create a different incentive. Parties will likely be required to be present. The mediator can ask each side critical questions and brainstorm for various alternatives. The parties, with the help of the mediator, might explore broader business concerns and consequently work together to fairly promote each other's legitimate interests in an agreement. Under the guidance of the mediator, both sides can make adequate apologies, and the parties can better judge the sincerity of the apologies. The parties can also better protect against attribution error (*see* chapter three).

Mediators are particularly useful to the parties in intractable disputes or in multiparty disputes.

When, then, should you counsel your client to consider the advantages of mediation? And how should you think strategically about mediation to implement your client's goals?

PROBLEM 9.1

Application to *Green v. Hall and Rose*

To illustrate the potential need to counsel your client about the advantages of using a mediator, think about how a mediator might facilitate a different kind of resolution of the dispute between the Greens with their realtor and the homeowner. Remember the Greens, who are African American, were assured by their realtor that their bid would be accepted. When it was not, and the Greens were not given a chance to raise their offer, the homeowner accepted the offer of a white buyer. Often, such cases are not resolved, and the parties end up going to court, although no one wants this. In the alternative, the Greens are paid close to $60,000, but only after Hall and Rose are cajoled into ponying up more money. Before a mediator-evaluator, the case often resolves at about the same point. But before a neutral mediator, who focuses on broader client goals and objectives, the chances improve that the parties can find some more creative and jointly beneficial solution.

If you understand how and why a mediator might facilitate such a better, tailored outcome, it might lead you to recommend, and your client choose, mediation.

For example, the Greens might have the following somewhat conflicting goals and objectives:

- an injunction to prevent future discrimination;

- damages to compensate for the loss of their bargain;

- damages to deter the realtor and homeowner from subjecting other African Americans to the treatment they received;

- a public apology from both of the other parties.

9.4 When to Mediate: Intractable Conflicts and Multiparty Disputes

In the business context in particular, where clients may more readily think in terms of transactions rather than disputes, these mediator-facilitated problem-solving solutions often work to the overall betterment of both sides. In litigation, the parties often resolve their disputes unassisted. Yet other times, the parties are not able to negotiate to an agreement unassisted. Perhaps there is bad blood between the clients, or their lawyers, or there is too much at stake, or it is a matter of principal.

Perhaps the size or complexity of the dispute prevents any approach other than a traditional litigation approach.

Peter Coleman, Director of the International Center for Cooperation and Conflict Resolution, wrote an article on intractable conflicts in the international political arena that sheds light on the intractability of conflicts in traditional litigation. His first factor of intractability is the *time and intensity* of the conflict. It is interesting to note how the standard litigation processes of complaint and answer, then interrogatories and depositions add time and intensity to the dispute between the parties and certainly to their lawyers. If the parties want to avoid intensifying the dispute, they should try mediation before filing their first pleadings.

The second factor is *issue centrality*, meaning that the conflict involves needs or values that are critical to the disputants' survival. Disputes over the purchase of a home that is denied on the basis of racism; spousal and child support payments; medical costs; or disputes that may result in a company going out of business might be of this type. Disputes with insurance companies shouldn't be of this type because one tenet of insurance companies is to pass on the costs in future premiums they charge to the client or other customers.

Third is *conflict pervasiveness*, meaning that the conflict affects the disputants in their everyday life and work.

Fourth is the feeling of *hopelessness* the parties share.

Fifth, some parties are *motivated to harm* the other side. In the litigation process, the parties so motivated have sought Rule 11 sanctions, made ethics complaints to the bar against the lawyers, and have stated intentions to "destroy," "put out of business," and "make sure that this never happens again."

Finally, the parties have repeatedly *resisted efforts to resolve* the dispute, but nothing seems to have worked.

In the above situations, you would be wise to consider whether a mediator ought to be employed. Your thoughts most often turn to the need for mediation where you have been involved in protracted and heated negotiations, with no movement between the parties.[2]

9.5   Social Science Teachings about Mediation

Knowing what social science literature suggests about how mediators might help resolve even intractable conflicts better prepares you and your clients to fit into these

---

2. Peter T. Coleman and Morton Deutsch, The Handbook of Conflict Resolution, Theory and Practice, 429–439 (2000).

processes.[3] This literature provides guidance to the ways that mediators are likely to see the process. As a result, it can help you plan when to mediate, know how the mediation will likely be conducted, and predict what processes the mediator might use to help the parties reach resolution.

Peter Coleman suggests a number of guidelines that mediators should employ to overcome the resistance the parties have to settlement, even with seemingly intractable conflicts. His guidelines are directed to intervenors or mediators. When you determine that either you (hopefully not the case) or the opposing side is unwilling to employ these guidelines, then you can bring in a mediator who can provide the missing ingredient. These guidelines are as follow.

9.5.1 Guideline 1: Conduct a Thorough Analysis of the Conflict System (Its History, Context, Issues, and Dynamics) Prior to Intervention

Mediators can design a process that ensures each side gets a chance to be heard as well as be assured that the mediator understands the perspective of each party. (Remember that Rusk's listening for understanding model is particularly good for fulfilling this guideline (*see* chapter three)).

9.5.2 Guideline 2: Mediator's Initial Concern Should Be to Establish or Foster an Authentic Experience of "Ripeness" Among the Disputants or Among the Key Representatives of Each of the Groups

You create this sense of ripeness by picking a skilled and fair mediator who has been successful in other difficult disputes by helping create a just and particularized solution to the dispute that lasts. Because of the reputation of the mediator, the parties may sense that the time is ripe to get the dispute settled. One variable that can help your timing to suggest the mediation can be a recent or near catastrophe. In addition, if you and the other side have recalculated the cost of stalemate and it is projected to raise unacceptable costs to both sides (for example, the likely number of plaintiffs in the future class will make it such that the existing plaintiffs will not receive fair compensation), then you should emphasize the time is ripe for mediation.

9.5.3 Guideline 3: Mediator Should Initially Orient the Disputants to the Primary Objective of Defining a Fair, Constructive Process of Conflict Engagement

What the mediator wants to steer the parties away from is are the objectives of achieving outcomes that resolve the conflict. Before resolving the conflict, the parties should focus on a fair process.

---

3. Peter T. Coleman, *Intractable Conflict*, MORTON DUETSCH & PETER T. COLEMAN, EDS., THE HANDBOOK OF DISPUTE RESOLUTION: THEORY AND PRACTICE, 428 (2002).

The 9/11 Commission experience is instructive here. Getting to this fair process requires input from the harmed party(ies) and flexibility from the mediator to hear the objections. Again, a skilled mediator is vital to this occurring, but you can "feed" the mediator suggestions regarding a fair process that will live within the limits of your client's goals and objectives.

9.5.4   Guideline 4: Given the Complexity of Intractable Conflict, Analysis and Intervention Must Be Embedded in a Multidisciplinary Framework

When you understand the social, psychological, economic, and justice implications involved in an intractable dispute, you can better prepare a process that will satisfy the parties. For example, where there are multiple parties and multiple interests—as in a mass tort setting—democratic theories require that each party has representation and a voice in the design of the process. In addition, you must design the economic analysis in a way that ensures that the process of valuing individual harms is reliable. Implement document retrievals and language searches that will ensure fairness. Draw experts need from different disciplines to advise and balance different biases within fields. The process needs to be open. You must clearly articulate the steps in each decision. Panels of decision-makers must be accountable for their decisions. While mediators can design these, you, your client, and the other side can suggest a structure that works and lasts.

9.5.5   Guideline 5: Approaches to Conflict Intervention, Particularly When Working across Cultures, that Elicit Input Tend to Be More Respectful of Disputants, More Empowering and Sustainable, and Generally More Effective than Prescriptive Approaches

The problem-solvers and facilitative neutral mediators are cheering! If the disputants can suggest the solution, they are more likely to own it and abide by it than if it is forced on them. Take, for example, the case of Congress in the 9/11 Commission dispute or that of the United States internal Iraqi disputes. What is true on a national or international political scale is true in private litigation. If the disputants can suggest, have input, and seem to have selected the process, they are more likely to live by it. (Again, you might propose a solution to the mediator, then suggest that she present it to the other disputants as her own demand to which the other side is "forced" to accede.)

9.5.6   Guideline 6: Short-Term (Crisis Management) Interventions Need to Be Coordinated with and Mindful of Long-Term Objectives and Interventions

This guideline is for the mediator, but it is yours to remind the mediator of the long-term goals of your client in mediation and ensure that these are not harmed.

9.5.7 Guideline 7: When Working with Conflicts between Large Groups (Such as Ethnic Groups and Communities), Concentrate Interventions on the "Midlevel" Leadership Representing Each Group

Coleman writes about this guideline in the context of international political disputes:

> The work of John Burton, Herbert Kelman, John Paul Lederach, and others has emphasized targeting for intervention with certain types of leaders with groups and communities engaged in protracted social conflicts. These leaders, labeled "track II diplomats" or "middle-range leaders," are typically influential, unofficial representatives (members of the media; former or potential government officials; leaders of business, educational, religious, union, and other local institutions) from opposing sides of a conflict who represent the mainstream of each community and reflect the attitudes and interests of their respective communities.

There are several advantages to working with such midlevel representatives. It is efficient because midlevel representatives have influence going up and down the ladder. Midlevel representatives are more realistic because they have seen the good and bad in the parties they represent. And usually their roles are such that they are not usually constrained to take the more extreme positions.

9.5.8 Guideline 8: The General Intervention Strategy Must Integrate Appropriate Approaches for Issues Rooted in the Past, Present, and Future

In mediations involving mass multiparty disputes, mediators worry that any short-term solution will be short term and leave future claimants without a remedy. Again, you must be prepared to show why your proposed resolution is designed to last.

9.6 Creative Solutions the Mediator Might Propose

Your client may question the utility and expense of employing a mediator if the client believes that you, the attorney, can the job yourself. Your client needs to understand, however, that your opponent or her client might resist your creative solutions if they come directly from you. As a result, using a mediator to deliver creative solutions might be the better choice. Of course, when you turn the negotiation process over to a mediator, you might lose some control over the agenda and find yourself dealing with a number of creative solutions that you and the client might not be prepared to discuss and evaluate. You should engage the client in a discussion about what might be proposed by a particular mediator. What creative solutions should you be on the lookout for if the client chooses to mediate?

9.6.1 General Litigation Disputes

As a way to help the parties reach fair resolution of their dispute, some mediators suggest classifying the level of fault that can be attributed to one or more of the parties. Drawing support from conflict resolution research, these mediators seek to help the parties determine whether the dispute is a simple misunderstanding, one that involves negligence or gross negligence, or one caused by a character flaw of one of the parties. If what caused the dispute is a simple *misunderstanding*, then minor compensation and an apology may be all it takes to resolve the dispute. If the dispute involves *ordinary negligence* (blame associated with not taking due care), then compensation is in order. If the behavior rises to *gross negligence* through *recklessness*, then compensation and some additional amount to deter future recklessness may be in order. And if the dispute involves a *character flaw*—racism, sexism, dishonesty or the like motivates the behavior—then compensation and punitive damages are in order.

The mediator might suggest ways to allow the parties to discover the true nature of what happened. Sometimes expedited discovery of key evidence may help resolve the dispute, especially if one of the parties has resisted discovery because of what it might bring to light— by inquiring directly about the facts and proof, the mediator may be able to break through the resistance.

Of course, motives are often mixed and subjected to recreation and narrative techniques (i.e., why someone makes a mistake is often unknowable). Thus, the mediator is left with trying to move the parties past extreme characterizations of the dispute so that the conflict can be resolved in favor of moving forward and ending the cost of the ongoing conflict.

Where the dispute is about the facts or *data*, what actually happened and what damage was caused, or the value of the item in dispute, the mediator might suggest ways to expedite finding the answers to these different data disputes, including the following:

- use the time value of money to narrow the value differences between the parties positions;

- create win-win solutions by suggesting areas of independent value as providing room for trade (e.g., in a divorce, valuing education as a means for helping a spouse return to the workforce may give rise to paying for tuition, when the kids leave the house);

- one side cuts the cookie, the other picks the half.

Where the dispute is about *principles* or *identity* or *meaning* each party ascribes to the event leading to the dispute, different solutions for resolution may include:

- helping the parties understand the complexity of interpreting the meaning of past events;

- helping the parties confront their own responsibility for what has happened;

- helping to the parties see that fear, anger, or resentment can cause paralysis and continuing harm to third parties;

- asking the parties directly what solutions they propose to help them engage in joint problem-solving (ask them to use their imaginations to see a future where the parties are no longer in dispute—what does such a future look like and what needs happen to make the future a reality);

- asking the parties if the mediator can suggest a solution that the mediator has seen used in similar cases.

9.6.2   Family Disputes

The interpersonal dynamics in family disputes cannot be underestimated. Years of slights and miscommunication, for example, can make in difficult for parties to agree. The fact that in many instances the "injury" felt by a party cannot be monetized makes a solution even more difficult. A mediator might suggestion the following:

- teach empathy by asking the parties whether what they propose is fair to other side or third parties (e.g., the children);

- introduce transformative strategies such as apologies and forgiveness;

- help the parties value apologies (trading money for apologies?);

- help parties understand that for an apology to be meaningful it must be sincere and cost something (public versus private); in addition, the party must admit what it did, why it did it, and what harm it caused;

- help the parties understand forgiveness;

- remind the parties that forgiving does not mean forgetting;

- help the party's understand that forgiving must be voluntary, not forced;

- help the parties understand of what was done, why it was done, and the harm it caused;

- if appropriate, help the parties put in place a mechanism to help ensure that the behavior will not reoccur;

- help the forgiving party to act as if the offending party is not responsible;

- suggest reconciliation be put off to future counseling sessions that the disputants agree to attend.

9.6.3 *Business Disputes*

In a business dispute, the mediator's own business experience might lead to the following proposals:

- renegotiate pricing discounts;

- explore loan forgiveness;

- explore market-sharing or territory noncompetition agreements (anti-trust concerns?);

- explore warranties or security agreements going forward;

- explore licensing agreements, partnerships, or joint ownership;

- discuss liquidated damages.

9.6.4 *Property or Succession Disputes*

Property and succession disputes often involve a mix of business and family disputes. A mediator might suggest the following:

- discuss options such as split ownership from control (owning through corporate form, sub-chapter S, limited partnership, joint-trust ownership, title held by third-party trustee);

- discuss substituted value;

- explore leaseback options;

- explore remainder interests or reversions;

- explore other options;

- discuss creative ways to hold title.

9.6.5 *International Political Disputes*

In disputes between nations, diplomats with experience in international negotiations might suggest the following:

- powersharing;

- transition agreements;

- new elections;

- interim constitution;

- referring matters to the International Criminal Court;

- amnesty;

- use of Truth and Reconciliation Commissions;

- hybrid courts or investigative proceedings to determine fault;

- agreements to hold new elections;

- third-party security force (UN);

- federal political structure with autonomous local control over specific matters;

- free enterprise zones.

9.7 Conclusion

To effectively think strategically about mediation, you must first determine what kind of mediator you want to mediate the session. If the mediator you choose is a retired judge or evaluative mediator, consider the following strategies:

- form an implied alliance with the mediator by making a concession that will communicate your good faith, your reasonableness, and your willingness to settle;

- use a concession pattern that communicates that your first offer was close to your bottom line;

- enlist the mediator to help you discover the weaknesses of the opposing side's case;

- use cooperative blocking techniques—i.e., over answering questions, setting up trades for information, and staggering offers in a way to ensure the good faith of the opposition;

- if your client is present, explain the importance of information exchange and the ability of the client to let the lawyer communicate the client's positions;

- if your client is present, teach the client how to block the mediator's questions or answer only on the condition of confidentiality.

If the mediator you choose is a neutral facilitator, consider these strategies:

- make sure the mediator understands the client's needs and goals;

- request that the mediator ask for information from the other side to insure that they are mediating in good faith;

- identify shared needs, independent needs, and conflicting needs;

- enlist the mediator to present creative solutions in a way that indicates those solutions came from the mediator—if the other side thinks the solutions were suggested by a neutral, she might accept them more readily.

For you to think strategically about implementing your client's goals and objectives, you must understand he theory choices and strategies that are likely to come into play. The two prominent strategies are position bargaining (or adversarial bargaining) and problem-solving. Position bargaining is the most common strategy employed by bargainers and involves taking positions to learn how your opponent likely sees his case and determining how to move the opposition into a solution that meets your client's goals. Problem-solving, on other hand, involves creating a relationship of trust and cooperation between the parties so together you can devise a better and more creative solution. Problem-solving strategies often require the involvement of a mediator for the promise of problem-solving to be fully implemented.

Understanding these strategy choices can help you better counsel the client about how he can achieve his goals. The strategies can also be useful for helping both you and your client understand the strengths, weaknesses, and risks involved in resolving his case, and finally, help your client make the best strategic moves to implement his goals.

Evaluative Mediator	Facilitative Neutral or Transformative Mediator
• Written submissions of facts and issues • May not ask for opening statement at session • Asks to go into caucus with each side • Asks for opening offer • Expresses opinion on offer and tries to suggest where offer overstates position • Tests proof of facts with confidentiality • Expresses opinion on chances of success at trial • Tries to generate concessions and more realistic bottom line • Does same with other side • Shuttle diplomacy till agreement	• Written commitment pre-session to cooperate and disclose and negotiate in good faith • Asks each side to describe their perspectives • Each side addresses other side, not the mediator, during their opening statement • Advocate should use the language of goals and needs, not offers and positions • Caucus used to ask for sensitive information and to ask about party's empathy for other side (How do you think the other side will react to your proposal? What should I use to convince them to understand our goals?)

Evaluative Mediator	Facilitative Neutral or Transformative Mediator
• If deadlock, uses persuasion on side out of line in evaluator's opinion	• Ask what is fair, in addition to what they want • Seeks to establish ethical understanding of each side • Seeks out and diffuses attribution and bias errors • Joint session asks parties what solutions they see • Brainstorm additional solutions • Facilitate party discussion underlying needs and goals • Asks parties to determine solutions • Where there is deadlock, suggest party processes for breaking deadlock that are objectively verifiable and fair • No evaluation given • Facilitates discussion of solutions for societal fairness • Sets up monitoring devices

Integrated Approach to Mediation
• A mediation process designed for the particular dispute and particular disputants • Written submissions of facts and issues • Written commitment up front to cooperate and disclose and negotiate in good faith • May not ask for opening statement at session if determines parties will not benefit but will become more intransient from making opening statement • May ask each side to describe their perspectives to facilitate empathy • Asks parties to describe broader goals and shared needs • Asks to go into caucus with each side

Integrated Approach to Mediation
• Refuses caucuses to promote trust and communication
• Or caucus used to ask for sensitive information and to ask about party's empathy for other side
• Tests proof of facts with confidentiality offer either in joint session or in caucus
• Asks parties to brainstorm possible solutions
• Facilitates conversation between the parties to develop understanding of economic, social, and psychological consequences
• Asks for opening offer
• Asks permission to express opinion on offer and to suggest where offer overstates position
• Asks permission, (Would it be helpful if I told you....) expresses opinion on chances of success at trial
• Tries to generate concessions and more realistic bottom line
• Does same with other side
• Shuttle diplomacy till agreement
• If deadlock, uses persuasion on side out of line (in mediator's opinion)
• Seeks to establish ethical understanding of each side
• Seeks out and diffuses attribution and bias errors
• Joint session asks parties what solutions they see
• Brainstorm additional solutions
• Facilitate party discussion underlying needs and goals
• Asks parties to determine solutions
• Where there is deadlock, suggest party processes for breaking deadlock that are objectively verifiable and fair
• No evaluation given or upon request suggest evaluation
• Facilitates discussion of solutions for societal fairness
• Sets up monitoring devices

Chapter Ten

Multiparty Negotiations

Up to this point, except for a brief foray during our discussion of mediation, our focus has been on two-party negotiations. As we have seen, there are a number of significant barriers to a negotiated settlement of a two-party dispute. There are biasing errors that each side must deal with. There are failures in trust and information exchange. There are game theory reasons why a particular party might want to withhold and conceal information to obtain a bargaining advantage. As a result, there are negotiation failures even when there are solutions that would provide an efficient, fair, and lasting resolution to a dispute.

As difficult as these barriers are in a two-party dispute, they become even more complex in a multiparty dispute. This is particularly true because even though some parties want to settle, others can gain advantages through *holding out* and *opting out* of the final agreement. These strategies threaten finality and place the fair resolution of a dispute into jeopardy. Consensus resolution is often unworkable, and so parties agree to resolve matters by majority voting or with reference to agreements by a "sufficient consensus" of the disputants. Some argue that where there is a "sufficient consensus," the "winners" can negotiate side agreements with the hold-outs, and everyone will reach resolution. In the end then, the resolution of multiparty disputes will likely be negotiated between two parties—the winners, or a sufficient consensus of winners, and the hold-outs.

While there are different strategic considerations that arise with multiple party negotiations, the two strategic frameworks we have already discussed inform those choices, and an integrative approach—one that blends adversarial and problem-solving strategies—can help you prepare for multiparty negotiations.

10.1 Criminal Context

Consider what happens when two alleged co-conspirators plea bargain with the state. If the negotiation starts at the interrogation stage, the state is looking to form an alliance with one of the defendants to get information about both of them. If one of the defendants is your client and can get a deal that is better than if the state gets the cooperation of the other co-conspirator against your client, it makes sense to accept the deal. If, however, the state's case against both defendants will fail if each refuses to cooperate with the state, then it makes better sense for the defendants to reach a joint-defense agreement and for your client to refuse to deal with the police. The "prisoner's" dilemma is that during the interrogation stage, neither suspect knows whether the other is cooperating; likewise, neither knows whether the other alleged co-conspirator sees the same likely success of a joint-defense agreement.

The case turns on the strategic control of information—both what each defendant gives and what the defendant can get from the state. You try to find out from the state what information they have and the likelihood that they will be able to either get the co-conspirator's cooperation or prove their case independent of your client's cooperation.

The lawyer bargainer's traditional strategy is to get the maximum from his own client about what the state knows. The bargainer then tries to get the most from the state about what it knows and seeks. Then he uses this information to perform a risk calculation to predict whether his client will do better by forming an alliance. The bargainer wants to go into the session with a clear understanding of his client's bottom line (understanding the worst result they will take) and by taking positions against the prosecutor to determine what the prosecutor has. From this he will decide whether reaching a deal with the prosecutor is the best way to ensure the client's bottom line.

The same basic calculations hold in a civil case for both position-bargaining plaintiffs and defendants. Where there are multiple plaintiffs, the plaintiffs may want to cooperate with each other if they believe they can do better with an average recovery. To do this, they would need to agree to block information about the particular weaknesses and contributory negligence or assumption of risk of their respective clients.

The single plaintiff, like the prosecutor, must determine whether his best shot at getting total maximum recovery is to form an alliance with one of the defendants (Mary Carter agreements). The defendants also are trying to determine whether it is better for them to form an alliance to reach a joint-defense agreement or for each to reach its own individual agreement with the plaintiff.

10.2 Mass Torts

The Ford Bronco roll-over cases and Firestone tire defect cases demonstrate the complexities where the defendants not only are trying to calculate how they will fare against an uncertain size class of plaintiffs, but also figure in the costs of their negotiations with government and any recall the government might order. As to any one defendant, the calculation depends on determining:

- the number of potential claimants;
- the average amount of their damages;

- the setoffs for each plaintiff's own behavior;

- the chances of success of the average case;

- the effect on the number of future claimants of settling with existing claimants;

- the cost of recall;

Defendants (or a combination of defendants and plaintiffs) can form alliances or coalitions to better assess the information needed to make the calculation. In addition, parties need to consider different procedures for getting information to assess the risks and values of the claims. So a defendant might consider:

- trying a sampling of representative cases to get better information with which to assess the number, size of damages, and setoffs;

- using class actions (for settlement purposes) as a vehicle for getting information about the number of claimants and classes of claimants;

- using Multidistrict Litigation (MDL) to get information through res judicata principles about causation, the ability of an expert to use certain kinds of expert testimony, and whether any defenses might bar all suits or certain classes of suits;

- using bankruptcy law to classify claimants and determine average recoveries, get rid of punitive damages claims, and/or preserve key business assets through Chapter 11 bankruptcy to sanitize the business from claims and avoid payments to unknown, future claimants.

10.3 Bankruptcy as Forum for Dispute Resolution

One of the common client misperceptions is that bankruptcy is not an option when thinking about dispute resolution. This is because there are a number of myths about bankruptcy that need to be looked at carefully.

10.3.1 Bankruptcy Myths

Myth 1. The corporate board may have obligations to equity holders and option holders that are likely lost when bankruptcy is declared.

At some point, because the fiduciary obligation runs to the corporation and not just to the equity holders, the board's obligations do run to the creditor. This may give the management the cover to protect key business assets from certain classes of claimants. As a result, management survives another day, protecting their own employment and future income. In fact, in a mass-tort situation, where there is ongoing liability, the existing claimants and creditors may have a conflict of interest with future claimants. They might join with management and not contest bankruptcy or bankruptcy plans if they determine it is better for their existing claimants and themselves to get a fee certain now and wash the debtor clean of future claims against it in its reformed state.

Myth 2. Bankruptcy hurts relationships with suppliers, creditors, and customers, which have an effect on the ongoing nature of the business.

Empirical studies on the effects of bankruptcy on the surviving business do not bear this out, at least not with the big players. Filing bankruptcy did not hurt United, or USAir, or Federal Mogul in its ongoing relationships with suppliers, creditors and customers, at least not as it affected their ability to secure the necessary supplies or credit, or maintain its customer base during the term of the bankruptcy proceeding.

Myth 3. Bankruptcy litigation costs—each party or group of parties gets an attorney and their costs get paid before other business costs to the detriment of the ongoing business.

The truth is that the trustee keeps a close eye on attorney fees and the court will also ensure that while the attorneys are fairly compensated the debtor is also protected.

Myth 4. When in bankruptcy, the business can only conduct normal business and mergers and acquisitions are outlawed. Other unusual business actions must be passed before committees. The business is less nimble and can't respond quickly enough in the market.

The truth is, bankruptcy can provide the flexibility to do these precise things, particularly if it is a reorganization.

Myth 5. Bankruptcy requires insolvency.

Note that some commentators think that the Constitution requires a finding of insolvency.[1] Bankruptcy legislation and bankruptcy practice suggests otherwise. Others are less sure, and the practice seems to be to the contrary.[2]

10.3.2 Bankruptcy Advantages

Advantages of the bankruptcy system you should consider are:

- bankruptcy may allow your client to protect key assets and scrub them from future liability;

- individual bankruptcy decisions cannot be reviewed;

---

1. Thomas E. Plank, *The Constitutional Limitations of Bankruptcy*, 63 Tenn. L. Rev. 487, 565 (1996).
2. George Kuney, *Bankruptcy and Recovery of Lost Damages*, 71 Tenn. L. Rev. 81 (2003).

- punitive damages may disappear, although fraud and intentional torts are not supposed to disappear in bankruptcy. The mere fact you are considering bankruptcy may communicate to the other party the seriousness of your actions.

10.4 Coalitions and Alliances

Setting aside for the moment the mass-tort situation, the conventional multiparty lawsuit seems to be simply a matter of controlling information, using position-bargaining techniques to control the opposition's view of the case, and maximizing the client's return. You should use alliances and agreements to cooperate to control information, maximize return, and minimize harm.

Yet there are a number of social and psychological effects from alliances and coalitions that need we need to examine.

First, there is a tendency for some coalitions, or "enclaves" of similarly-situated decision makers, to polarize or take extreme positions. For example, institutional defendants, like tobacco companies and families of persons who died from smoking, might initially meet and agree to share information, but gradually become more extreme in the positions they take. They may tend to demonize the opposition and miss the legitimacy of the competing claims.

Second, coalitions can sow mistrust. Our experience observing three-party negotiations, where parties are permitted to form alliances, bears witness to the strong psychological affects that pre-negotiation coalitions have on causing mistrust and deadlock, even when the clients have given their lawyers plenty of authority to settle the case.

The problem-solver would predict as much. Position bargainers who stonewall will not engender a communication process that will lead to a fair resolution of the dispute. Not only will the parties be highly skeptical of the information they get from the other side, they will likely attribute wrongful intent on both parties, raising the stakes on both sides of the table. In addition, position bargaining will more often lead to making deals with the wrong party, with the result that parties lose at trial.

It is better, say the problem-solvers, to design a negotiation process that will build trust and the frank and full sharing of information, while will lead to a fair, just, particularized, and lasting result. If you can, try to employ advanced empathy strategies of agreeing to the benefits of the problem-solving process.

Each party should present his case in a manner that tries to fairly describe how he sees the situation. To the extent that all parties can either concede weakness or admit to the strength of the other parties' positions, they can build trust. Also, to the extent that each bargainer can demonstrate that he is listening to the others and open to changing his view of the case, if a fair problem-solving approach can be reached, the bargainers will be better able to reach a particularized result that maximizes the creative win-win solutions that are possible.

10.5 Democratic Theory and Multiparty Dispute Resolution

Problems-solvers in a multiparty negotiation setting are more interested in setting up a process that places great faith in the principles of representative democracy. They argue that coalitions and enclaves of like-minded, fear-driven bargainers are likely to engage in "group tough" talk and polarize the discussions by taking extreme positions. Problem-solver believe it is better to let the deliberative process take place, informed by the reasoned positions of all the diverse interests in the outcome so the parties can reach a creative and lasting solution.

Once again, the adversarial position bargaining and problem-solving distinction will help you determine whether a mediator might help the parties design a fair process that will bring about the best result. When a mediator is a skilled position-bargainer as well as an expert evaluator, then she can help position-bargainers and start to assess the value of the case and risks at the end game. These mediators can also help the parties form coalitions to move an intransient bargainer to settlement. (Professor Francis McGovern, who mediates classes of asbestos cases, is the classic example of this kind of mediator. In the asbestos litigation, his success occurred in delivering classes of claimants to the defendants. He negotiated fixed numbers of claimants and average amounts of plaintiff's damages in exchange for certainty and finality for the defendants.)

The neutral problem-solving mediator brings other skills to the mediation. The neutral problem-solver will bring a process that builds trust. The parties may be asked to sign an agreement that they will engage in a full and complete exchange of information. The neutral problem-solver may suggest that other parties be brought into the negotiation to insure that representative democracy really takes place. (An agreement reached between the state government and a polluter that does not take into account the interests of those who live downstream in a different state will not last very long.) The information exchange will include an exchange of the underlying goals and objectives of the parties. The neutral problem-solving mediator will then engage the parties in brainstorming alternative solutions and help them get the information they need to predict consequences. The neutral problem-solving mediator will be interested in designing a monitoring system for whatever solution is selected to ensure that the solution is being implemented in the fair and reasonable way according to the parties.

Such a process of joint deliberation also avoids the problems that arise from the phenomenon of *group polarization*. Group polarization occurs when those who think similarly discuss their views of what happened only with each other. They tend to become more convinced of their view, less tolerant of other views, and less empathetic to the perspectives and concerns of those who are not in their group. It is important for parties to realize the potential biasing effects of entering into alliances or side deals with other like-minded defendants or plaintiffs. The loss of the other sides' trust, coupled with the polarizing biased and radical presentation of the case can lead to deadlock. That is why it may be better to engage all the affected parties in a negotiation about the democratic process they will use to explore the facts and fairly attribute responsibility rather than seek strategic combinations that may lead to deadlock and distrust.[3]

PROBLEM 10.1

In the *Green v. Hall and Rose* negotiation, the plaintiff is a black couple seeking damages, an apology, and assurances that the discrimination they experienced will not happen again. They had submitted an offer through Hall to Rose, for Rose's home. Hall, the broker, communicated the Greens' offer and assured the Greens it would be accepted. Rose received a second higher bid from another prospective buyer. The prospective buyer was white. Rose accepted the higher bid without giving the Greens a chance to counteroffer. In depositions of Hall and Rose, each blames the other for what happened, attributing racist motives to the other. If you represented Hall, would you now still seek to reach a coalition with Rose before you entered into negotiations with Green? In the alternative, what process might Green, Rose, and Hall agree to that would fairly lead to the resolution of the dispute? How might this negotiated process differ from traditional adjudication?

Multiparty Negotiations Adversarial Approaches	Multiparty Negotiations Problem-solving Approaches
• Enter coalitions or joint defense agreements	• Identify, research salient features, history of dispute
• Position, bargain, and block information exchanged	• Use principles of democratic theory to identify all stakeholders' representatives, and design a process that will likely produce a fair result
• Test opposition through classic position bargaining	
• Use representative adjudications, focus group results to predict and persuade outcomes	• Select fair, distinguished mediator
	• Make early concession to demonstrate good faith
• Use bankruptcy to protect key assets, dismiss punitive damages, and limit future claimants	• Look for win-win creative solutions
	• Enlist mediator in proposing solutions
• Suggest solutions that party controls (arbitration before sympathetic arbitrator)	• Cooperative and participate in monitoring settlement solution(s)

---

3. Cass R. Sunstein, *Deliberative Trouble: Why Some Groups Go to Extremes*, YALE L.J. 71 (2000).

Chapter Eleven

Cultural Considerations and Negotiations

In an increasingly global marketplace, it is vital that lawyer negotiators understand the role that cultural differences can play in conducting negotiations. There is a great deal of evidence that suspicion and hostility between parties from different cultures can inadvertently be fueled by remarks and actions that negotiators interpret as insulting and offensive and reflecting badly on their honor. The ability to implement your client's ends will often depend on your ability to anticipate these differences and choose the right approach for the right setting.

In general, part of preparing for your understanding of cultural considerations includes examining your own cultural chauvinism. A party is chauvinistic if her view is egotistic and self-centered—the view that a toddler has of the world, that he is the center of attention and that the world revolves around his happiness. On a related matter, you need to examine your ethnocentrism. By this, we mean you need to examine not only your ethnic perspectives, but also your religious, racial, or national characteristics, especially your subconscious beliefs about the importance of the individual and the particular values imbedded in your ethnicity.

One of the most important values to examine is the tolerance of each party for the other's cultural differences. Inherent cultural differences are often viewed through the lens of each party, and each party creates a bias that it is more practical and realistic about the way the world works. Each may appear to minimize differences, but lack real understanding of how the particular cultural lens will distort each party's position to the other. Examining your own stereotypes of the other party will help prepare you to be sensitive to cultural differences and their impact on your strategic decision-making.

11.1 The Japanese Experience as a Paradigm

In the decades when the Japanese economy was booming, American business and U.S. government entities were particularly enamored with Japanese business. In trade negotiations between the U.S. and Japan to open Japanese markets to U.S. manufacturers, the experience of U.S. negotiators was cited as a reason to take cultural differences seriously when negotiating with foreigners. In a gross oversimplification of the negotiations between the parties, the negotiations went something like this: The head of the U.S. delegation led off and made persuasive statements in support of why the Japanese needed to give equal shelf space to U.S. products as they gave to Japanese products, how the U.S. did the same with Japanese goods, how free trade demanded fair goods placement, and how everyone was better off because the market would then be better able to make quality and price comparisons for the betterment of the customers in both countries.

All during the presentations, the Japanese negotiators listened respectfully. They nodded in apparent agreement. They even said "yes" with enthusiasm as the American negotiators made their points. The U.S. delegation went back to their rooms that night fully believing that they had convinced the Japanese of their positions. In the days and weeks that followed, however, the Americans determined that the Japanese delegation was not persuaded. They, in fact, learned that the Japanese delegation was not calling the shots, that there was an "undisclosed principal negotiator" who was behind the scenes and refusing to move. The U.S. delegation announced agreements, only to learn that there had been no agreement. Similar experiences were reported in negotiations between U.S. and Japanese businesses.

At first, the cultural differences were described in somewhat racist terms—that you could not trust the Japanese, that they were tricky and inscrutable. But over time, the American negotiators discovered a number of cultural differences that explained the negotiation experience. Seen in the light of our position-bargaining and problem-solving paradigms, they became quite understandable.

Commentators have written books explaining the different cultural values that underlie the Japanese business experience.[1] At the heart of the difference between negotiation styles and strategies is the Japanese concept of *wa*. *Wa* is a deeply ingrained system of principles designed to promote interpersonal harmony, mutual trust, respect, responsibility, unselfish cooperation, and loyalty among groups. While it can be seen similarly to religion (that the cynic would say oppresses the masses for the betterment of the few, powerful, and extremely wealthy), the Japanese promote *wa* as a means of establishing the trusting relationships necessary for creativity, personal growth, and responsible, accountable action that drive Japanese productivity and quality of product.

If *wa* is the goal of any business relationship, then the Japanese negotiating style is understandable.

- First meetings should not include talk about business and should be purely social, emphasizing the start of a new relationship between the parties and

---

1. YUMI ADACHI, BUSINESS NEGOTIATIONS BETWEEN THE AMERICANS AND THE JAPANESE, GLOBAL BUSINESS LANGUAGES (1997); ROBERT M. MARCH, THE JAPANESE NEGOTIATOR: SUBTLETY AND STRATEGY BEYOND WESTERN LOGIC (1990); KAZUO NISHIYAMA, DOING BUSINESS WITH JAPAN: SUCCESSFUL STRATEGIES FOR INTERCULTURAL COMMUNICATION (2000); ALAN GOLDMAN, DOING BUSINESS WITH THE JAPANESE: A GUIDE TO SUCCESSFUL COMMUNICATION, MANAGEMENT, AND DIPLOMACY (1994); BOYE DEMENTE, JAPANESE ETIQUETTE & ETHICS IN BUSINESS (1994).

the importance of getting to know each other and understand each other's values.

- Exchanging business cards is a ritual.

- Any decision the Japanese reach will be a product of a business consensus. The parties to this consensus will include people drawn from every level of the business, including line workers, middle managers, and the highest officers. Each of these groups needs to understand the decision and feel right about it.

- A U.S. business delegation should also include members from all levels of the U.S. business. If these are people who will be in relationship with the Japanese business, then the Japanese need to get to know them. (A part of the business-card ritual is to help the Japanese delegation understand that there is representation and relationships at all levels of the business.)

- Longevity of a negotiator, or party representative, with a business is especially important. It shows the importance of loyalty and commitment to the business that is necessary to enhance *wa*.

- Japanese don't mean "yes" when they say "yes," or "no" when they say "no." The Japanese are more interested in reaching understanding and promoting a good feeling during presentations of ideas. They do not want the opposing negotiator to be interrupted, embarrassed, or become defensive. The Japanese give agreeable responses, or *aizuchi*, to make the other side's communication go smoothly and avoid making the other side feel embarrassed. In fact, it is common for the Japanese negotiator to lead off with "yes," even when they disagree—the disagreement will come in what follows the "yes," as a refinement, modification, or reversal of what the other side said. Saying "no" is too confrontational and hurts the relationship. For a Japanese negotiator, it is far better to change the subject than to say "no."

- Eye contact is disrespectful. It interrupts the speaker, who becomes concerned about the listener, and affects the speaker's train of thought.

- Silence is respect. It allows the speaker to think and gather words and ideas to promote better understanding.

- Negotiations take time, as the goal is *wa*, even where no deal can be reached. *Ningen kankei* (warm interpersonal relationship) requires time and trust and is put off by aggressive position bargaining by parties with a limited understanding of or longevity with the business.

These commentators then suggest that American negotiators adopt the following tactics, if they want to be successful.

- Start slow. Develop relationships and trust first, then talk business.

- Take a team approach and include negotiators from all levels on your team.

- Recognize the persons with authority may not even be present at first and that any big business decision will likely be made by consensus and needs to be supported by reasons appealing to those in all levels of the business.

- American negotiators should develop a vague and general style up front. They should speak in terms of goals and broad objectives. (They should develop the language of problem-solving.)

11.2 The Chinese

Imagine doing business in the following environment. There is no "rule of law." If a person breaks a promise, there are little real consequences. If you would go to court, the judge would not likely be legally trained. The judge would be open to being directly influenced by the political party in control of national and local government. The contract law provides for freedom of contract, but makes an exception for the enforceability of the contract if "public policy" dictates otherwise. (On its face, not all that different from U.S. contract law, except that there is no developed system of case precedent that describes unconscionability, when a contract might be unenforceable and there is no common practice whereby a U.S. judge will call the "party" to determine whether this is a "policy" against or in favor of the contract, as there is in the Chinese setting.) Your lawyer would not be allowed in court. You are entitled to a "friend," as is your opposition. Of course, a party might pick a friend to whom the judge is beholden for their job, or who runs the local government, or who knows how any judgment might negatively affect the community. Even if you got a judgment from the court, the finality of the judgment would be open to question. In addition, the enforcement of the judgment would be open, as the official tasked with enforcement is its own entity with limited notions of private property. Levying on assets would also raise its own set of questions.

Imagine further that business practices provide little in the way of transparency and does not have a mechanism for a bargainer to know the financial condition of the person with whom they are bargaining. There is little in the way of accounting records. Relationships with creditor and financiers (state banks) are hard to document and are very uncertain because the lending institutions themselves are hard to examine for their financial condition.

If you want to do business in these circumstances, your bargainer is left to bargain out of the shadow of the law or in anything like the conditions that most businesses in the West are used to dealing. In these situations, one can see why the Japanese-like style of negotiation, based on the *wa*, would develop.

When you enter into a relationship without the automatic enforcement mechanisms of contract damages or specific performance, you are left in a state of continued negotiation. Even if you have agreed on a dispute resolution forum and/ or choice of law for enforcement that is more predictable (i.e., international arbitration in Hong Kong, where principles of English common law have developed a body of Hong Kong Chinese case law), you still have problems of enforcing those decisions on mainland China. Whatever you "agree" to up front is just a starting point if either side does not perform. Your only remedy is to "renegotiate" the terms of the relationship in light of whatever new conditions have arisen. This is what negotiators contend with in China.

Of course, the situation in China is evolving. China has a new constitution. It is developing a system of laws that can be known by its judges. It is developing a role for lawyers. It is "committed" to the development of the rule of law by training its judges. Because its businesses want to do business in the West (for example Chinese furniture businesses want to sell furniture in California), it needs its own lawyers to understand Western law and Western-style negotiations. As these businesses do business with the West, they develop models of contract that are influenced by the Western understanding of efficient enforcement and rule of law. China has joined the WTO and seems to understand that International UCC and rule-of-law principles lower transaction costs, encourage investment, and allow the globalization of the marketplace to take place. Still, until the rule of law advances sufficiently in China, the problems of gathering information, judging risk, and managing gains necessitates a "Japanese" style of negotiation. People seeking to do business in China must develop a relationship of trust. They must go slow and understand the underlying goals and aspirations of the business persons they are dealing with. They must learn who controls the business and who makes the decisions. They must develop either enough trust, or a set of processes to build trust, that the risks they entail are balanced by the gains they can expect.

As with the Japanese paradigm (and maybe Chinese experience helps us understand how the Japanese models of negotiation developed), the advice for U.S. negotiators is to develop a more problem-solving approach.

- Develop first the process of gathering information and communicating about and dealing with expected income and costs rather than on pricing the deals.

- Prepare a clear understanding of your own goals.

- Seek a relationship that will help you get information about the opposing side's goals and objectives.

- Take the time to get to know the other side's business, and for them to get to know yours.

- Lengthen the time you expect to take to reach a deal.

Do not start with an extreme offer and expect that the other side will be used to position bargaining and that you will not lose credibility if you move off your opening position.

- Make an early initial concession as a demonstration of your good faith.

- Seek to learn from each other how to best fulfill the shared goals of each side.

- Brainstorm alternative arrangements and their consequences.

- Initially, state positions tentatively and hypothetically so that you do not lose face either by accepting the term and later be unable to live up to it, or by rejecting the term in its initial offering.

- Cooperate in reaching a consensus on what would work best. Involve decision-makers at all levels in both your businesses.

- Look at joint-paying arrangements for employees.

- Offer positions to prominent Chinese business persons on the board of your company, just as you might with a major U.S. business who was important to your business.

- Use national Chinese negotiators (trained in the U.S. in the ways of U.S. business) as the face of your business.

- Develop monitoring mechanisms with the Chinese business to get both sides' information about how well the deal is working. This will allow you to adjust the terms of the deal before a dispute arises and the relationship of trust is affected by the dispute itself.

11.3 The Russians

Doing business in Russia raises all the considerations of the need for cultural sensitivities that we have discussed with regard to Asian cultures that are in the process of developing rule of law systems for more efficiently and fairly deciding business disputes. In Russia, commercial disputes are decided by a specialty business court call an Arbitrage Court. Until recently, disputes making their way up through the arbitrage courts were decided by a Supreme Court of Arbitration. In 2014, National Supreme Court took over jurisdiction at the highest level of appellate review of commercial disputes. Some see this as a way for the Putin government to exercise more control over business disputes that potentially could have an impact on the Russian economy.

Even where the parties have agreed to International Arbitration of any disputes that can arise between the parties, the Russian National Courts retain jurisdiction over any disputes whose outcome could have an impact on the governance systems in place in any Russian business. If one of the parties would contest the outcome of such a dispute, the Court could make the determination that the Arbitration decision changes the power over the company and its assets and set aside the decision. If the parties haven't made provisions for security and enforceability of judgments through assets held outside of Russia, the decision of the Arbitration court would have no effect on the Russian corporation.

In other words, the parties may be left to negotiate only in the shadow of law and with remedies usually prescribed to the parties. They with then be forced to create future-oriented problem-solving solutions if they are going to maintain any hope of securing a rightful return when a dispute arises.

11.4 The Palestinians

Image you are Palestinian. You grew up learning about the way that your parents and grandparents were treated when Israel was established. The version you were told is that when U.S. and Europe offered Israel a homeland, your parents were promised, when they were moved from their homes, that they would soon be able to return. Since then, through a number of wars with Egypt, Syria, Jordan, and Lebanon, various promises were made by the West that your family would return to their homeland. None of these promises have been kept. You understand that the reasons given for why they have not been kept are issues of security and the right of Israel to exist. You believe the right of Israel to exist depends first on the return of your family to the land unlawfully taken from them. You do business in this cultural environment. How would it affect your strategy and tactics of negotiation?

On the one hand, you might take your lesson from how you were treated, especially when dealing with the West. You make promises when it is convenient to get what you want. You believe it is unnecessary to fulfill your promises if it is inconvenient for you do so. You are not lying. You believe in the principles of efficient breach.

Your level of distrust is great. You are only willing to enter into deals with people you trust. Trust is much more than taking positions and making promises. Trust has to borne out by action and sacrifice. But once that trust is earned, the loyalty will be worth the time spent in building the trust.

To the Westerner, with Western expectations, the Palestinian bargainer displays a more adversarial and position-bargaining strategy than they do. The culture helps explains where the Westerner's stereotype of the Palestinian might come from—that Palestinians lie; that they go back on their promises; that they are angry and emotional bargainers, taking exceptions to the mildest threats and are quick to escalate the bargaining and resort to deadlock and violence if need be. Issues of saving face are of utmost importance.

Some argue that the only way to deal with position bargainers is by positioning bargaining and insisting on strictly enforced agreements. Others believe that problem-solving strategies offer more hope, especially where the time is taken to build trust by building principles and processes for dealing with future disputes (*see* intractable disputes; cf. Ireland and Dayton Peace accords).

11.5 The Caution of Black South Africans

In the mid-1990s, after apartheid ended in South Africa, the U.S. State Department and USAID developed a program to develop business and government leaders among black South Africans. The program was designed to bring groups of forty to fifty black South Africans to the U.S. for special training. They started at the Wharton School for instruction in finance, then they went to New York and Wall Street, and then to Washington, DC, for a course in negotiation training.

One of us had the privilege of teaching a course in negotiation, and on a number of occasions during that course, some version of the following experience was relayed that raises a significant caution for problem-solving negotiators:

> I'm so happy to be taking this course. I'm in desperate need of learning how to negotiate like you in the West. You see, my family has long run a business in South Africa. After apartheid ended, we were approached by a Western business. They told us they were very interested in seeing us succeed. They want black South African business to lead Africa into prosperity. They asked us how they could help. They wanted to know all about our business: our suppliers, our customers, our marketing approaches, our sources of finance, our manufacturing process, everything about our business. After we spent an enormous time with them, they left. We did not hear from them. After about a year we came across them again. It turns out that they had taken the information we gave them and used it to set up a competing business here in South Africa. Sure, they may have hired a black South African to be the face of the business, but in reality, they were never negotiating with us in good faith at all. We want to learn those techniques so that we can protect ourselves and use them on others.

The warning for all bargainers is clear. There are risks to "problem-solving" strategies if the other side is not negotiating in good faith. Trust is not something that is developed risk-free. And a lie dressed up like trust looks like trust. So, too, a position-bargainer dressed up like a problem-solver looks and acts like a problem-solver. In the words of the immortal George Burns, "Once you learn how to fake sincerity, everything else comes easy."

So we recommend, in the end, a functional approach to bargaining, whether in the international arena, public or private, or in litigation or national or local business setting. Just as cultural differences form the lens through which each bargainer sees the bargaining process, so does the personality of the individual bargainer and the strategy they have adopted form the lens by which they act and respond to the bargaining process.

Both strategies need to be used to control the flow of information—what you give and what you get. Position bargaining does not depend on trust and derives information from the moves people make. Deadlines and threats, deadlocks and walk-outs, strikes, and even violence reveal information about the other side's strengths, weaknesses, goals, and objectives.

Problem-solvers can cut through the inefficiencies of bargaining in the context of distrust, where the rule of law provides an after-the-fact deterrence on the behavior of the parties. It allows the parties the potential to grow to *wa* and experience the harmony and joy of long-term creative relationships built on trust. At risk, however, is a bet on your judgment of human nature. Does the other side really care about your growth and happiness? What if it is better for them financially or otherwise to enter into a different relationship with someone else? Can you ever really trust them to not cause you harm whenever a combination of a better offer and "getting away with it" arises? For these reasons, the problem-solver needs to be able to access the probabilities and risks and determine what position needs to be their bottom line. Just as an abused spouse needs to be able to walk out as a matter of personal integrity, so too the problem-solver needs to understand position bargaining to enforce and maintain his integrity.

CHAPTER TWELVE

ETHICAL CONSIDERATIONS

Usually, negotiators prefer not to disclose everything at a negotiation's outset and want to influence the direction the negotiation goes to some extent. Even cooperative problem-solvers do not initially disclose everything and are interested in steering the negotiation—or at least the process the negotiation follows—in a particular direction. Competitive adversarial negotiators might be more blunt. They seek to mislead the other side—at least as to their real bottom line—and they seek to manipulate the other side to achieve their goals. Given this setting, negotiation raises a number of ethical issues that should not be a surprise. Chief among the ethical issues in negotiation is how truthful you must be. In this chapter, we will discuss this issue and raise additional ethical considerations of which you should be aware.

12.1 Truthfulness

The most troubling ethical issue in negotiation is lying. A fundamental assumption of negotiation is that the participants resist revealing at least some information to the other side. To be sure, during information bargaining, adversarials emphasize seeking and hiding information whereas problem-solvers emphasize seeking and revealing information. In chapter six, we discussed the tactics associated with "blocking" the disclosure of information. At what point does this attempt to avoid disclosure become unethical? Unfortunately, no clear answer exists.

PROBLEM 12.1

The lawyers for the Greens have been authorized to settle the lawsuit with Hall and Rose for $10,000, plus a public apology. During face-to-face negotiations, may the lawyers for the Greens ethically state: "My client has authorized to settle for nothing less than $250,000. That's our bottom line. Accept it or we will see you in court."?

Problem 12.1 raises the basic question of whether negotiation statements about what your client will find acceptable are subject to a truthfulness standard.

The American Bar Association Model Rules of Professional Conduct provide only general statements about the obligation to be truthful. Model Rule 4.1 provides:

In the course of representing a client a lawyer shall not:

(a) Knowingly make a false statement of fact or law to a third person; or

(b) Knowingly fail to disclose a fact to a third person when:

(1) In the circumstances failure to make disclosure is equivalent to making a material misrepresentation;

(2) Disclosure is necessary to prevent assisting a criminal or fraudulent act, as required by Rule 1.2(d); or

(3) Disclosure is necessary to comply with the law.

Model Rule 4.1(b) provides little more guidance than the admonition that lawyers shall not fail to disclose when such failure is in violation of legal requirements to disclose. Subparagraph (a), however, with its broad prohibition against making a false statement, has significantly more potential for suggesting ethical restrictions. What the drafters actually contemplated by the phrase "knowingly make a false statement" is, however, not at all clear. A comment to Rule 4.1, in fact, states: "Under generally accepted conventions in negotiation, certain types of statements ordinarily are not taken as statements of material fact. Estimates of price or value placed on the subject of a transaction and a party's intentions as to an acceptable settlement of a claim are in this category . . . ."

Under the commentary to the Model Rules, it appears clear that counsel's statements in Problem 12.1 are ethically permissible. However, relying on conventions—as the community does—to determine what is permissible is problematic at best. A number of problems are readily apparent. What community of lawyers should we look at to determine the conventions? Do the conventions in one geographical area apply across the country, much less the state or the city? Even within a geographical area, do lawyers in different types of practices have different conventions? Are the conventions different for criminal defense attorneys, for example, than for securities lawyers?

In light of the ambiguity of the standard, we must make a couple of points. First, you should not assume that your interpretation of existing conventions is the same as opposing counsel's. A little skepticism is not a bad thing. Certain conduct crosses the line and constitutes unethical or even illegal behavior. However, you should recognize that negotiation is among the most private activities a lawyer does, and you cannot count on the bar ethics committee to be looking over your opponent's shoulder.

Second, some guidance is nonetheless available. The Model Rule's commentary that "[e]stimates of price or value placed on the subject of a transaction and a party's intentions as to an acceptable settlement of a claim are in this category . . . ." suggests that you can make a useful distinction between statements concerning historical facts and interpretations, inferences, or intentions. A statement that a client has received twenty stitches as a result of the accident when he only received ten concerns a historic, objectively verifiable fact, and is a lie. A statement that the client will not accept less than $250,000 in satisfaction of his claim, when, in fact, the client has indicated he would accept as little as $10,000 plus a public apology, is puffing and would generally be considered permissible.

12.2 Other Ethical Considerations

You should keep in mind a number of other professional responsibility issues, none unique to negotiation.

Model Rules of Professional Conduct Rule 1.1 provides that "[a] lawyer shall provide competent representation to a client. Competent representation requires the legal knowledge, skill, thoroughness, and preparation reasonably necessary for the representation." The obligation to provide competent representation obviously is not unique to negotiation. You should remember, however, that competence is more than facility with doctrinal analysis. Competence in the context of a negotiation requires negotiation skill, just as competence in the context of a trial lawyer requires courtroom skill.

PROBLEM 12.2

Assume in Problem 12.1, plaintiff's counsel responds by saying: "That offer is insulting. I'm not even going to dignify it by taking it back to my client." Is there an ethical problem?

To the extent that the lawyer in Problem 12.2 does not take the settlement offer back to the Greens, there appears to be an ethical problem. Model Rules of Professional Conduct Rule 1.2(a) provides that "[a] lawyer shall abide by a client's decision whether to accept an offer of settlement of a matter. In a criminal case, the lawyer shall abide by the client's decision, after consultation with the lawyer, as to a plea to be entered, whether to waive jury trial and whether the client will testify." The Model Rules clearly make the decision on whether to accept a legitimate settlement offer the client's—not the lawyer's. Indeed, the Model Rules make it clear that the lawyer has an affirmative obligation to ensure that the client has sufficient information on which to base this decision: "a lawyer negotiating on behalf of a client should provide the client with facts relevant to the matter, inform the client of communications from another party and take other reasonable steps that permit the client to make a decision regarding a serious offer from another party." Model Rules of Professional Conduct Rule 1.4.

PROBLEM 12.3

Assume that in Problem 12.2, defense counsel is convinced that plaintiff's counsel has not communicated the $250,000 offer to the Greens. May defense counsel contact them directly with the offer?

As just discussed, Model Rules 1.2 and 1.4 require the client to decide about a serious settlement offer. Problem 12.3, however, raises the question of what opposing counsel can do if she believes the offer has not been communicated to the other party. On occasion, a lawyer will feel frustrated, thinking that a legitimate offer she put on the table has not been taken back to the client. The solution is, however, not to bypass opposing counsel and communicate directly to the opposing party. Model Rules of Professional Conduct Rule 4.2 states: "In representing a client, a lawyer shall not communicate about the subject of the representation with a party the lawyer knows to be represented by another lawyer in the matter, unless the lawyer has the consent of the other lawyer or is authorized by law to do so."

Your options to get the offer to an opposing party are therefore limited. Asking your client to contact the other client is not an option in a litigation setting, because you cannot circumvent an ethical proscription through the actions of a third person. If suit has been filed and the jurisdiction has a provision similar to Federal Rule of Civil Procedure 68's offer of judgment, invoking the rule may provide some help in this situation. Rule 68 provides in part: "[a]t any time more than 10 days before the trial begins, a party defending against a claim may serve upon the adverse party an offer to allow judgment . . . against the defending party . . . for the money . . . specified in the offer." If the offer is not accepted, and the offeree ultimately recovers less than the offer, the offeree must pay all costs subsequent to the offer. The effect of the provision for our purposes is that it increases the likelihood opposing counsel will at least communicate an offer made subject to Rule 68.

General provisions concerning confidentiality and conflict of interest, of course, affect the lawyer in negotiation. In particular, Model Rules of Professional Conduct Rule 1.8(g) provides that "[a] lawyer who represents two or more clients shall not participate in making an aggregate settlement of the claims of or against the clients . . . unless each client consents after consultation, including disclosure of the existence and nature of all the claims . . . involved and the participation of each person in the settlement." This Rule makes clear what should probably already be clear from general provisions governing conflicts of interest and the client's right to accept or reject settlement offers.

A final consideration concerns Model Rules of Professional Conduct Rule 4.4, which prohibits conduct intended to humiliate and harass. Competitive negotiators, in particular, must be aware of the line between aggressive advocacy and harassment. Crossing that line may not only affect your effectiveness, but be unethical.

PROBLEM 12.4

Assume that negotiations in *Green v. Hall and Rose* have been conducted over a number of weeks. You are approaching trial. You represent Hall. Remember that Hall has had her deposition taken and has denied having a racial motive for not taking the Greens' offer. In recent conversations with Hall, she refuses to pay more and expresses that part of her reasoning was and is racist. May Hall's attorney settle the case without revealing that Hall lied during her deposition?

Traditionally, lawyers have taken the position that the risk of a deposition was that no automatic duty arose to supplement if facts testified to in a deposition changed after the deposition and before trial. If a witness admitted giving false testimony, the remedy was to settle the case without revealing the fact of the false testimony.

Recent changes to the Model Rule 3.3 have called this practice into question. Model Rule 3.3 speaks to Candor toward the Tribunal. It provides:

(a) A Lawyer shall not knowingly:

(1) make a false statement of fact or law to a tribunal or fail to correct a false statement of material fact or law previously made to the tribunal

(2) . . .

(3) offer evidence that the lawyer knows to be false. If a lawyer, the lawyer's client, or a witness called by the lawyer, has offered material evidence and the lawyer comes to know of its falsity, the lawyer shall take reasonable remedial measures, including, if necessary, disclosure to the tribunal.

While early Model Rules were unclear about whether a statement in a deposition was a statement to a tribunal, the comments recently enacted make it clear that a deposition is a statement to a tribunal.

Comment 1 to 3.3 provides:

> [1] This Rule governs the conduct of a lawyer who is representing a client in the proceedings of a tribunal. See Rule 1.0(m) for the definition of "tribunal." It also applies when the lawyer is representing a client in an ancillary proceeding conducted pursuant to the tribunal's adjudicative authority, such as a deposition. Thus, for example, paragraph (a)(3) requires a lawyer to take reasonable remedial measures if the lawyer comes to know that a client who is testifying in a deposition has offered evidence that is false.

As a result, the Model Rule 3.4 specifies the action that the lawyer is supposed to take if he learns that false testimony has been given in a deposition. The lawyer is to remonstrate with the client and take reasonable remedial measures. If the client does not agree to reveal the fraud to the other side, the lawyer must move to withdraw. The implication is that the lawyer cannot settle the case without withdrawal or revealing to the other side the false statement at the deposition.

PROBLEM 12.5

Assume that negotiations in *Newman v. Popchek* have been conducted over a number of weeks. You are approaching trial. You represent Ms. Newman. Counsel for Mr. Popchek has called and says that his client is deeply embarrassed by the lawsuit and is desperate for his wife not to learn about the suit. He wants to explore whether Ms. Newman might be willing to hear his apology and if that might help settle the case for a reasonable amount. You think that if Mr. Popchek might be able to persuade Ms. Newman to take substantially less than what he might pay otherwise and that this would have an impact your fee. Do you have to discuss Mr. Popchek's offer to apologize with Ms. Newman?

Model Rule 1.7 warns the lawyer against allowing personal interest to affect his advice and tactics in the lawyer's representation of the client. Comment 1 addresses the loyalty required of the lawyer,

> [1] Loyalty and independent judgment are essential elements in the lawyer's relationship to a client. Concurrent conflicts of interest can arise from the lawyer's responsibilities to another client, a former client or a third person *or from the lawyer's own interests*. (author's emphasis.)

It is important for the lawyer to be sufficiently self-aware to realize that she is in a conflict situation. Not communicating the offer is probably unethical under the provisions of Model Rule 1.2 (client controls the objectives of the litigation) and Model Rule 1.4 (client should be kept informed). The question for the lawyer becomes how best to deal with the conflict and counsel the client, now that the conflict is made manifest.

There are two models the lawyer should consider in handling the conversation the client.[1] First is a client-centered model, which requires that the lawyer provide a neutral evaluation of the opposing offer, exploring its strengths and weaknesses without regard to how it might affect the lawyer's fee. The second option would be

---

1. *See* PAUL J. ZWIER AND ANTHONY J. BOCCHINO, FACT INVESTIGATION: A PRACTICAL GUIDE TO INTERVIEWING, COUNSELING, AND CASE THEORY DEVELOPMENT, ch. 7 (2d ed. 2015) (for a discussion of a client-centered model and friendship model for lawyer-client counseling).

to admit that the lawyer has an interest in the client's decision, but let the client off the hook for considering the impact of their decision on the lawyer.

Where the lawyer decides to attempt a neutral presentation of the Popchek offer, she must take some care must in how the discussion will take place. The conversation requires a careful and neutral discussion of the strengths and weaknesses of the case, including the legal, economic, moral, and psychological consequences of considering a settlement. The choice is the clients, and while the lawyer has a certain right to recover costs the client has agreed to pay in pursuing the litigation, the "contingency" fee risk is otherwise borne by the lawyer. Perhaps the lawyer can be steeled in her neutrality by the fact that happy clients make referrals. The lawyer must ask not only how the client will "feel" about having forgone money when she is strapped for cash, is in a lower paying less prestigious job and the baby gets sick, but also explore how she will "feel" if she learns that Mr. and Mrs. Popchek's marriage breaks up or he loses his position in the firm; or she gets more money, but never is able to work in a prestigious firm.

Still, the lawyer may decide that the best option for dealing with the client's offer is to be transparent.

> Ms. Newman, I know you have come to me for objective neutral advice, and to provide you with that advice, I need to remind you of what you already know, that my fee is based on the amount of the total dollars paid in this case. I am afraid it may subconsciously color my advice to you about what you should do. Still, I remind you this is your decision, and you should not worry about my fee in deciding what to do. That is a risk I took in deciding on our fee arrangement. Having said that, my advice is to not get mired in a discussion of apologies. It is often a way for him to play on your sympathies and good graces in attempt to get away with what he did. In my view, the money is evidence of wrongdoing and should be seen by you as an apology from firm for what they did.

12.3 Conclusion

As much, if not more, than anything else a lawyer does, negotiation is usually a very private activity. The client is counseled in private, and the lawyers sit down face-to-face in private. The result may be public, but the process is quite closed. As such, inappropriate behavior will not likely be subject to outside review. Just imagine, for example, the difficulty of filing a complaint with a state bar ethics group and then proving that opposing counsel has lied to you during the negotiation. Negotiation, like so much else a lawyer does, therefore, relies heavily on the individual ethics of the participants involved. You should keep in mind that your ethical conduct with a client or an opponent in a negotiation will pay dividends to both your professional reputation and your future dealings with these people.

Adversarial Approaches to Ethical Dilemmas	Problem-Solving Approaches to Ethical Dilemmas
• Counsel client to not give negotiator "knowledge" of bad fact • On questions of intent to settle, represent the party's intent in whatever way best serves the negotiator's position-bargaining strategy • On questions of value, represent value in whatever way best serves the negotiator's position-bargaining strategy • Using agenda control and multiple blocking strategies • Rule questions out of bounds • Refer to what is on the record or "before the court" in answer to questions concerning vulnerabilities	• Investigate facts to discover vulnerabilities before formal discovery starts • Use client counseling to get permission to reveal vulnerabilities as a strategy of showing good faith and reasonableness • Trade information on vulnerabilities • Brainstorm with clients about creative solutions to resolve dispute and produce fair results • Think strategically for how to protect what is vital and essential and deal fairly with opponent's legitimate needs

Appendix A

Preparation and Planning Worksheet

Your goals

— What do you wish to accomplish?

— What are you willing to accept?

Their goals

— What do you believe the other party seeks to accomplish?

— What do you believe the other party would be willing to accept?

Adversarial or problem-solving or a combination?

— What advantages do each strategy have in this particular negotiation?

— If you are going to approach the negotiation from an adversarial perspective, what is your bottom line at this point?

— What will you use as a starting position?

— What facts do you have that might indicate

the likely starting position of the other side?

the likely bottom line of the other side?

— Can you plot the potential bargaining ranges on each side?

— What information do you have available that would suggest the other side's probable strategy (adversarial, problem-solving, or some mix)?

— What facts do you have that might indicate

the underlying needs, interests, and desires of the other side?

the probable proposals the other side might make?

— Are you aware of any social or psychological facts that might have an impact on this negotiation?

— **If you are willing to shift strategy during the negotiation, what factors will motivate you to switch? How will you make the switch?**

> For example, if you wish to move from adversarial to problem-solving, what actions can you plan to take to increase trust or decrease the risk associated with problem-solving?

—**What information can you seek from sources other than a face-to-face meeting with the other person?**

— **Is this negotiation best accomplished face-to-face, by telephone, by letter, or some combination? Why?**

— **If the negotiation is face-to-face, where will it take place? Why?**

— **If you control the setting of the negotiation, how will you arrange the location?**

— **How long will the negotiation take? Why?**

— **In this particular phase of the negotiation do you seek to accomplish all of your goals or do you have a more limited purpose? For example, is this meeting only to obtain information or merely to begin developing a rapport?**

— **Are there any conventions or controlling principles you need to consider in this negotiation?**

— **How will you establish the agenda?**

> — How will you establish what to negotiate?
>
> — How will you establish the manner in which you negotiate?

—**What type of ice-breaking will you use, if any? Why?**

—**What information do you need to get from the other person? Why?**

> — How will you get this information?
>
> — What questions will you ask to get information from the other person?
>
> — In what order will you ask the questions?
>
> — What information is the other side likely to seek from you?
>
> — What information is the other side likely to try and avoid giving you?

— What will you do if the other person asks you for information you do not want to reveal?

— What will you do if the person refuses to give you a piece of information either by blocking or outright refusal?

— What will you do if the person tells you what you know to be a lie?

— What information do you need to give the other side and how will you give it?

— What type of persuasive statements will you make?

— Can you identify objective criteria that support the likely positions you will take or proposed solutions you will make?

— What are the possible criteria to be used by the other side?

— How will you respond to them?

— What are the details of your persuasive elements?

— Can you make your persuasive statements multidimensional? balanced? emphatic?

— Are there any points that must be subtle?

— Do you anticipate any threats?

— How will you respond to threats?

— What type of concessions are you willing to consider?

— What will you need to convince you a concession is appropriate?

— How will you respond if any of the following tactics is used against you?

Anger

Aggression

Boulwareism

Uneven number of negotiators

False demands

Attempts to get you to make the first offer

Attempts to get you to negotiate against yourself

Time pressure

— Will you use any of these tactics? Why?

— If it appears you are going to deadlock, what might you do?

— When will you likely end this negotiation?

— How will you likely end this negotiation?

— Is one of your goals to monitor how the settlement is working?

    If so, how will this be done?

    Who will report to whom about what?

    What happens if they don't report?

    What happens if a dispute arises?

— Do the parties want to decide now on how future disputes will be resolved?

APPENDIX B

POST-NEGOTIATION WORKSHEET

Did you accomplish your goals? Why? Why not?

Were you able to set the tone that you desired for the negotiation? Why or why not?

Did you control the agenda? Why or why not?

Did you find as much information as you wanted? Why or why not?

Did you reveal too much information? Why or why not?

Did you fail to reveal information you should have? Why or why not?

If you did not agree, was it appropriate given the context of this particular negotiation? Why or why not?

If you have deadlocked, what might you be able to do to break that deadlock?

If you have deadlocked, might any of the issues in dispute profit from mediation? Would you want a neutral facilitative mediator or an evaluative mediator?

If you agreed, is the result fair, just, and equitable from everyone's perspective? Why or why not?

For each stage of the negotiation process you conducted, what did you learn from this negotiation?

    Preparation and Planning

    Ice-Breaking

    Agenda Control

    Information Bargaining

    Offers/Demands/Proposals

    Persuasion

    Concessions/Reformulations

    Crisis

    Closing

    Memorialization

What is the one thing you will do differently in the next negotiation? Why?

APPENDIX C

SELECTED BIBLIOGRAPHY

The following list of articles and books is not meant to be an exhaustive bibliography. Also, the list is not meant to imply we agree with what the material has to say about negotiation. In fact, we do not agree with everything that is said in these books and articles, but they provide additional detail and sometimes a different perspective that can further your understanding of the negotiation process.

Articles

Robert S. Adler & Elliot M. Silverstein, *When David Meets Goliath: Dealing With Power Differentials in Negotiations*, 5 Harv. Negot. L. Rev. 1 (2000).

Ian Ayres & Barry J. Nalebuff, *Common Knowledge as a Barrier to Negotiation*, 44 UCLA L. Rev. 1631 (1997).

John Barkai, *Teaching Negotiation and ADR: The Savvy Samurai Meets the Devil*, 75 Neb. L. Rev. 704 (1996).

Gary S. Berman, *Facilitated Negotiation: An Effective ADR Technique*, 50 Disp. Resol. J. 18 (1995).

Gary S. Berman, *Facilitating Construction Negotiations*, 50 Disp. Resol. J. 23 (1995).

Richard Birke and Craig R. Fox, *Psychological Principles in Negotiating Civil Settlements*, 4 Harv. Negot. L. Rev. 1 (1999).

Wayne D. Brazil, *Protecting the Confidentiality of Settlement Negotiations*, 39 Hastings L.J. 955 (1988).

Marshall J. Breger, *Should an Attorney be Required to Advise a Client of ADR Options?*, 13 Geo. J. Legal Ethics 427 (2000).

Jennifer Gerarda Brown, *The Role of Hope in Negotiation*, 44 UCLA L. Rev. 1661 (1997).

Cash and Janda, *The Eye of the Beholder*, Psychol. Today 46, Dec. 1984.

Jonathan R. Cohen, *Reasoning Along Different Lines: Some Varied Roles of Rationality in Negotiation and Conflict Resolution*, 3 Harv. Negot. L. Rev. 111 (1998).

Robert J. Condlin, *Bargaining in the Dark: The Normative Incoherence of Lawyer Dispute Bargaining Role*, 51 MD. L. REV. 1 (1992).

Robert J. Condlin, *"Cases on Both Sides": Patterns of Argument in Legal Dispute-Negotiation*, 44 MD. L. REV. 65 (1985).

John W. Cooley, *The Geometries of Situation and Emotions and the Calculus of Change in Negotiation and Mediation*, 29 VAL. U. L. REV. 1 (1994).

Charles B. Craver, *Negotiation Ethics: How to be Deceptive Without Being Dishonest/ How to be Assertive Without Being Offensive*, 38 S. TEX. L. REV. 713 (1997).

Charles B. Craver, *Effective Legal Negotiation and Settlement*, CB55 ALI-ABA 1 (1996).

Joseph L. Daly, *International Commercial Negotiation and Arbitration*, 22 HAMLINE J. PUB. L. & POL'Y 217 (2001).

Andrew F. Daugherty & Jennifer F. Reinganum, *Settlement Negotiations with Two-sided Asymmetric Information: Model Duality, Information Distribution, and Efficiency*, 14 INT'L REV. L. & ECON. 283 (1994).

Luis Miguel Diaz, *Notes on Negotiation and Unlearning Legal Thinking*, 688 PLI/ LIT 505 (2003).

W. Donohue, *An Empirical Framework for Examining Negotiation Processes and Outcomes, Communication Monographs,* Vol. 45, August (1978).

Lynn A. Epstein, *Cyber E-mail Negotiation vs. Traditional Negotiation: Will Cyber Technology Supplant Traditional Means of Settling Litigation*, 36 TULSA L.J. 839 (2001).

Mary Jo Eyster, *Clinical Teaching, Ethical Negotiation, and Moral Judgment*, 75 NEB. L. REV. 752 (1996).

Amy Farmer & Paul Pecorino, *Pretrial Negotiations with Asymmetric Information on Risk Preferences*, 14 INT'L REV. L. & ECON. 273 (1994).

A. FOROUGH, ET AL., AN EMPIRICAL STUDY OF AN INTERACTIVE, SESSION-ORIENTATED COMPUTERIZED NEGOTIATION SUPPORT SYSTEM, GROUP DECISION AND NEGOTIATION 4 (1995).

Lawrence J. Fox, *Those Who Worry About the Ethics of Negotiation Should Never be Viewed as Just Another Set of Service Providers*, 52 MERCER L. REV. 977 (2001).

Clark Freshman et al, *The Lawyer-Negotiator as Mood Scientist: What We Know and Don't Know About How Mood Relates to Successful Negotiation*, 2002 J. DISP. RESOL. 1 (2002).

Donald G. Gifford, *The Synthesis of Legal Counseling and Negotiation Models: Preserving Client centered Advocacy in the Negotiation Context*, 34 UCLA L. REV. 811 (1987).

Portor Goltz, *Settling the Score: Good Negotiation Skills Pave the Way for Better Settlements*, 82-AUG A.B.A. J. 90 (1996).

Samuel R. Gross & Kent D. Syverud, *Getting to No: A Study of Settlement Negotiations and the Selection of Cases for Trial*, 90 MICH. L. REV. 319 (1991).

Thomas F. Guernsey, *Truthfulness in Negotiation*, 17 U. RICH. L. REV. 99 (1982).

Milton Heumann & Jonathan M. Hyman, *Negotiation Methods and Litigation Settlement Methods in New Jersey: "You Can't Always Get What You Want"*, 12 OHIO ST. J. ON DISP. RESOL. 253 (1997).

Michael R. Hogan, *Judicial Settlement Conferences: Empowering the Parties to Decide Through Negotiation*, 27 WILLAMETTE L. REV. 429 (1991).

James R. Holbrook & Laura M. Gray, *Court-annexed Alternative Dispute Resolution*, 21 J. CONTEMP. L. 1 (1995).

Shi-Ling Hsu, *A Game-Theoretic Approach to Regulatory Negotiation and a Framework for Empirical Analysis*, 26 HARV. ENVTL. L. REV. 33 (2002).

Jonathan M. Hyman, *Trial Advocacy and Methods of Negotiation: Can Good Trial Advocates Be Wise Negotiators?*, 34 UCLA L. REV. 863 (1987).

Peter R. Jarvis & Bradley F. Tellam, *A Negotiation Ethics Primer for Lawyers*, 31 GONZ. L. REV. 549 (1995-96).

Peter A. Joy & Kevin C. McMunigal, *Disclosing Exculpatory Material in Plea Negotiations*, 16-FALL CRIM. JUST. 41 (2001).

Russell Korobkin, *A Positive Theory of Legal Negotiation*, 88 GEO. L.J. 1789 (2000).

Bailey H. Kuklin, *The Asymmetrical Conditions of Legal Responsibility in the Marketplace*, 44 U. MIAMI L. REV. 893 (1990).

The Law Lists: The Art of Negotiating, 81-JUN A.B.A. J. 90 (1995).

Alain Lempereur, *Negotiation and Mediation in France: The Challenge of Skill-based Learning and Interdisciplinary Research in Legal Education*, 3 HARV. NEGOT. L. REV. 151 (1998).

Lisa G. Lerman, *Lying to Clients*, 138 U. PA. L. REV. 659 (1990).

Patrick Emery Longan, *Symposium, Ethics in Settlement Negotiations: Foreword*, 52 MERCER L. REV. 807 (2001).

Gary T. Lowenthal, *A General Theory of Negotiation Process, Strategy and Behavior*, 31 U. KAN. L. REV. 69 (1982).

Kate Marquess, *Point, Click—Settle Quick: Online Negotiations Hailed for Efficiency, but Some Prefer Face to Face*, 86-APR ABA J. 82 (2000).

Craig A. McEwen & Roselle L. Wissler, *Finding Out if it is True: Comparing Mediation and Negotiation Through Research*, 2002 J. DISP. RESOL. 131 (2002).

Kevin C. McMunigal, *Disclosure and Accuracy in the Guilty Plea Process*, 40 HASTINGS L.J. 957 (1989).

Carrie Menkel Meadow, *Toward Another View of Legal Negotiation: The Structure of Problem solving*, 31 UCLA L. REV. 754 (1984).

Robert H. Mnookin, *Strategic Barriers to Dispute Resolution: A Comparison of Bilateral and Multilateral Negotiations*, 8 HARV. NEGOT. L. REV. 1 (2003).

Eleanor Holmes Norton, *Bargaining and the Ethic of Process*, 64 N.Y.U. L. REV. 493 (1989).

Curtis Nyquist, *A Spectrum Theory of Negotiability*, 78 MARQ. L. REV. 897 (1995).

K. O'Connor, *Motives and Cognitions in Negotiation: A Theoretical Integration and an Empirical Test*, THE INTERNATIONAL JOURNAL OF CONFLICT MANAGEMENT (1997).

K. O'Connor & A. Adams, *What Novices Think About Negotiation: A Content Analysis of Scripts*, NEGOTIATION JOURNAL, April (1999).

David Brainerd Parrish, COMMENT, *The Dilemma: Simultaneous Negotiation of Attorneys' Fees and Settlement in Class Actions*, 36 HOUS. L. REV. 531 (1999).

Rex R. Perschbacher, *Regulating Lawyers' Negotiations*, 27 ARIZ. L. REV. 75 (1985).

Don Peters, *Mapping, Modeling, and Critiquing: Facilitating Learning Negotiation, Mediation, Interviewing, and Counseling*, 48 FLA. ST. L. REV. 875 (1996).

Don Peters, *Forever Jung: Psychological Type Theory, the Myers Briggs Type Indicator and Learning Negotiation*, 42 DRAKE L. REV. 1 (1993).

Geoffrey M. Peters, *The Use of Lies in Negotiation*, 48 OHIO ST. L.J. 1 (1987).

Lynne H. Rambo, *Impeaching Lying Parties With Their Statements During Negotiation: Demysticizing the Public Policy Rationale Behind Evidence Rule 408 and the Mediation-privilege Statutes*, 75 WASH. L. REV. 1037 (2000).

N. Reiches & H. Harral, *Argument in Negotiation: A Theoretical and Empirical Approach*, Speech Monographs, Vol. 41 (March 1974).

Alvin B. Rubin, *A Causerie on Lawyers' Ethics in Negotiation*, 35 LA. L. REV. 577 (1975).

Ernest P. Sachs, 25-JUN VT. B.J. & L. DIG. 46 (1999) (reviewing GREGG HERMANN, THE JOY OF SETTLEMENT: THE FAMILY LAWYER'S GUIDE TO EFFECTIVE NEGOTIATIONS AND SETTLEMENT STRATEGIES (1997)).

Andrea Kupfer Schneider, *Shattering Negotiation Myths: Empirical Evidence on the Effectiveness of Negotiation Style*, 7 HARV. NEGOT. L. REV. 143 (2002).

Roy Stuckey, *Understanding Casablanca: A Values-based Approach to Legal Negotiations*, 5 CLINICAL L. REV. 211 (1998).

L. Thompson, *Negotiation Behavior and Outcomes: Empirical Evidence and Theoretical Issues*, PSYCHOLOGICAL BULLETIN (1990), Vol 108, No 3, pg 515

S. Weiss-Wik, *Enhancing Negotiator's Successfulness - Self-help Books and Related Empirical Research*, JOURNAL OF CONFLICT RESOLUTION, Vol 27 No. 4 (Dec. 1983).

Gerald Wetlaufer, *The Ethics of Lying in Negotiations*, 75 IOWA L. REV. 1219 (1990).

Williams W. Wilkins, Jr., *Plea Negotiations, Acceptance of Responsibility, Role of the Offender, and Departures: Policy Decisions in the Promulgation of Federal Sentencing Guidelines*, 23 WAKE FOREST L. REV. 181 (1988).

Zakeria Mohammed Yacoob, Salient Features of the Negotiating Process, 52 SMU L. REV. 1579 (1999).

Douglas H. Yarn, *Lawyer Ethics in ADR and the Recommendations of Ethics 2000 to Revise the Model Rules of Professional Conduct: Considerations for Adoption and State Application*, 54 ARK. L. REV. 207 (2001).

Marguerite Zoghby, *The Prohibition of Communication with Adverse Parties in Civil Negotiations: Protecting Clients or Preventing Solutions?*, 14 GEO. J. LEGAL ETHICS 1165 (2001).

Selected Books

HAROLD I. ABRAMSON, MEDIATION REPRESENTATION: ADVOCACY IN A PROBLEM-SOLVING PROCESS (2004).

JEAN ALBERT, NEGOTIATION SKILLS: A HANDBOOK (1986).

KARL ALBRECHT & STEVE ALBRECHT, ADDED VALUE NEGOTIATING: THE BREAKTHROUGH METHOD FOR BUILDING BALANCED DEALS (1993).

TOM ANASTASI, PERSONALITY NEGOTIATING: CONFLICT WITHOUT CASUALTY (1993).

KARE ANDERSON, GETTING WHAT YOU WANT: HOW TO REACH AGREEMENT AND RESOLVE CONFLICT EVERY TIME (1993).

JOSEPH AUER & CHARLES EDISON HARRIS, COMPUTER CONTRACT NEGOTIATIONS (1981).

KENNETH J. ARROW ET AL., BARRIERS TO CONFLICT RESOLUTION (1995).

ASSOCIATION OF LABOR RELATIONS AGENCIES, LABOR-MANAGEMENT RELATIONS IN THE PUBLIC SECTOR: REDEFINING COLLECTIVE BARGAINING (John L. Bonner ed., 1999).

EILEEN F. BABBITT, JIMMY CARTER: THE POWER OF MORAL PERSUASION IN INTERNATIONAL MEDIATION, IN WHEN TALK WORKS: PROFILES OF MEDIATORS (Deborah M. Kolb ed., 1994).

Samuel B. Bacharach & Edward J. Lawler, Bargaining: Power, Tactics, and Outcomes (1981).

Ginny Pearson Barnes, Successful Negotiating: Letting the Other Person Have Your Way (1998).

Ginny Pearson Barnes, 8 Steps for Highly Effective Negotiation: Letting the Other Person Have Your Way (1995).

Robert M. Bastress & Joseph D. Harbaugh, Interviewing, Counseling, and Negotiating (1990).

Max H. Bazerman & Margaret A. Neale, Negotiating Rationally (1992).

Bureau of National Affairs (Washington, D.C.), What's New in Collective Bargaining Negotiations & Contracts: Patterns in Union Contracts (1989).

Bureau of National Affairs (Washington, D.C.), Collective Bargaining Negotiations and Contracts (1979).

Neal W. Beckmann, Negotiations: Principles and Techniques (1977).

Gary Bellow & Bea Moulton, The Lawyering Process: Negotiation (1981).

Alfred Benjamin, The Helping Interview (1974).

Jacob Bercovitch, Social Conflicts and Third Parties: Strategies of Conflict Resolution (1984).

Eric Berne, Games People Play: The Psychology of Human Relationships (1964).

Sissela Bok, Lying: Moral Choice in Public and Private Life (1978).

Steven J. Brams & Alan D. Taylor, The Win-Win Solution: Guaranteeing Fair Shares to Everybody (1999).

Wayne D. Brazil, Effective Approaches to Settlement: A Handbook for Lawyers and Judges (1988).

Ed Brodow, Negotiate with Confidence (1996).

Earl Brooks & George S. Odiorne, Managing by Negotiations (1984).

Jimmy Carter, Negotiation: An Alternative to Hostility (1984).

Jimmy Carter, Talking Peace: A Vision for the Next Generation (1993).

Pierre Casse, The One-hour Negotiator (1992).

Ralph Charell, How to Get the Upper Hand (1978).

David Churchman, Negotiation: Process, Tactics, Theory (2d ed. 1995).

David Churchman, Negotiation Tactics (1993).

HERB COHEN, NEGOTIATE THIS!: BY CARING, BUT NOT T-H-A-T MUCH (2003).

HERB COHEN, YOU CAN NEGOTIATE ANYTHING (1980).

LAURIE S. COLTRI, CONFLICT DIAGNOSIS AND ALTERNATIVE DISPUTE RESOLUTION AND MEDIATION (2004).

CHARLES CRAVER, THE INTELLIGENT NEGOTIATOR: WHAT TO SAY, WHAT TO DO, AND HOW TO GET WHAT YOU WANT—EVERY TIME (2002).

CHARLES CRAVER, EFFECTIVE LEGAL NEGOTIATION AND SETTLEMENT (4th ed. 2001).

JOHN G. CROSS, THE ECONOMICS OF BARGAINING (1969).

MORTON DEUTSCH & PETER T. COLEMAN, THE HANDBOOK OF CONFLICT RESOLUTION: THEORY & PRACTICE (2000).

JOHN PATRICK DOLAN, NEGOTIATE LIKE THE PROS (1992).

TED A. DONNER & BRIAN L. CROWE, ATTORNEY'S PRACTICE GUIDE TO NEGOTIATIONS (2d. ed. 1995).

DANIEL DRUCKMAN, NEGOTIATIONS: SOCIAL-PSYCHOLOGICAL PERSPECTIVES (1977).

DANIEL DRUCKMAN ET AL., NONVERBAL COMMUNICATION: SURVEY, THEORY AND RESEARCH (1982).

JOEL EDELMAN & MARY BETH CRAIN, THE TAO OF NEGOTIATION: HOW YOU CAN PREVENT, RESOLVE, AND TRANSCEND CONFLICT IN WORK AND EVERYDAY LIFE (1993).

JULIUS FAST, BODY LANGUAGE (1970).

ROGER FISHER & WILLIAM URY, GETTING TO YES: NEGOTIATING AGREEMENT WITHOUT GIVING IN (Bruce Patton ed., 2d ed. 1991).

XAVIER M. FRASCOGNA, JR. & H. LEE HETHERINGTON, THE LAWYER'S GUIDE TO NEGOTIATION: A STRATEGIC APPROACH TO BETTER CONTRACTS AND SETTLEMENTS (2001).

XAVIER M. FRASCOGNA, JR. & H. LEE HETHERINGTON, NEGOTIATION STRATEGY FOR LAWYERS (1984).

DONALD G. GIFFORD, LEGAL NEGOTIATION: THEORY AND APPLICATIONS (1989).

MALCOLM GLADWELL, BLINK: THE POWER OF THINKING WITHOUT THINKING (2005).

MALCOLM GLADWELL, THE TIPPING POINT: HOW LITTLE THINGS CAN MAKE A BIG DIFFERENCE (2000).

STEPHEN B. GOLDBERG ET AL., DISPUTE RESOLUTION (1985).

ALVIN L. GOLDMAN, SETTLING FOR MORE: MASTERING NEGOTIATING STRATEGIES AND TECHNIQUES (1991).

ADAM GRANT, GIVE AND TAKE (2014).

FRANCIS GREENBURGER & THOMAS KIERNAN, HOW TO ASK FOR MORE AND GET IT: THE ART OF CREATIVE NEGOTIATION (1978).

JULIAN GRESSER, PILOTING THROUGH CHAOS: WISE LEADERSHIP, EFFECTIVE NEGOTIATION FOR THE 21ST CENTURY (1995).

P.H. GULLIVER, DISPUTES AND NEGOTIATIONS: A CROSS-CULTURAL PERSPECTIVE (1979).

EDWARD TWITCHELL HALL, THE SILENT LANGUAGE (1959).

JUDITH A. HALL, NONVERBAL SEX DIFFERENCES: COMMUNICATION ACCURACY AND EXPRESSIVE STYLE (1984).

ANN HALPERN, NEGOTIATING SKILLS (1992).

FEN OSLER HAMPSON & MICHAEL HART, MULTILATERAL NEGOTIATIONS: LESSONS FROM ARMS CONTROL, TRADE, AND THE ENVIRONMENT (1995).

JOSEPH D. HARBAUGH, NEGOTIATION: WINNING TACTICS AND TECHNIQUES (1988).

ROBERT GALE HARPER ET AL., NONVERBAL COMMUNICATION: THE STATE OF THE ART (1978).

DENNIS A. HAWVER, HOW TO IMPROVE YOUR NEGOTIATION SKILLS (1992).

ROGER S. HAYDOCK, NEGOTIATION PRACTICE (1984).

JOHN M. HAYNES & GRETCHEN L. HAYNES, MEDIATING DIVORCE: CASEBOOK OF STRATEGIES FOR SUCCESSFUL FAMILY NEGOTIATIONS (1989).

ROBERT D. HELSBY ET AL., THE EVOLVING PROCESS: COLLECTIVE NEGOTIATIONS IN PUBLIC EMPLOYMENT (1985).

ROBERT D. HELSBY, PORTRAIT OF A PROCESS: COLLECTIVE NEGOTIATIONS IN PUBLIC EMPLOYMENT/PUBLIC EMPLOYMENT RELATIONS SERVICES (Muriel K. Gibbons et al. eds., 1979).

NANCY HENLEY, BODY, POLITICS, SEX, AND NONVERBAL COMMUNICATION (1986).

GREGG M. HERMAN, THE JOY OF SETTLEMENT: THE FAMILY LAWYER'S GUIDE TO EFFECTIVE NEGOTIATIONS AND SETTLEMENT STRATEGIES (1997).

JEAN M. HILTROP & SHELIA UDALL, THE ESSENCE OF NEGOTIATION (1995).

FRED CHARLES IKLÉ., HOW NATIONS NEGOTIATE (1964).

JOHN ILICH, DEALBREAKERS AND BREAKTHROUGHS: THE TEN MOST COMMON AND COSTLY NEGOTIATION MISTAKES AND HOW TO OVERCOME THEM (1992).

JOHN ILICH.& BARBARA SCHINDLER JONES, SUCCESSFUL NEGOTIATION SKILLS FOR WOMEN (1981).

Norbert S. Jacker, Effective Negotiation Techniques for Lawyers (1984).

Fred Edmund Jandt, Win Win Negotiating; Turning Conflict into Agreement (1985).

Ralph A. Johnson, Negotiation Basics: Concepts, Skills, and Exercises (1993).

Daniel Kahneman, Thinking, Fast and Slow (2011).

Chester Louis Karrass, Give and Take: The Complete Guide to Negotiating Strategies and Tactics (1993).

Chester Louis Karrass, The Negotiating Game (1970).

Karrass, G., Negotiate to Close (1985).

Gavin Kennedy, The Perfect Negotiation (1994).

Gavin Kennedy, Pocket Negotiator (1987).

Robert C. Knee & Robert C. Knee, Jr., Collective Bargaining Clauses: Guideline Forms for Use in Labor Negotiations (1975).

Deborah M. Kolb & Judith Williams, Everyday Negotiation: Navigating the Hidden Agendas in Bargaining (rev. ed. 2003).

Deborah M. Kolb & Judith Williams, The Shadow Negotiation: How Women Can Master the Hidden Agendas That Determine Bargaining Success (2000).

Korda, M., Power! How to Get It, How to Use It (1975).

Russell Korobkin, Negotiation Theory and Strategy (2002).

Stephen Kozicki, Creative Negotiating: Proven Techniques for Getting What You Want from Any Negotiation (1998).

Henry S. Kramer, Game, Set, Match: Winning the Negotiations Game (2001).

Roderick M. Kramer & David M. Messick, Negotiation as a Social Process (1995).

Victor A. Kremenyuk et al., International Negotiation: Analysis, Approaches, Issues (1991).

Phyllis Beck Kritek, Negotiating at an Uneven Table: Developing Moral Courage in Resolving Our Conflicts (2d ed. 2002).

Robert Lawrence Kuhn, Dealmaker: All the Negotiating Skills and Secrets You Need (1988).

Amos Lakos, International Negotiations: A Bibliography (1989).

Arthur Samuel Lall, Multilateral Negotiation and Mediation: Instruments and Methods (1985).

ARTHUR SAMUEL LALL, MODERN INTERNATIONAL NEGOTIATION (1966).

DAVID A. LAX, THE MANAGER AS NEGOTIATOR: BARGAINING FOR COOPERATION AND COMPETITIVE GAIN (1986).

LEN LERITZ, NO-FAULT NEGOTIATING: A SIMPLE AND INNOVATIVE APPROACH FOR SOLVING PROBLEMS, REACHING AGREEMENTS, AND RESOLVING CONFLICTS (1990).

PAUL LESTI ET AL., STRUCTURED SETTLEMENTS (1986).

RACHELLE L. LEVITT & JOHN J. KIRLIN, MANAGING DEVELOPMENT THROUGH PUBLIC/PRIVATE NEGOTIATIONS (1985).

ROY J. LEWICKI ET AL., ESSENTIALS OF NEGOTIATION (3d ed. 2004).

ROY J. LEWICKI ET AL., NEGOTIATION: READINGS, EXERCISES, AND CASES (4th ed. 2003).

ROY J. LEWICKI ET AL., THINK BEFORE YOU SPEAK: THE COMPLETE GUIDE TO STRATEGIC NEGOTIATION (1996).

DAVID V. LEWIS, POWER NEGOTIATION TACTICS AND TECHNIQUES (1981).

PAUL MICHAEL LISNEK, A LAWYER'S GUIDE TO EFFECTIVE NEGOTIATION AND MEDIATION (1993).

GRANDE LUM ET AL., EXPAND THE PIE: HOW TO ADD VALUE TO ANY NEGOTIATION (2003).

FRANCES MAUTNER-MARKHOF, PROCESSES OF INTERNATIONAL NEGOTIATIONS (1989).

BERNARD S. MAYER, THE DYNAMICS OF CONFLICT RESOLUTION: A PRACTITIONER'S GUIDE (2000).

BRAD MCRAE, NEGOTIATING AND INFLUENCING SKILLS: THE ART OF CREATING AND CLAIMING VALUE (1998).

ALBERT MEHRABIAN, SILENT MESSAGES: IMPLICIT COMMUNICATION OF EMOTIONS AND ATTITUDES (2d ed. 1981).

ALBERT MEHRABIAN, NONVERBAL COMMUNICATION (1972).

LEE E. MILLER & JESSICA MILLER, A WOMAN'S GUIDE TO SUCCESSFUL NEGOTIATING: HOW TO CONVINCE, COLLABORATE, AND CREATE YOUR WAY TO AGREEMENT (2002).

GEORGE J. MITCHELL, MAKING PEACE (1999).

ROBERT H. MNOOKIN, BEYOND WINNING: NEGOTIATING TO CREATE VALUE IN DEALS AND DISPUTES (2000).

ROBERT H. MNOOKIN ET AL., NEGOTIATING ON BEHALF OF OTHERS: ADVICE TO LAWYERS, BUSINESS EXECUTIVES, SPORTS AGENTS, DIPLOMATS, POLITICIANS, AND EVERYBODY ELSE (1999).

Ian E. Morley & Geoffrey M. Stephenson, The Social Psychology of Bargaining (1977).

Morrison, W., The Prenegotiation Planning Book (1985).

William F. Morrison & Henry H. Calero, The Human Side of Negotiations (1994).

J. Keith Murnighan, Bargaining Games: A New Approach to Strategic Thinking in Negotiations (1992).

J. Keith Murnighan, The Dynamics Of Bargaining Games (1991).

Margaret A. Neale & Max H. Bazerman, Cognition and Rationality in Negotiation (1991).

Richard G. Neal, Negotiations Strategies: A Reference Manual for Public Sector Labor Negotiations (1981).

Richard G. Neal, Bargaining Tactics: A Reference Manual for Public Sector Labor Negotiations (1980).

Richard G. Neal, Retrieval Bargaining: A Guide for Public Sector Labor Negotiations (1981).

Wade J. Newhouse, Public Sector Labor Relations Law in New York State: The Law Relating to Public Employee Organization, Negotiations, Resolution of Disputes, and Enforcement of Agreements (1978).

Richard P. Nielsen, The Politics of Ethics: Methods for Acting, Learning, and Sometimes Fighting with Others in Addressing Ethics Problems in Organizational Life (1996).

Gerard I. Nierenberg, The Complete Negotiator (1991).

Gerard I. Nierenberg, The Art of Negotiating (1987).

Gerard I. Nierenberg, Fundamentals of Negotiating (1973).

Gerard I. Nierenberg & Henry H. Calero, How to Read a Person Like a Book (1971).

Juliet Nierenberg & Irene S. Ross, Negotiate for Success: Effective Strategies for Realizing Your Goals (2003).

Louise Nieuwmeijer, Negotiation: Methodology and Training (1992).

Personal Injury Valuation Handbooks (Jury Verdict Research, Inc.).

Stephen M. Pollan & Mark Levine, The Total Negotiator (1994).

Peter J. Poulopoulos, Negotiating Tips: A Practical Guide to Be a Successful Negotiator and Obtain Results (1996).

PROGRAM ON NEGOTIATION AT HARVARD LAW SCHOOL, NEGOTIATION: STRATEGIES FOR MUTUAL GAIN (Lavinia Hall ed., 1993).

DEAN G. PRUITT, NEGOTIATION BEHAVIOR (1981).

DEAn G. PRUITT & PETER J. CARNEVALE, NEGOTIATION IN SOCIAL CONFLICT (1993).

HOWARD RAIFFA, THE ART AND SCIENCE OF NEGOTIATION (1982).

HOWARD RAIFFA ET AL., NEGOTIATION ANALYSIS: THE SCIENCE AND ART OF COLLABORATIVE DECISION MAKING (2002).

BERNARD A. RAMUNDO, EFFECTIVE NEGOTIATION: A GUIDE TO DIALOGUE MANAGEMENT AND CONTROL (1992).

BERNARD A. RAMUNDO, EFFECTIVE NEGOTIATION: A PRIMER (1984).

L.N. RANGARAJAN, THE LIMITATION OF CONFLICT: A THEORY OF BARGAINING AND NEGOTIATION (1985).

ROSS R. RECK & BRIAN G. LONG, THE WIN-WIN NEGOTIATOR (1985).

LINDA RICHARDSON, WINNING NEGOTIATION STRATEGIES FOR BANKERS (1987).

ROBERT J. RINGER, WINNING THROUGH INTIMIDATION (1974).

JEFFREY Z. RUBIN & BERT R. BROWN, THE SOCIAL PSYCHOLOGY OF BARGAINING AND NEGOTIATION (1975).

RAYMOND SANER, THE EXPERT NEGOTIATOR: STRATEGY, TACTICS, MOTIVATION, BEHAVIOUR, LEADERSHIP (2000).

NICHOLAS REID SCHAFFZIN, NEGOTIATE SMART (1997).

NICHOLAS REID SCHAFFZIN, DON'T BE A CHUMP!: NEGOTIATING SKILLS YOU NEED (1995).

TOM RUSK,M.D., THE POWER OF ETHICAL PERSUASION: WINNING THROUGH UNDERSTANDING AT WORK AND HOME, (1993)

MICHAEL SCHATZKI & WAYNE R. COFFEY, NEGOTIATION: THE ART OF GETTING WHAT YOU WANT (1981).

MARK K. SCHOENFIELD & RICK M. SCHOENFIELD, LEGAL NEGOTIATIONS: GETTING MAXIMUM RESULTS (1988).

G. RICHARD SHELL, BARGAINING FOR ADVANTAGE: NEGOTIATION STRATEGIES FOR REASONABLE PEOPLE (1999).

SIDNEY SIEGEL & LAWRENCE E. FOURAKER, BARGAINING AND GROUP DECISION MAKING: EXPERIMENTS IN BILATERAL MONOPOLY (1977).

JAMES R. SILKENAT & JEFFREY M. ARESTY, A GUIDE TO INTERNATIONAL BUSINESS NEGOTIATIONS: A COMPARISON OF CROSS-CULTURAL ISSUES AND SUCCESSFUL APPROACHES (2d ed. 2000).

MICHAEL SPANGLE & MYRA WARREN ISENHART, NEGOTIATION: COMMUNICATION FOR DIVERSE SETTINGS (2003).

DONALD B. SPARKS, THE DYNAMICS OF EFFECTIVE NEGOTIATION (1982).

PHILIP SPERBER, ATTORNEY'S PRACTICE GUIDE TO NEGOTIATIONS (1985).

MIKE R. STARK, THE POWER OF NEGOTIATING: STRATEGIES FOR SUCCESS (1996).

DOUGLAS STONE, BRUCE PATTON & SHEILA HENN, DIFFICULT CONVERSATIONS: HOW TO DISCUSS WHAT MATTERS MOST (1999)

ANSLEM L. STRAUSS, NEGOTIATIONS: VARIETIES, CONTEXTS, PROCESSES, AND SOCIAL ORDER (1978).

LARRY L. TEPLY, LEGAL NEGOTIATION IN A NUTSHELL (1992).

O.C. TIRELLA & GARY D. BATES, WIN-WIN NEGOTIATING: A PROFESSIONAL'S PLAYBOOK (1993).

TRIAL LAWYERS SECTION AND THE COMMITTEE ON CONTINUING LEGAL EDUCATION OF THE NEW YORK STATE BAR ASSOCIATION, SECRETS OF SUCCESSFUL EVALUATION NEGOTIATION AND SETTLEMENT TECHNIQUES IN CIVIL CASES (1985).

WILLIAM URY, GETTING PAST NO: NEGOTIATION YOUR WAY FROM CONFRONTATION TO COOPERATION (1993).

WILLIAM URY, GETTING PAST NO: NEGOTIATING WITH DIFFICULT PEOPLE (1991).

ROGER J. VOLKEMA, THE NEGOTIATION TOOLKIT: HOW TO GET EXACTLY WHAT YOU WANT IN ANY BUSINESS OR PERSONAL SITUATION (1999).

JOHN VON NEUMANN & OSKAR MORGENSTERN, THEORY OF GAMES AND ECONOMIC BEHAVIOR (1944).

JAMES A. WALL, JR., NEGOTIATION, THEORY AND PRACTICE (1985).

MICHAEL A. WALKER & GEORGE L. HARRIS, NEGOTIATIONS: SIX STEPS TO SUCCESS (1995).

TESSA ALBERT WARSCHAW, WINNING BY NEGOTIATION (1980).

ROBERT A. WENKE, THE ART OF NEGOTIATION FOR LAWYERS (1985).

GERALD R. WILLIAMS, LEGAL NEGOTIATION AND SETTLEMENT (1983).

GERALD R. WILLIAMS, A LAWYER'S HANDBOOK FOR EFFECTIVE NEGOTIATION AND SETTLEMENT (1981).

GERALD R. WILLIAMS, HANDBOOK ON EFFECTIVENESS IN LEGAL NEGOTIATION: A SYSTEM FOR MAXIMIZING NEGOTIATOR EFFECTIVENESS (1977).

DONALD H. WOLLET & ROBERT H. CHANNIN, THE LAW AND PRACTICE OF TEACHER NEGOTIATIONS (1974).

ORAN R. YOUNG, BARGAINING: FORMAL THEORIES OF NEGOTIATION (1975).

I. WILLIAM ZARTMAN, THE NEGOTIATION PROCESS: THEORIES AND APPLICATIONS (1978).

I. WILLIAM ZARTMAN & MAUREEN R. BERMAN, THE PRACTICAL NEGOTIATOR (1982).

PAUL J. ZWIER, PRINCIPLED NEGOTIATION AND MEDIATION IN THE INTERNATIONAL ARENA: TALKING WITH EVIL (2013).

INDEX

National Institute for Trial Advocacy